# Interviews with Writers of the Post-Colonial World

# Interviews

### WITH

# Writers

### OF THE

# Post-Colonial World

*Conducted and Edited by*

Feroza Jussawalla and Reed Way Dasenbrock

UNIVERSITY PRESS OF MISSISSIPPI
*Jackson & London*

Picture credits: Ngũgĩ wa Thiong'o, Michael Marsland, Yale University, Office of Public Information; Chinua Achebe, Michael Weisbrot; Raja Rao, News & Information Service, University of Texas at Austin; Anita Desai, Jerry Bauer; Zulfikar Ghose, Helena de la Fontaine; Bapsi Sidhwa, Milkweed Editions; Rudolfo Anaya, University of New Mexico; Rolando Hinojosa, Larry Murphy, News & Information Service, University of Texas at Austin; and Sandra Cisneros, Rubén Guzmàn.

95  94  93  92    4  3  2  1

The paper in this book meets the guidelines for permanence and durability of the Committee on Production Guidelines for Book Longevity of the Council on Library Resources.

Library of Congress Cataloging-in-Publication Data
Jussawalla, Feroza F., 1953-
    Interviews with writers of the post-colonial world / conducted and edited by Feroza Jussawalla and Reed Way Dasenbrock.
    p. cm.
    Includes index.
    ISBN 0-87805-571-1 (cloth). — ISBN 0-87805-572-X (paper)
    1. Commonwealth of Nations literature (English) — History and criticism.   2. American literature — Mexican American authors — History and criticism.   3. Authors, Commonwealth of Nations — 20th century — Interviews.   4. Mexican American authors — 20th century — Interviews.   5. Commonwealth of Nations — Intellectual life.
    6.  Mexican Americans — Intellectual life.   7. Decolonization in literature.   I. Dasenbrock, Reed Way.   II. Title.
    PR9080.J87   1992
    820.9'9171241—dc20                                                    91-48022
                                                                                  CIP

British Library Cataloging-in-Publication data available

For each other, our families,
the writers and their families,
and the larger family of world literature written in English

*tandaroosti*

# Contents

# Acknowledgments

First of all, we need to acknowledge and thank all of the writers interviewed here, for agreeing to be interviewed, for their generous hospitality and graciousness throughout the interview process, and for helping us prepare the transcripts for publication by reading and editing them. We also need to thank Ben Lindfors and Bapsi Sidhwa for helping to put us in touch with several of the writers interviewed here. Our son Homi patiently travelled with us while we interviewed most of the writers. A small army of transcribers helped turn tapes into writing, among them Diana Burke, Harold Green, Lisa Hartfelder and Michele Auzenne, and Li-Ying Wu helped with the index. Our thanks to all. Some of the travel costs associated with the book were paid for by a University Research Institute Grant from the University of Texas, El Paso and a minigrant from New Mexico State University, and New Mexico State University enabled Reed to use Crimson Scholar research assistants to do some of the transcribing. Raja Rao and Bapsi Sidhwa's visits to El Paso with some financial assistance from UTEP helped complete their interviews. The creative writing program of the University of Texas, El Paso enabled us to continue our dialogues with Anaya and Hinojosa which were conducted in Albuquerque and Austin respectively. We also interviewed Sandra Cisneros on her visit to UTEP. Finally, we need to thank the journals where earlier versions of some of these interviews appeared— *Transition*, *The Review of Contemporary Fiction*, *Chelsea*, and *Puerto del Sol*— for permission to reprint.

Interviews with Writers of the Post-Colonial World

# Introduction

The single most important development in literature written in English over the past century has been its increasingly international—indeed, global—nature. Once the language of a few million people on a small island on the edge of Europe, English is now spoken and written on every continent and is an important language inside at least one-quarter of the world's one hundred sixty countries. As English has become an important international language, it has also become an important international literary language. Significant writing in English is now being done all over the world, not just in North America and the British Isles, but also in the English-speaking countries of the West Indies, including one country in South America, Guyana, and one country in Central America, Belize, in Malta, all over Africa, particularly but not just in Nigeria, Kenya and South Africa, in the South Asian countries of India, Pakistan, and Sri Lanka, in the South-East Asian countries of Malaysia, Singapore, and the Philippines, and across the Pacific, in New Guinea, Samoa, and Fiji as well as in Australia and New Zealand. These "new literatures in English," as they are sometimes called (though some of them are not so new), now threaten to eclipse the older literatures in English in prominence. English recipients of England's most prestigious literary prize, the Booker Prize, are virtually an endangered species, as in recent years the prize has gone to writers from Australia, New Zealand, India, Trinidad, and South Africa. Comparably, in the United States, the hegemony of writers from the mainstream has been sharply challenged in two directions, first from the exciting writing being done by "minority" writers and second from a renewed influx into the United States of talented emigré writers from all over the world, writers from Asia and Africa as well as the Eastern European writers who have given us our last three Nobel Laureates.

A complete history of how English became an international literary language would of course involve a history of how English became an international language, how it has ceased to be just the language of the English.

It is, paradoxically, precisely the English who are responsible for this, who through trade and conquest across many centuries built the most extensive empire the world has ever seen. The sun may now have set on the British Empire, but that Empire, in establishing English as a language of trade, government, and education in that sizable part of the world ruled by the British, helped create what may be a more enduring "empire" of the English language. For though English is an important foreign language in many parts of the world never colonized by the British or the Americans, widespread use of the language for imaginative literature has been restricted to former colonies of Britain and the United States. This process by which English was accepted as a language was a deliberate result of British Imperial policy from the time of Macaulay, as it has been of American policy. Macaulay wanted the Indians to be educated in English precisely to put them in connection with Western civilization, and this means that writing in English often has political connotations and implications, something which we will return to below and which many of the writers we interview have decided positions on.

Thus the precondition for the birth of world writing in English was colonialism, yet with a very few exceptions significant writing in English from the former colonies dates not from the colonial but from the post-colonial period. During the period of colonialism, the dominant voices were writers from the Imperial power writing about the colonial peoples: Kipling and Forster, on a more popular level Rider Haggard and A. Conan Doyle. After independence, to use Salman Rushdie's phrase, "The Empire writes back." It uses the language of the former colonial power, but it speaks in its own independent and quite original voice, often contesting the way it has been represented by the earlier writers. The writing that emerges in this process issues from a remarkably complex combination of cultures, as the post-colonial writers draw on indigenous traditions and languages of their own as well as on the resources of the tradition of writing in English. That complexity has been and continues to be tremendously enabling, as we can see from the explosion of great writing in English from around the world.

What we have done in this book is to interview some of the best writers from the new literatures in English, bringing together writers from former British colonies in Africa, the Caribbean, and the Indian Subcontinent, as well as minority writers from New Zealand and the United States. These writers have a good deal more in common than their diverse countries of origin might indicate, and sketching what they have in common explains something about the situation of these writers as well as about the nature of our approach to them.

First of all, these writers are novelists. They may write in other forms: Chinua Achebe, Zulfikar Ghose, and Sandra Cisneros are poets as well as prose writers; Ngũgĩ wa Thiong'o, Nuruddin Farah, and Rudolfo Anaya have written plays as well as novels; and most of the writers have written essays and criticism. Moreover, some of these writers have branched out into other forms: Witi Ihimaera, for instance, has written an opera. However, all these writers are known primarily for their fiction, and most of them for their novels. We have focused on fiction, not just because the most impressive achievement of the new literatures is to be found in the novel (despite some conspicuous exceptions such as the poetry of Derek Walcott and the plays of Wole Soyinka), but also because the novel is the site of the most complex cultural encounter in the new literatures. The novel is of course a Western form, so it would seem that the spread of the novel to the non-Western world was simply an extension of European culture comparable to the spread of European languages. Macaulay did not envision Indians writing novels in English, but this certainly fits in with his program of Europeanization through the use of the English language. Yet neither the European language nor the European form remains unchanged as it finds new homes around the world, and as theorists of the novel such as Bakhtin have pointed out, one of the characteristics of the novel is its lack of rigid criteria, its comparative formlessness. This makes it easy to adapt to the experience of different cultures and modes of narration. The novel is always novel, always being reinvented anew, and its most spectacular reinventions over the past several decades have come from the non-Western world.

This leads to the second distinguishing feature of the group of writers gathered together here. We have not aimed at an inclusive survey of writing in English from around the world, for we have included no writers from Canada and Australia, and from New Zealand, we have interviewed only the Maori writer Witi Ihimaera. This is not to say that no interesting writing is coming from these countries, but its character is radically different from the writing coming from the former colonies in Asia, Africa and the West Indies, and there are some powerful historical reasons for this. The British Empire was made up of two very different kinds of places: dominions where the majority of the population were European, largely British, settlers; and colonies, where the majority of the population were the people who had always been there. The literature and culture of the dominions understandably demonstrate a much greater degree of continuity with that of Britain. After all, until very recently "Home" in these countries meant Britain, and even though this orientation towards Britain has inevitably weakened across time, the literature and culture of the dominions remain essentially European in form and spirit. In this respect, they closely resemble the United States as English-speaking countries who have left Europe physically but not culturally behind. The New Englands and New Brunswicks of North America find their parallel in the New South Wales and New Zealand of the antipodes, and the literature of all these countries shares a common heritage of exploration and a sense of being on the "frontier" of a great outward wave of European settlement. The critic Peter Alcock, writing about the preconceptions found in early New Zealand literature, has caught this sense nicely with his term "informing the void."

But of course nowhere the British went, bringing their language and art forms as well as their ships and flag, was there really a void. There was always someone there first who spoke a different language, had a different culture, and saw the world rather differently. The literature we are most interested in and concentrate on here is not the writing of the European newcomers but rather that of the descendants of those who were there before the British came. These are the writers who live in the most complex cultural space, inheriting the English language and much more from their former rulers, yet in many cases drawing on their own received forms and languages as well. These are the post-colonial writers who now make up an "Empire" that is "writing back." But this is not always a distinction between European invaders and non-Europeans: if the United States is the first of the "dominions," Ireland is surely the first of the colonies. Seven hundred years of colonization changed Ireland but never subdued it, and the rich literature of the Irish Literary Revival is in important respects a prototype for the explosion of writing in countries formerly colonized by the British around the world. Irish literature today is at a different moment of its historical evolution, but were one able to travel back in time, interviews with James Joyce and Flann O'Brien would have fit in perfectly with the concept of this book.

However, it is important to realize that this distinction between informing the void and the empire writing back is not a rigid distinction between two given sets of countries. The dominions and the United States are places where the newcomers eventually attained an overwhelming preponderance over the indigenous population; the colonies are where the newcomers gained political control but never overwhelmed the inhabitants. Nonetheless, there are writers from indigenous and colonized peoples in all the former dominions and in the United States as well as in the former colonies of Asia, Africa and the West Indies. These writers are represented in this collection by the Maori writer Witi Ihimaera and three Chicano writers, Rudolfo Anaya, Rolando Hinojosa, and Sandra Cisneros. In the United States, these writers are sometimes called ethnic or, more recently, minority writers and though that is a term we will revisit later, these writers ought to be seen as having important elements in common with writers in English from around the world, not just considered an unusual aspect of American or New Zealand literature. What they share with the other writers interviewed here is precisely their multilinguality and their multiculturalism. They, too, draw on a complex mixture of European and non-European cultural traditions and forms; and they, too, come to English with another language—in Ihimaera's case, Maori; in the case of the Chicano writers, Spanish. They share the experience of a form of colonialism, the colonialism of a dominant language and a dominant culture, and the experience of the breaking of that colonialism, which is something both Sandra Cisneros and Rudolfo Anaya speak to. They too represent the empire writing back. These commonalities, which we explore in the interviews that follow, seem too important to let national differences prevent us from seeing and investigating, more important than the fact that the Maoris and the Chicanos— unlike the other writers—represent a "nonwhite" minority population in largely white countries. What does it mean to write in a language that is not one's own? What does it mean to have more than one language to write in? How does this affect one's approach to English? These questions and a related set of questions about culture are questions that all these writers—

no matter what part of the English-speaking world they are from—have had to grapple with.

Given the fact of the empire writing back, given the explosion of post-colonial writing in virtually every part of the world, what approach should we use in studying this rich and complex literature? Everyone we interviewed had an answer—some explicit, some implicit—to this question, but the variety of answers indicates no clear consensus. Nor is there any consensus on this matter among the scholars and critics of the new literatures, and in fact controversy has raged, particularly in the study of African literature, over the proper critical approach. This does not mean that every scholar of the new literatures has felt the need to enter the fray; on the contrary, many scholars—particularly the generation that was the first to study this literature—have concentrated on explicating and promoting the literature, making sure it won the hearing it deserved. In contrast, the next generation of critics of the new literatures have felt it essential to develop theoretical approaches, and this has sometimes taken precedence over a thorough acquaintance with the literature. Here, as elsewhere, an Aristotelian mean combining the initial scholars' thorough knowledge with the more recent critics' theoretical sophistication ought to be the goal and has been the goal we have aimed at in these interviews. Our point of departure has been an interest in the work of the writers themselves, and our concern in the interviews that follow was always to let the writers themselves speak, to let their voices come through. Nonetheless, we are also concerned with the question of formulating an adequate theoretical model of these new literatures; while not highlighting theoretical issues in the interviews, nonetheless the questions we ask and the way we have organized the collection imply a position on this important issue.

The controversy in African literature has centered on the question of whether—and to what extent—European critical criteria need to be modified in order to study African literature. The initial generation of critics, largely Western and all inevitably trained in the methods of Western criticism, tended to posit that the methods that worked for other literatures would work for the new literature emerging from Africa in English and other European languages as well. It was initially the African writers themselves who contested this. Chinua Achebe labelled such critics "colonialist critics," and reacting particularly against the assumption that one "universal" approach should be used, Achebe wrote that "I should like to see the word *universal* banned altogether from discussions of African literature until such a time as people cease to use it as a synonym for the narrow, self-serving parochialism of Europe, until their horizon extends to include all the world" (11). A later generation of critics, of whom the Nigerian Chinweizu is perhaps the best known, generalized Achebe's insights into a critical method, arguing that the approach to African literature must be "afrocentric," not "eurocentric," that it must be based on a full understanding of the cultural context of African literature. That is hard to disagree with, at least taken that far, but Chinweizu carried it a stage further, attacking many of the modern African writers for their "euromodernism," for their failure to be sufficiently African. Hence, while Achebe modestly called for the decolonization of the criticism of African writing, Chinweizu called for the decolonization of African literature, arguing that it was still in thrall to European forms. Chinweizu's particular object of attack has been the Nigerian playwright, Wole Soyinka, and when Soyinka was the first African to win the Nobel Prize in 1987, Chinweizu insisted that Soyinka and the Nobel Prize deserved each other, that Soyinka's winning the Nobel just showed how European in spirit his work really was. Leaving aside the details of whether Soyinka is as "eurocentric" as Chinweizu insists (Soyinka has been eloquent in his own defense), it is obvious that Chinweizu has seen something, which is that contemporary African writing in European languages is indebted to the European forms and languages in which it is expressed. That does not make it "eurocentric" as much as—in our terms—multicultural, combining aspects of African and European culture in a complex mix and synthesis. An "afrocentric" criticism must feel uncomfortable with this multiculturalism, preferring something closer to a uniculturally African mode of cultural expression. But to be truly afrocentric, one should go back to writing in African languages, not writing in a European language such as English, and it has been the Kenyan writer Ngũgĩ wa Thiong'o—not Chinweizu—who has carried this to its logical conclusion. Ngũgĩ, as we discuss in our interview with him, is one of the great novelists in English of our time but he has turned back to his own Gĩkũyũ (or Kikuyu) for his recent novels. Ngũgĩ's choice has stirred widespread debate, not just in Africa, as a number of the interviews show, because his choice is one that could be made by many of the other writers interviewed here.

So one response to post-colonial literatures has been this repudiation of European critical norms (and sometimes languages) which in the African context is called afrocentrism. If one wanted a general term for this position, one could call it localism, which we would define as the belief in using critical criteria derived from the region or locale itself to understand and judge the literature of that region. Such an approach invariably stresses the Africanness of African literature in English, the Indianness of Indian literature in English, the ways in which the new literary expression reflects the culture that existed before the arrival of the colonial powers. Now, no one can argue against the localist critique of eurocentric "universalism," and there can be no dispute both that contextually informed criticism is important and that indigenous cultural forms often have a strong influence on post-colonial cultural expression. Yet localism—whether afrocentric or whatever—hardly generates a full theory of the post-colonial situation. This can be seen in the way Chinweizu has to argue with African writers, to chastise them for not fitting his model. When a criticism becomes prescriptive, that is a sign that there is something out there it can not quite make sense of and feels uncomfortable with. Chinweizu can see the multiculturalism of contemporary African literature, but he cannot accept it.

One problem with any version of localism is defining the locale which is seen to be decisive. The noted American Marxist literary critic Fredric Jameson, in his widely cited essay "Third-World Literature in an Era of Multinational Capitalism," urges what is essentially a localist methodology, arguing that the central concern of contemporary Third World literature has been the nation: "All third-world texts are necessarily, I want to argue, allegorical, and in a very specific way: they are to be read as what I will call *national allegories*. . . . Third-world texts, even those which are seemingly private and invested with a properly libidinal dynamic—necessarily project a political dimension in the form of national allegory" (69). Jameson suggests therefore that if these works are to be read correctly, they need to be read with this political background in mind, which is to say by a reader informed about these contexts and subtexts. As the example of Jameson and Ngũgĩ alike should show, localist approaches tend to be political, in the sense that they valorize the struggle against the colonial power as the defining moment of post-colonial culture. However, though no one could dispute the thorough politicality of much post-colonial writing, defining the nation as the determining locale is fraught with problems, and in this respect one could criticize such an approach in fact for its "eurocentrism," for its mechanical application of a nation-centered model of literature derived from Europe to the very different post-colonial situation.

Any nation-centered model of writing in English today is going to come into conflict with two important features of the post-colonial situation: first, the arbitrariness and in many places the fragility of the post-colonial states, the fact that they are not nation-states in the older European sense; and second, the migrations and displacements created both by colonialism and by what has taken its place. Both of these factors have shaped the lives and work of all of the writers interviewed here and help indicate what an appropriate methodology for the study of those writers might be. The first is exemplified most fully in Africa, the second in the Caribbean, but both come into play all over the world. The first point should be relatively obvious. E. D. Hirsch makes the claim in *Cultural Literacy: What Every American Needs to Know* that "one of the most important features of the modern world" is "the linguistically homogeneous populations of the industrial nations" (71), and he supports this claim by the example of the abrupt change at the border between France and Italy from a French-speaking population to an Italian-speaking one. And he considers the link between language, nationhood and statehood to be crucial: a viable nation-state for Hirsch is where the people share a language and a culture as well as live under a shared government. But this state of affairs simply does not obtain for most of the non-Western world. (It does not obtain for much of Europe either, as one could see from substituting other neighbors of France such as Spain, Switzerland and Belgium for the neighbor of France Hirsch chooses, and if it clearly obtained in the United States, Hirsch would not have to make the arguments he does in *Cultural Literacy*.) In most of the non-Western world, the original nations or peoples who may have been self-governing and cohesive entities before the arrival of the colonial powers were shoved together into colonies by the Europeans without much regard for the preexisting political arrangements or the wishes of the inhabitants, and these colonies have provided the basis for the subsequent post-colonial countries that followed. Mount Kilimanjaro is in Tanzania today, not in

Kenya, largely because Queen Victoria thought her cousin Kaiser Wilhelm ought to have a mountain in his colony, then German East Africa, and she could afford to give him one since she would still have Mount Kenya in her colony, Kenya.

Our earlier contrast between "minority writers" in New Zealand and the United States and the writers from Africa, Asia and the Caribbean is therefore far from absolute, for writers from the post-colonial countries are often also minorities, members of groups sharply distinct from and often at odds with the majority or plurality population of the countries in which they live. There are only a few post-colonial countries where a single language and people make up the preponderance of the population. This situation has impinged on the life and work of all the writers included in this book, most obviously and tragically on the life and work of Chinua Achebe: Achebe's Igbo (or Ibo) people were one of the African nations who tried to secede from the artificial state Nigeria, seeking to create their own nation of Biafra. Their attempt was brutally crushed, and the Biafran experience served as a warning for the rest of Africa not to try to undo the map-making of the colonial powers. Kenya's borders were obviously drawn with no consideration for the people who lived there, and though it is one of the few countries in Africa with an African language, Swahili, as the official language, Ngũgĩ does not write in Swahili but instead in his own language Gĩkũyũ. Even where a country has a homogenous population that shares a language, as in Somalia, the area of the state may diverge widely and tragically from the area in which the people live. Large numbers of Somalis live in Ethiopia and Kenya as well as in Somalia, and this is an important theme in the work of the Somali writer Nuruddin Farah, brought up in the Somali-speaking part of Ethiopia. So the original nation of the precolonial culture may not be— almost inevitably is not—the reconstituted state of the post-colonial culture, and this has profound consequences for a "localist" criticism. If we need to understand Achebe's cultural context to understand his work, what is that context? Is it an Igbo context, for Igbo is his mother tongue? Or is it a Nigerian context, for Nigeria is the country in which he lives? If the answer—as we think it is—is both, then we must speak of formative contexts, not *the* formative context, and there is no reason for Achebe's Western education, commitment to the heritage of literature in English, and residence abroad not to be other, crucial formative contexts. Localism then becomes "multilocalism," which is something else entirely.

The other thing the colonial powers did was to move lots of people around, and this is another reason why our distinction between the colonies made up of the indigenous inhabitants and the dominions made up of settlers needs refining. Virtually the entire indigenous population of the Caribbean was destroyed in the centuries following European contact, and the islands and coastlands were repopulated, first with slaves brought from Africa and then with indentured workers brought from Asia, preeminently from India. Indians constitute 32 percent of the population of Trinidad and 57 percent of the population of Guyana. This is a little known but important fact about the Caribbean that, as one can see from our interviews with the Trinidadian and East Indian writer Sam Selvon as well as with the Guyanese writer Roy Heath, has had a real impact on the literature of the area. The British encouraged Indian settlement not just in Trinidad and Guyana but also in East and South Africa, in Malaya, in Fiji, which means that there is an Indian diaspora created by colonialism all over the world. This process of migration did not end with the end of colonialism; as a result of the political and economic problems the new states of the nonWestern world experienced after independence, the former colonial powers are seeing an influx of immigrants from their former colonies. So Britain now has a large Asian and West Indian population, and the very France Hirsch describes as a cohesive nation-state now has a large black African and North African population from its former colonies. Though we tend to ignore and be made uncomfortable by such parallels, the United States is certainly not isolated from any of these developments either: the Chicano or Mexican-American population of the Southwest resulted from the cultural and racial fusion of the Spanish and Indian populations that created Mexico, and that population moved north over the centuries for a complex mixture of political and economic reasons. And our other minority populations—though not directly represented in this collection—have been created by comparable historical forces.

All of these factors can be seen at work in the lives as well as in the work of the writers interviewed here. Many of them are themselves migrants or immigrants, permanently resident in Britain or the United States or moving back and forth between the West and their native countries. Many of them are also members of communities sharply divergent from the majority population of their countries. And all of these historical factors make it extremely problematic to fix on a single aspect of their cultural make-up as decisive.

Our sense is therefore that these writers cannot be understood or placed exclusively in a narrow regional or local focus. This is reflected, of course, in the organization of this collection, in which we have interviewed writers from every continent and from many different countries in each continent. We feel—and we hope that the interviews show—that these writers have a good deal in common. They have a common heritage of colonialism and post-colonialism, a common heritage of multilingualism and multiculturalism, a common heritage of displacement and migration. What this means is that it is much more illuminating to study these writers together than it is to study them in isolation. The study of distinct national literatures may work well enough in a European context, but it does not make much sense of the post-colonial world. What we need instead to make sense of the richness of literature in English from around the world today is a comparative approach. Comparative literature is customarily taken to be the study of literature in different languages, but what we need to develop today is comparative literature within English, studying and comparing the different literatures in English, looking both for their similarities and commonalities but also for their differences. This is why we have brought together these writers from around the world together in one book: their lives cross borders and their work does as well, so we need to cross borders freely as well if we are to understand their work.

It is important, therefore, to realize just how large a conceptual revolution is needed in order to make sense of this literature. Most of our ways of studying literature are based on the nation, on a sense of a single, cohesive national literary tradition: we study English literature, the literature of the English, or French literature, the literature of the French. This assumption that literature in a given language and the literature of a given nation are compatible and readily combinable ways of studying literature breaks down in the face of the multilinguality of so many countries in the world and the global reach of writing in a number of European languages, French, Spanish, and Portuguese as well as English.

George Steiner has gone so far as to argue in *Extraterritorial* that writers such as Faulkner who are "housed" in a given region and locality may well be the last of their type, that the great writing not just of the present but also of the future will be multilingual and extraterritorial, fitting neither into the literature of a single country nor the literature of a single language. And though his privileged examples come from the great European modernists such as Joyce and Kafka to the later generation of Borges, Nabokov and Beckett, his discussion of these writers remains applicable to the post-colonial writers we have focused on here. Joyce remains a central figure for many of the post-colonial writers in English because of the way he comes to the English tradition as an outsider and bends the English language to fit his Irish subject matter and culture. Stephen's conversation with the dean of studies of his college in *A Portrait of the Artist as a Young Man* about the meaning of the word tundish leads him at first to some pessimistic thoughts about his ability to control and master the English language:

> —The language in which we are speaking is his before it is mine. How different are the words *home, Christ, ale, master,* on his lips and on mine! I cannot speak or write these words without unrest of spirit. His language, so familiar and so foreign, will always be for me an acquired speech. I have not made or accepted its words. My voice holds them at bay. My soul frets in the shadow of his language.                                    (189)

And this passage bears a remarkable resemblance to a passage Steiner quotes from Kafka's diaries in which he is reflecting on the difference between his apprehension of German, as a trilingual German, Czech and Yiddish speaker living in the trilingual society of Prague, and that of a typical German speaker:

> Yesterday it occurred to me that I did not always love my mother as she deserved and as I could, only because the German language prevented it. The Jewish mother is no "Mutter," to call her "Mutter" makes her a little comic. . . . For the Jew, "Mutter" is specifically German. . . . The Jewish woman who is called "Mutter" therefore becomes not only comic but strange.                                                                        (16)

Nor should this resemblance occasion any surprise, as Kafka and Joyce were writers whose lives are closely parallel (and closely parallel to contemporary post-colonial writers), both citizens of an empire in a state of decay whose native countries became independent in their own lifetimes. But the fact that Stephen feels that it is not his language ultimately gives him a sense of freedom from convention and a sense of power over the language. As he reflects towards the end of *A Portrait*,

> 13 April: That tundish has been on my mind for a long time. I looked it up and find it English and good old blunt English too. Damn the dean of studies and his funnel! What did he come here for to teach us his own language or to learn it from us? Damn him one way or the other!    (251)

Here, his sense that English was the dean of studies's language—not his—is enabling, not disabling. This discovery by the young Stephen Dedalus presumably echoes the discovery by his creator, James Joyce, that his outsider status was in fact a powerful position from which to write. Comparable passages from the writings of many post-colonial writers could be found. V. S. Naipaul echoes Joyce when he reflects in *The Overcrowded Barracoon* that "the English language was mine; the tradition was not."

Steiner's point is that it is the ability of writers from outside England to draw on other languages which is crucial in their ability to transform the language and the literary forms. Flann O'Brien made the same point in a letter to Sean O'Casey:

> I agree absolutely with you when you say that the Irish language is essential, particularly for any sort of literary worker. It supplies that unknown quantity in us that enables us to transform the English language—and this seems to hold good for people who know little or no Irish, like Joyce.                                          (qtd. in Clissman 238)

Achebe echoes O'Brien in a number of his critical essays defending the African use of English as a creative medium:

> Most African writers write out of an African experience and of commitment to an African destiny. For them that destiny does not include a future European identity for which the present is but an apprenticeship. And let no one be fooled by the fact that we may write in English, for we intend to do unheard of things with it. Already some people are getting worried.                                                         (9)

Certainly part of the reason for the vitality of contemporary world writing in English can be connected to its multilinguality, to the power it gains from these "multilingual imaginings," to use Steiner's phrase, and the multilingualism of these writers is one of our central concerns in the interviews. Yet the stress Achebe places here on African experience shows that a focus just on multilingualism is insufficient, for as Achebe realizes, it is the different culture behind him as well as the different language that accounts for his productive difference from the English tradition.

Now, for some reason no one has connected Steiner's work on the multilingual European writers to non-Western writing in English, possibly because of his stress on the European tradition and on a kind of cosmopolitanism that few if any of the non-Western writers aspire to. These writers are, after all, in many cases as "housed" in a locality as Faulkner; it is just that the locality in which they are housed is itself multilingual and multicultural. But the French theorists Gilles Deleuze and Felix Guattari in their discussion of Kafka seize on exactly the same aspect of Kafka's achievement, and the terms of their discussion—remarkably close to Steiner's though perhaps more attuned to the cultural as well as the purely linguistic aspects of his situation—have had a growing influence and resonance in the critical discussions about post-colonial writing.

Deleuze and Guattari, like their compatriot Jacques Derrida, have a marvellous gift for introducing terms that catch on. Their chapter "What is a Minor Literature?" in *Kafka: Toward a Minor Literature*, introduces two that are particularly relevant to our discussion, deterritorialization and the concept of minor literature. By deterritorialization, they mean something very close to Steiner's "extraterritoriality," but what they mean by "minor literature" needs more careful definition. The distinction is sometimes made between major and minor languages, and this has essentially to do with the size of the populations that speak them: hence, English, German and French would be major European languages, Dutch, Danish, Slovenian would be minor. But Deleuze and Guattari mean something quite different; as they say, "A minor literature does not come from a minor language; it is rather that which a minority constructs with a major language" (16). So Kafka, as a Jewish resident of Prague, writes from a very different position than, say, his contemporary Thomas Mann, and a writer in such a "minor" position as Kafka's must challenge and contest the established literature of that language. Deleuze and Guattari insist that in minor literatures in this sense, "everything in them is political" (17). The "cramped space [of a minor lit-

erature] forces each individual intrigue to connect immediately to politics."
This way of putting it returns us to Jameson's insistence on the politicality
of non-Western literature without Jameson's limiting insistence on that politics being the politics of the national situation. The writing of minorities
may or may not extend its political concerns to the national situation; it
may instead restrict its political concerns to the situation of the minority
itself. And this formulation of Deleuze and Guattari seems remarkably appropriate for the work of many post-colonial writers.

This appropriateness has led a number of critics to extend their work to
the post-colonial world, most notably in a collection of essays edited by
Abdul JanMohamed and David Lloyd, *The Nature and Context of Minority
Discourse*. Here, the concept of minor literature is extended to writing from
the post-colonial world and writing by minority populations within the
"metropolitan" countries. An extension of Deleuze and Guattari in this way
does help define the coherence of our project here in several attractive ways.
First, when critics consider writing from many different countries and situations together, one tendency—as indeed JanMohamed and Lloyd remark
in their introduction—is to ask, what do all of these different literatures
have in common? After all, they do not descend from a common root as one
could say the European literatures do. What they have in common in a sense
is the condition they are trying to avoid, the condition of dominance by the
colonizing center. But that condition of "writing back," of reacting against
a colonizing center, does provide an important element of commonality. As
JanMohamed and Lloyd say, "Cultures designated as minorities have certain
shared experiences by virtue of their similar antagonistic relationship to the
dominant culture, which seeks to marginalize them all" (1). These non-
Western writers may not have a specific cultural background of their own
in common, but they have a situation in common, a situation of marginality
and politicality. The second advantage the work of Deleuze and Guattari
would bring to a consideration of these new literatures is that the language
of "minor literature" enables us to see a common element between the minority writers from countries such as the United States and New Zealand
and the literature of Asia and Africa written in English: they are not all the
literature of demographic minorities, for the population of India alone is
over three times that of the United States and Britain combined. But they
can be seen to be minor literature in the sense that they are writing in some

respects against the grain and against the conventions of mainstream Anglo-American writing. This is surely part of their power, just as it was for Joyce or Kafka.

That said, there are some losses as well as gains from accepting the entire thrust of the minor literature argument. First, though Deleuze and Guattari work energetically to reverse the normal evaluation of the terms major and minor, the negative associations of minor with lesser inevitably remain. We guarantee that the writers interviewed here would not welcome being told that they were "minor writers" or part of a minor literature, no matter how thoroughly one explained the concept, and their objections would not be irrelevant. The perspective they would be justifiably objecting to can be illustrated by the opening of Fredric Jameson's essay, where he claims that it is "peculiarly self-defeating because it borrows the weapons of the adversary" to try "to prove that these texts are as 'great' as those of the canon itself." He goes on to say that "the third-world novel will not offer the satisfactions of Proust or Joyce" (65). Of course, the "third-world novel" will not offer the satisfactions of Proust or Joyce. No one but Proust or Joyce offers the satisfactions of Proust or Joyce, though it should be clear enough that Joyce is a good deal closer in spirit to these writers than Proust. But we see no reason why this literature must be considered minor or permanently outside the canon. Jameson then goes on to compare this question of canonicity to the question of whether Dashiell Hammett "is really as great as Dostoyevsky," but this is an extremely misleading comparison. The distinction between "high" and popular Western literature is very different from a distinction between Western and non-Western literature. One of the great debates in the American academy today is over the "canon," and it is always assumed that these writers from around the world are part of the challenge to the canon and to the very possibility of a canon. Our sense, in contrast, is that they are part of a challenge to a particular canon but not to canonicity itself simply because they are rapidly constituting a new canon. By now, if there is major contemporary literature in English, it is written by those who would be considered minor in Deleuze and Guattari's terms. The question of evaluation may be less important here than the question of tradition. The term minor literature implies a certain stability in the relation between major and minor, but it is our sense that what we are seeing is a real shift of energy and centrality away from the traditional centers. What happens when the margin becomes the new center? When the minor becomes major? For even if the power of these writers lies to some extent in how they write against the grain, nonetheless because of that power, they are inaugurating traditions and being imitated in turn. The term minor assumes a continuing status of marginality and therefore does not seem sufficiently attuned to the possibility of change, sufficiently historical. The very centers against which these writers are seen to be marginal were themselves marginal once and may in turn be "re-marginalized" by the globalization of writing in English.

A later work by Deleuze and Guattari has been less quickly absorbed into discussions of non-Western literature but has in it a concept that is particularly appropriate for the peregrinations of the writers we interview here. *A Thousand Plateaus* is a treatise on what they call nomadology, and nomadology—though an elusive concept—is their attempt to find a way of talking about the migratory nature of human culture. Most of our concepts for mapping literature, in as much as they depend on the concept of the national literature, basically depend on writers staying put, staying in one place. That is one thing writers historically have not done and the postcolonial writers we are concerned with here have not done at all. Nuruddin Farah, for instance, grew up in Somalia and the Somali-speaking part of Ethopia; he went to college in India which is where he was living when his first novel was published. He subsequently returned to Somalia, left a political exile, and has subsequently lived in Nigeria, the Gambia, the Sudan, and Uganda in Africa, in Germany and Italy in Europe, and in the United States. When we interviewed him, he was on his way from the United States to the Sudan by way of Britain and Germany; our paths crossed briefly in London. Our older localist concepts will not make much sense of a writer like Farah, and nomadology would seem to have some promise.

But of course it would be easy to imagine what Chinweizu would say about most of the attempts to apply concepts from contemporary theory to non-Western writing in English. He would say that all of this is simply one more manifestation of eurocentrism. Even though he would agree with Jameson and Deleuze and Guattari at least on the inherent politicality of this work, he would wonder why the source of concepts is again Europe, why critics once again turn to Europe for ideas and approaches. And he would have a valid point, one well worth keeping in mind while reading the interviews that follow. If Chinweizu's version of localism is incomplete because it insists on the relevance of only the local context or originating culture of these writers, other more theoretical approaches may well err in the other direction, insisting only on the nomadic, international, "deterritorialized" elements of their work. Some of these writers have stayed quite close to their "roots," others have moved very far from them. The closer the writer has stayed to his or her point of origin, the more appropriate a variety of localism will be; the further he or she has moved, the more appropriate the language of European critical theory is likely to be. Again this is not without precedent: James Joyce and Samuel Beckett "deterritorialized" themselves and found artistic sustenance on the European continent but J. M. Synge and Flann O'Brien "reterritorialized" themselves and made greater use of local Irish traditions. A comparable distinction runs throughout all of the new literatures, with writers like Zulfikar Ghose, Nuruddin Farah, and others writing in a way that seems close to the language of "deterritorialization" and "nomadology" (no matter what they might think of such jargon), while others such as Ngũgĩ, Raja Rao and Witi Ihimaera writing in ways that resist such descriptions. We would like to think that the proper response of critics to this complex and confusing situation is reflected in the interviews that follow: we think the appropriate methodology is an informed eclecticism that takes its guidance from the writing itself and from the writers themselves. What we need to be able to do is not overwhelm these works and writers with our own perspectives but somehow to listen patiently and carefully to what they have to tell us.

It seems important *now* more than ever, as critics from the left and right squabble over the merits of the literary production in English by writers who are multilingual and multicultural, that we let these writers speak for themselves about their work, their politics and the traditions—both Western and non-Western—that made them who they are. Scholars and teachers can then make up their own minds about which writers they wish to include when they teach and study a new and developing multicultural literature. Recently, the media has been flooded by conservative complaints about the inclusion of non-Western and minority writers in the curriculum in an effort at teaching multiculturalism. This is ironic given how all the writers we have interviewed inevitably speak about how a Western canon helped to shape their writing. It can be argued that ascribing a political agenda to all Third World writers has caused their work to be misunderstood. Letting the writers speak for the value of their work can show how exaggerated are the complaints of the traditionalists that a radical left is engaged in a conspiratorial takeover of the hearts and minds of young Americans by replacing tried and true classics with untried Third World material of considerably less significance.

We believe that presenting this collection of interviews as "archival" material to be consulted by those who may wish to develop theoretical/political paradigms as well as those who may just turn to them for interest is a useful endeavor in expanding the horizons of literary study. It is not "mere affirmation of achievement" that causes us to present these interviews largely unmediated by our own theoretical perspectives but the fact that each one of the writers has his or her own theoretical perspective (though as in the case of Zulfikar Ghose or Anita Desai this can take the form of a desire to avoid overly theoretical or scholarly interpretation).

What all of these writers seem to be asking for is to be evaluated within their particular cross-cultural traditions. As Ngũgĩ talks about a turn to orature, Anita Desai asks to be seen in the particular cross-cultural context of Urdu literature and European traditions that made up the colonial India she grew up in, while Zulfikar Ghose would prefer to be evaluated according to modernist and postmodernist critical values. Relevant here is Henry Louis Gates' caution, "No critical theory—be it Marxist, feminist, poststructuralist, Kwame Nkrumah's 'consciencism' or whatever—escapes the specificity of value and ideology, no matter how mediated these may be. To attempt to appropriate our own discourses by using Western critical theory uncritically is to substitute one mode of neocolonialism for another" (87). Each of the writers included in this volume would like to be seen within his or her specific "contexts of situation" and to be read by a criticism that stems from those contexts.

Doing this book of interviews for us has been an experience of learning to listen to and learning to learn from their different voices, and we hope the same will be true for its readers. There is a world of exciting writing being done in English around the world, and this collection will have served its purpose if its readers turn (or return) to that body of writing with new enthusiasm and new knowledge.

## *Works Cited*

Achebe, Chinua. *Morning Yet on Creation Day.* 1975; rpt. Garden City: Anchor, 1976.

Alcock, Peter C. M. "Informing the Void: Initial Cultural Displacement in New Zealand Writers." *Journal of Commonwealth Literature* 6, No. 1 (1971): 84–102.

Chinweizu, Onwuchekwa Jemie & Ihechukwu Madubuike. *Toward the Decolonization of African Literature.* 1980; rpt. Washington: Howard University Press, 1983.

Clissmann, Anne. *Flann O'Brien: A Critical Introduction to His Writings.* Dublin, 1975.

Deleuze, Gilles & Felix Guattari. *Kafka: Toward a Minor Literature.* Trans. Dana Polen. Minneapolis: University of Minnesota Press, 1986.

———. *A Thousand Plateaus: Capitalism and Schizophrenia.* Trans. Brian Massumi. Minneapolis: University of Minnesota Press, 1987.

Gates, Henry Louis, Jr. "Authority, (White) Power, and the (Black) Critic: It's All Greek to Me." In *The Nature and Context of Minority Discourse.* Eds. Abdul R. JanMohamed & David Lloyd. New York: Oxford University Prss, 1990. 72–101.

Hirsch, E. D. *Cultural Literacy: What Every American Needs to Know.* Boston: Houghton Mifflin, 1987.

Jameson, Fredric. "Third-World Literature in the Era of Multinational Capitalism." *Social Text* 15 (Fall 1986): 65–88.

JanMohamed, Abdul R. & David Lloyd, eds. *The Nature and Context of Minority Discourse.* New York: Oxford University Press, 1990.

Joyce, James. *A Portrait of the Artist as a Young Man.* 1916; rpt. New York: Viking, 1964.

Naipaul, V. S. *The Overcrowded Barracoon.* London: André Deutsch, 1971.

Ngũgĩ wa Thiong'o. *Decolonising the Mind: The Politics of Language in African Literature.* London: James Currey, 1986.

Rushdie, Salman. "The Empire Writes Back with a Vengeance." *The Times [of London]* (3 July 1982): 8.

Steiner, George. *Extraterritorial: Papers on Literature and the Language Revolution.* New York: Atheneum, 1971.

# Ngũgĩ wa Thiong'o

The Kenyan novelist Ngũgĩ wa Thiong'o, born in 1938, is the chief propo-
nent of African literature in African languages. After a remarkably successful career of writing such English novels as *Weep Not, Child* (1964), *The
River Between* (1965), *A Grain of Wheat* (1967), *Petals of Blood* (1977), and
of creating and translating such politically powerful plays as *The Trial of
Dedan Kĩmathi* (1976) and *I Will Marry When I Want* (1982 translation of
*Ngaahika Ndeenda* produced in 1977 in Gĩkũyũ), Ngũgĩ has abandoned the
English language in favor of Gĩkũyũ, his mother tongue, as the medium of
his creative expression.

In London, in June 1988, at the launching of *Storms of the Heart: An
Anthology of Black Arts and Culture*, Ngũgĩ made a firm restatement of his
personal and literary conviction that African literatures must be written in
African languages. This is a position that Ngũgĩ has held since 1977 and
continues to restate, despite the fact of his exile in England and now in the
United States and the criticism that his reading public is primarily in England. In his *Decolonising the Mind* (1986) he traces the processes through
which he came to this conclusion, notably his reaction to the 1962 "Conference of African Writers of African Expression." This conference had accepted what Achebe had called "the fatalistic logic of the unassailable position of English in our literature" (*Decolonising* 7). Ngũgĩ began to rethink
this acceptance of English across the years, first by calling for the use of
Kenyan languages as the medium of education. With *Caitaani Mũtharabainĩ*
written during his 1978 detention, Ngũgĩ abandoned writing in English as
the medium of his creative expression and began to use Gĩkũyũ. However,
he did translate *Caitaani* as *Devil on the Cross* (1980) himself. With his latest
novel, *Matigari Ma Njirũũngi* (1987), Ngũgĩ has stopped translating his own
work and says, "I have lost interest in the use of the English language."

Ngũgĩ's position has attracted much attention. He summarizes the debate
over his position as follows:

> A debate has been raging around my book *Decolonising the Mind*, which
> deals with the politics of African language literatures. Some participants
> in the debate are clearly in support of the challenge in the book, that
> African writers should stop serving foreign/colonial and neo-colonial lan-
> guages such as French, English and Portuguese, and turn to the develop-
> ment of African languages by writing in them. Other participants in the

debate form a group which feels embarrassed at even the slightest mention of African languages. (*Storms* 225)

In the following interview, Ngũgĩ articulates his conception of the future of African literatures in African languages despite the banning of some of his works in Kenya, the only area where a Gĩkũyũ-speaking audience is likely to be. Yet he also maintains that his position is that of *one* writer committed to *one* position and is by no means an ideology that he wishes to impose on all African writers or, for that matter, all writers from recently independent nations. In this interview Ngũgĩ lays out his position apropos the political and literary questions that have risen as a result of the stand he has taken. And the way the interview moves from the abstract taking of positions to a discussion of Ngũgĩ's own work is true to the spirit of Ngũgĩ's recent work. He is a good deal more interested in discussing political and cultural questions than he is in discussing the nuances of his own works, thinking perhaps that they can speak for themselves. What follows is actually a composite of several interviews over the years, initially with Feroza Jussawalla at Duke University in North Carolina and then later with both editors in London.

**Feroza Jussawalla**: I want to ask you first about the choice of language. Should English be the medium of expression for African writers or, as you have been advocating since 1977, should African writers only write in African languages?

**Ngũgĩ wa Thiong'o**: I believe that it is very important for African writers to use African languages for their creative expression. The situation in Africa is a little absurd when you take into account that the majority of the African people speak African languages and that only a tiny minority speak French or English or Portuguese. This means that when Africans write in these languages, they are basically addressing themselves only to that very tiny minority.

**Reed Dasenbrock**: I don't know if you're aware what an impact you've had with that position. Almost everyone we have interviewed for this book has had a definite, strong response to your position. In some cases, they have brought up your name saying, "Ngũgĩ says we should do this." The West Indian writer, Roy Heath, was saying that your work was a real inspiration to him, in choosing to write more in Creole or nation language in the West Indian situation.

Perhaps we could start with some questions about the implications of that position. You've made it clear that you're going to be doing your own writing in Gĩkũyũ. But what about a black writer in Britain, like some of the other writers in the anthology *Storms of the Heart*, who may be trying to reach people in Britain. What's the language option there?

Ngũgĩ: Individual writers must use whatever language best suits their particular situation. I was thinking more of a collective position. I see what is typically necessary for Africa. Obviously the position of writers will be determined by the audience they want to reach and by the language at their individual and collective disposal. Every situation will vary. I don't expect to see a writer brought up in Britain and who has learned the English language all his life to start learning another language at age forty or fifty and start writing in it. But just as Caribbean writers or Afro-Americans are going more and more to the roots of their own language, the young black writers in Britain will go to the roots of the language as spoken by, say, the black community in Britain. But for African writers, I'm very clear about the necessity of the use of African languages. After all, nearly all African writers have a choice. I can only think of a handful of African writers who could not use an African language and write as well as, if not better than, their contributions in the English language.

This is also true all over the world. Writers write in their own languages for their own communities and nations. I'm not saying anything Dante didn't say. I am embarrassed when I get a very strong, and at times hostile, response to what is so obvious.

R.D.: What do you think of Achebe's new novel, *Anthills of the Savannah*? Were you disappointed that he didn't write it in Igbo?

Ngũgĩ: No, no, no. Mine is a general argument, not a moral judgment on the practice of any individual. As I said, writers will respond to situations according to their own circumstances, but whatever the path taken, it does not alter the general argument that I've been trying to advocate in my book, *Decolonising the Mind*. Ninety percent of the population in Africa today speak only African languages, and we need to reach that 90 percent.

F.J.: Does the banning of your work in Gĩkũyũ change your attitude even a little bit?

**Ngũgĩ**: The basic argument remains whether my book was banned or not. If anything, it strengthens the case for writing in African languages. If there are such strong reactions from the government, then writing in Gĩkũyũ must be doing something which writing in English does not do. Writing in an African language enables me to reach a certain social stratum that was always bypassed by my works in English. Rather than being discouraged by that kind of government reception, I should become more encouraged by the reception of my work in African languages by the people.

**F.J.**: But isn't there a danger that this will cause greater language fragmentation in Africa? Will the Gĩkũyũ be able to communicate with the Igbo, and the Igbos be able to communicate with the Zulus?

**Ngũgĩ**: Why not? It is the actual practice in the world today. Gorbachev and Reagan met in summit meetings, deciding the fate of the world, talking and smiling and trading jokes, even though one used American English and the other Russian. They did not have to abandon either English or Russian; they just had to accept that one spoke Russian and the other English. They were able to find a means of communicating with that fact as the starting point. The truth of the matter is that the vast majority of African people speak different languages today. And therefore the starting point for any writer is that reality, the language spoken by the people. If I am writing for this audience, I have to use the language they use. I persuade them into my vision of Kenya, Africa and the world in the only language that they can understand. We must not forget that many languages in the world comunicate through translations.

**F.J.**: This is essentially the statement you made at the book launch of *Storms of the Heart*, when you said that to achieve decolonization of the mind you need to work in the African context.

**Ngũgĩ**: Yes. The real language that one is looking for is the language of struggle, the language of transformation of our various societies. Eventually, this language can only be found in the actions and feelings and thoughts and experiences of the working people. Therefore to discover that real language of struggle is to find an identity, to identify oneself with the struggles of the working people. When one discovers that real language of struggle, whichever formal language one may be using, whether English or Gĩkũyũ or Swahili or Igbo or Hausa or American or Chinese or Russian, then it will be reflected in one's work.

**F.J.**: I understand that in South Africa, the government is trying to promote local languages and cultures, the Zulu versus the Xhosa, to break down communication in English among the various groups. Isn't there a kind of reversal there, where if the people start speaking in their own languages, they stop communicating with the revolutionary cultures? That seems to suit the government just fine.

**Ngũgĩ**: It doesn't, because speaking one's language does not stop people from communicating with each other. People putting their language first doesn't mean that they don't know or must not know other languages. When the English learn English, it does not stop them from learning French and German and Chinese on top of their national tongue. So in the same way, making African languages primary doesn't prevent Africans from learning other languages of the world. The South African people will learn English, they will learn German, French, and they will speak their national languages, using them according to their circumstances and their needs. I am sure that if the South African people use South Africa's languages to call for the unity of the people against apartheid, the South African government would be the first to ban these books. Already, in terms of cultural resistance, when I've seen South African people singing songs of revolution, they sing them in the different African languages. One of the most famous songs is *Nkosi Sikelel' i Africa*, an anthem composed in Zulu. It is a song which any person who comes from the continent, whether north, south, central, east, west, responds to. The South African regime doesn't like that song and does not encourage it being sung in Soweto or in Johannesburg.

**F.J.**: What are the politics of language specifically in Kenya?

**Ngũgĩ**: English was always a colonial language in the sense that English came with the colonization of Kenya. It was the language used in the schools, it was the language of education and of administration. This is still the case. In Kenya, even today, English is the language of education, of administration, of trade, of commerce, of everything. But Kiswahili is the all-Kenya national language, understood by a large section of each of the nationalities in Kenya. And traditionally each of the nationalities have their own national language, like Gĩkũyũ and so on. Most of us were educated in English. The books we read, the literature we were exposed to was mostly in English. So when it came to writing, it was almost inevitable that we would write in English, unless we were very conscious of the opposite, or unless we were very conscious of the implications of what we were doing. It was easy for people to write in the language of their colonization because it was the language of their conceptualization, the language of education, the language in which they attempted to intellectually grasp the world around them.

I believe that the language issue is a very important key to the decolonization process. What is really happening now is that African thought is imprisoned in foreign languages. African literature and African thought, even at their most radical, even at their most revolutionary, are alienated from the majority. In English, this thought is not available to the majority, it is not vitalized through its communication with the majority, the people.

If you take the Gĩkũyũ-speaking nationalities alone, we have about five million people, but only five percent of that five million people can effectively read, understand, and use the English language. Ninety-five percent have the Gĩkũyũ language as their only means of communication. I know that when I'm writing in Gĩkũyũ, I'm reaching many more people within that nationality than if I wrote in English. But in addition to that, I believe that it is important that such works as I may write in Gĩkũyũ be made available in other *African* languages. Translation among African languages is important; that means that the African languages will be communicating with one another. And if a literature develops from that communication, that literature will be reaching many more readers over all than if we're using only English, French, or Portuguese, as is the case for most African writers today.

F.J.: How about the urban majority, though? Would the urban majority in Africa, in major cities like Nairobi and maybe in various West African cities such as Lagos, be speaking English and the various pidgins? Do you think that would be a relevant medium of communication?

Ngũgĩ: Every language spoken by a people, even when it's borrowed, has its own validity. But in this case, I ask myself why should an African writer go out of his way to be using other people's languages when he or she has his own language? For everyone who speaks pidgin, there are thousands who speak their own languages, and even those who speak pidgin English or other sorts of English nevertheless have their own fully fledged national language to which they have access.

F.J.: I wonder if we could talk about how this complex linguistic situation in Kenya has shaped your own work. Your first few books are all in straight standard English. Then, while you have narrative in standard English in *Petals of Blood*, you begin to incorporate some words and phrases in African languages, in Gīkūyū or in Kiswahili. It seems to me that in *Petals of Blood* you were already in transition towards writing in Gīkūyū.

Ngūgī: *Petals of Blood* was a transitional novel, my last novel in English, but language experimentation was only a small part of this novel. I was writing about peasants and workers and their struggle against colonialism and other forms of foreign domination. This was true not just of *Petals of Blood* but of all my novels. And yet none of the people who formed the subject matter of my novels could possibly read them because the novels were encased in a language to which they had no access. My change from English and towards African languages as a means of my creative writing came in 1976–77 when I worked at the Kamīrīīthū Community Educational Center. Kamīrīīthū is a small rural village, about thirty kilometers from Nairobi. There I was trying to develop a community center to develop resources, skills, and also culture with theatre at the center. I have told the story of that experience in my book, *Detained: A Writer's Diary* and in *Decolonising the Mind*. As we confronted the struggles of the people, we found that we no longer could avoid the issue of language. When you work in a village, you know what language you've got to communicate with. The only way to do theatrical performances in a village, for instance, is to use the language of the people. In this case it was the Gīkūyū language. When the play was successful, it was banned by the government, and I myself was put in political detention for a year. That was 1977–78.

F.J.: Why were you sent to jail? Was it because of *I Will Marry When I Want*?

Ngūgī: They didn't explain anything, but I'm sure it had something to do with the play, *I Will Marry When I Want*, which was scripted together with the peasants from Kamīrīīthū. The play talked about the history of struggle against colonialism, particularly the peasants' history of struggle as led by Dedan Kimathi, the leader of the Kenya Land and Freedom Army Mau Mau. But the play also reflected the social conditions under which they worked after independence. All these factors probably made a neo-colonialist state like Kenya feel uncomfortable about a play by the people, which seemed to be critical of what had been happening since independence.

**F.J.**: Sometimes in your early work, too, there's a sense of "our own people betray us." Did you have the feeling that the people who should have been making the changes you dreamed about, let you down?

**Ngũgĩ**: Oh, yes, of course they let the *people* down. The people expected real economic, political and cultural changes after independence. They didn't expect to continue being producers who produced but did not control that which they produced. They did not want to continue being the people who fed and clothed every other person but themselves. They did not really expect the kind of political repression which, I'm afraid, has come to Kenya, particularly since 1982, with the detention without trial of university lecturers and students, and other people who are deemed to be holding views which are contrary to that of the neo-colonial regime of Moi. And then there have been so many killings by the government! So, for all those reasons, I would say that the people felt let down, but nevertheless, I think the struggle has to continue, and the struggle continues, even up to today.

**F.J.**: Do you see a parallel between the Kenyan and the South African situations? Do you think that despite a change in the Apartheid regime there will still come another period of transition where the people of South Africa will still have to suffer?

**Ngũgĩ**: Well, obviously the two situations are dissimilar, and also similar in the sense that the real powers behind South Africa are the western financial interests from New York, Bonn, Paris, Tokyo, and so on. Those financial powers are still also the powers behind most of the repressive neo-colonial regimes in not only Africa but in the Third World as a whole, in places like South Korea, Marcos's Philippines, El Salvador, Pinochet's Chile, and so on. But despite the fear of a possible neo-colonial outcome, it is *absolutely* the right of the South African people to make their own history, just as it is the right of the Kenyan people to make their own history. And whatever errors, whatever shortcomings, it's still their right to make their history and no foreigners, however generous, however brilliant, or however stupid even, have the right to control the affairs of another people.

**F.J.**: Now that you're a writer living in exile, does your sense of audience change? Are you still trying to reach people in Kenya?

**Ngũgĩ**: I am continuing to attempt to reach the people in Africa. Even my children's stories, the *Njamba Nene* stories, are meant to raise the consciousness of children in Kenya.

**F.J.:** How effectively do you think you can continue inspiring the struggle from overseas?

**Ngũgĩ:** These are the hazards of being in exile. A writer needs his own home and the society around him. To be able to function effectively, a writer needs the inspiration of his own community. I should, for instance, be where the language I use is being spoken. Being away from Kenya has its limitations. But it is also a challenge. One can see some problems much more clearly. In that sense, one can get strength and stamina from the continuous struggle to meet the challenges of exile.

**F.J.:** How does it feel to be writing Gĩkũyũ where there are not many Gĩkũyũ-speaking people around you?

**Ngũgĩ:** As I said, there are always limitations in writing in exile, but the attempt to keep up with the language while being away is a challenge for me as a writer.

**F.J.:** Because Gĩkũyũ itself is changing in its own context, and you're not catching the current idioms?

**Ngũgĩ:** Yes, it is changing, you know, all the time. A writer needs to catch that phrase which is being used in a bar, that phrase which is being used in a restaurant, in a taxi, in the market place, in the shopping center. He needs all that and more. He needs to be in touch with the *feel* of the language, the rhythm, the music and all that. A writer misses all that when he is far away from where the language is located.

**F.J.:** Was writing *Matigari Ma Njirũũngi* very different from writing in English when you used to?

**Ngũgĩ:** Well, it was much more enjoyable. My novels in Gĩkũyũ have a strange irony. The first one, *Caitaani Mũtharabainĩ*, was written in prison and the second in England, so in a way both were written in exile.

**R.D.:** You translated *Devil on the Cross* yourself, but Wangui wa Goro is translating *Matigari*. What differences are there between translating your own work and having it translated by someone else?

**Ngũgĩ:** For me, translating my own work was very difficult.

**F.J.:** Why? Did you find yourself rewriting parts of it?

**Ngũgĩ:** No, when I was translating it, I tended to become impatient, because I had gone over the same material before during the original creation process. And now I was going over the same novel, but just doing the translation. There was no real excitement. But I have also lost interest in the use of the English language. By this I mean that there was a time when I was very fascinated with what I could do with the English language. Make it sing, for instance. The nuances. But not now, in that way. Another frustration is the inability to render the satiric dimensions of the novel in English. Gĩkũyũ readers of *Caitaani* feel that the original was better than the translation was.

**R.D.:** At a number of points you indicated through italics that the words were in English in the original. These are things you can't get in English.

**Ngũgĩ:** Yes, the play on words is difficult to convey in translation. This is because of the three-language situation in Kenya. English is the official language, Swahili is the national lingua franca, as it were. And then there are the nationality languages like Gĩkũyũ, Luo, and so on. By playing with this language situation, you can get another level of meaning through the interaction of all three languages.

**R.D.:** It seemed to me that you did more of that in *Petals of Blood*, where there's a fair amount of Gĩkũyũ and Swahili, than in *Devil on the Cross*, at least in the English translation, where more of it gets translated.

**Ngũgĩ:** The difference is that, in *Petals of Blood*, the characters are speaking English and occasionally using Gĩkũyũ. In *Devil on the Cross*, you get the correct perspective, where the character is actually speaking Gĩkũyũ or another African language, with occasional phrases or words in Kiswahili or in English or French or German or any other language. That's how it would be in the real life of such characters. So you lose that in translation. You would lose that also in my play, which has not been published, *Maitũ Njugĩra (Mother Sing For Me)*, in which I deliberately made use of the three-language situation in Kenya in which different classes use different languages.

**R.D.:** So you have some characters speaking in English and some characters speaking in Kiswahili.

**Ngũgĩ:** Yes. A worker on a settler plantation is in the perfect situation for the use of three languages. The settler would be using the English language. The overseer would be using Swahili. And the different workers from different language groups would use their own languages. So the mediating language would be Kiswahili. That kind of situation is reproduced in *Devil on* *the Cross*, I think, and also on a small scale in *Matigari Ma Njirũũngi*. Most readers of *only* Gĩkũyũ or *only* English would lose the satiric dimensions of the other languages. Of course it's possible to code-switch, but that loses some readers as also the resulting irony.

F.J.: Is *Matigari* available in Gĩkũyũ in Kenya?

Ngũgĩ: The book has not been formally banned, but it was seized by the police. The story goes that the president, Moi, heard people talking about a man called Matigari who was going around the country preaching revolution. He asked for the arrest of that man. The police were going around the country asking for Matigari, but then they came back and told him, "No, he's not a real man, he's only a character in a book." The book came out in October 1986. For four months Moi let "Matigari" roam around the country, preaching revolution. Then he was stopped in February of 1987. The book was seized from all the bookshops in the country.

F.J.: But can the book still circulate?

Ngũgĩ: It is difficult to tell. Three to four thousand copies had been sold by the time it was seized. Whether those three thousand copies are circulating or not is difficult to tell. But there is much borrowing and even copying of books in Kenya, so people probably still borrow and pass along copies.

R.D.: When they banned the book, did they destroy all the copies that were for sale?

Ngũgĩ: They didn't make a formal announcement when it was banned. They just seized the book in all the bookshops. And they went to the warehouse of the publisher and took all the copies in the warehouse. So they won't dare publish the book again. The regime must of course have actually burned the books seized.

R.D.: That didn't happen to *Devil on the Cross*, did it?

Ngũgĩ: No, *Devil on the Cross* went scot-free.

R.D.: What's the difference, do you think? *Devil on the Cross* is just as radical, just as political.

Ngũgĩ: I don't really know, I can only guess. I think what happened is this. *Devil on the Cross* is a very satiric and metaphorical novel. Some of the characters have such outrageous names and behaviors and characteristics, in scenes like when the robbers in the cave are competing for the honor of being the greatest robber, that if they had banned it, then people might be

thinking that the regime identified with the characters who were being sat-
irized, that they were accepting that they were the robbers being depicted
in the book. So I think they were probably embarrassed and silenced by the
nature of the book.

R.D.: Your novels in English were never banned, were they? Was *Petals of
Blood* ever in trouble?

Ngũgĩ: No, but it is discouraged in the schools. In Kenya, they allow *Weep
Not, Child, The River Between*, and *A Grain of Wheat* to be taught in the
schools, but they discourage the teaching of *Petals of Blood, Devil on the
Cross* and subsequent writings. They make a distinction between my first
three novels, which are supposed to be "artistic," and my other novels,
which are supposed to have "abandoned art for politics." That's how some
of the intellectual henchmen of the regime explain it.

F.J.: What do they mean by "abandoned art for politics"? Because they
provoke revolt?

Ngũgĩ: They're saying the first three books are artistic, but the later books
are no longer artistic, just politics.

R.D.: Do you think that if you were still writing in English that your
books wouldn't be banned? Do you think it is because you're writing in
Gĩkũyũ?

Ngũgĩ: It's a combination of factors. It's a question of audience, but it's a
question of the content of the books, obviously, because if the book or
books were praising the regime in power, I'm sure they wouldn't mind it
being written in Gĩkũyũ or Swahili or some of the other African languages.
But if the book is written in the language of the people and is critical of the
existing order and is addressed to and is being received by the peasantry, by
the working people of Kenya, then the government fears that this might give
the people "wrong ideas."

R.D.: Is there a greater tolerance for publication in English because it is
less likely to reach working-class people? Certainly, *Petals of Blood* was as
revolutionary as your later books, yet it's had no difficulty.

Ngũgĩ: Yes, this is true. That's why the language factor is important.
When you're talking of the English language, you're talking about five percent of the population. And of that five percent, probably only one percent
read books. So anything in English is reaching only one percent of the
population. Essentially, this is why the government can tolerate what is

written in English, whereas for them writing in Gĩkũyũ is a bit more dangerous. If I sell a thousand copies of a book in Gĩkũyũ, I know the readership would not be just a thousand. It might be ten thousand, because normally the books would be read by many people. A lot of people line up and say, "I'm next" and "I'm next." It is also read in families and in groups. This is why they are much more fearful of works written in African languages.

R.D.: What about *A Grain of Wheat*? That book seems to be an attack on Kenyatta and on the people who took over in Kenya after independence. It's set on Independence Day, and the man who is going to be celebrated, Mugo, turns out to be the traitor. I have always read that as a kind of allegory about the bourgeoisie in Kenya, that they got the credit for independence but didn't really do the work. It seems to me that Mugo is the figure for Kenyatta there: he took the credit for the struggle, but didn't really engage in it.

Ngũgĩ: It may not have been conscious, but obviously there is an element of Kenyatta in Mugo. By the time I was writing *A Grain of Wheat*, I was already very critical of what was happening in Kenya and saw the seeds of what has now become common knowledge. But in 1966 or 1967, when I wrote the novel, what I was saying was heretical.

R.D.: Is that why you created the character Mugo in the way you did? At least by the end of the novel, I think most readers—at least today—would see a certain kind of equation between Mugo and Kenyatta.

Ngũgĩ: That's correct; there's a parallel.

R.D.: But you have to read the whole book to see that. Did you do that indirectly because you knew that to attack Kenyatta directly at that point would put people off.

Ngũgĩ: No, it wasn't as conscious a criticism of Kenyatta as that, but there were those implications. In the original draft, I ended with a chapter, a simple radio announcement, that the people, the freedom fighters, who had come down from the forest and mountains, had returned to the mountains to continue their fight. Then, in another draft, I changed this to the beginning. I had this statement at the very beginning of the novel, as a radio announcement, so that the whole novel was going to be a kind of an explanation as to why they were returning to the mountains.

R.D.: So you backed away from that a little bit.

Ngũgĩ: Yes, I cut out the radio announcement. I would have had to write many more chapters of the novel to show the connection between their return to the forest and what was happening in Kenya.

**R.D.:** Is that why you did it indirectly?

**Ngũgĩ:** The main body of the novel remained. It was only the radio announcement that I had removed. But nevertheless I did write a small preface which said quite categorically that what the peasantry had fought for had been betrayed. It's still there in the novel. I don't think by 1966–67, when I wrote that, many people were thinking of the betrayal of the peasantry in Kenya. And for that reason, I suppose it was so outrageous, it didn't seem to make an impact, it didn't seem real. It *was* fiction.

**R.D.:** So they just brushed it aside, you think?

**Ngũgĩ:** The novel was just slightly ahead of its time in its critical perceptions of the post-colonial regime in Kenya. Too ahead for the regime to have noticed the implications.

**R.D.:** But if there is this criticism of the status quo already in *A Grain of Wheat*, then how can it be seen with the first two novels as nonpolitical?

**Ngũgĩ:** There are real differences between the early and the later novels. The first novels, although they are political, are not as clear about the class dimensions of the struggle. The connection between the national and the class oppression is clear in *Petals of Blood*, *Devil on the Cross*, and in *Matigari*.

**R.D.:** Both *Petals of Blood* and *Devil on the Cross* also differ from the first three novels because they have less one individual protagonist than a group who functions as a protagonist.

**Ngũgĩ:** Yes, they are based on the collective struggle.

**R.D.:** Here, too, *A Grain of Wheat* seems transitional. I see a critique of leadership working in *A Grain of Wheat*. The novel seems to say, "Don't trust leaders entirely, people need to struggle on their own." Hence the move in the latter novels towards a more collective sense of narrative, a group of characters rather than just one protagonist. So why, in your most recent novel, *Matigari*, has there been this return to a hero or single protagonist?

**Ngũgĩ:** The protagonist in this case is a kind of collective protagonist; he's a collective leader, as it were. The novel opens with an address to the reader, "You see, this, too, is fictitious, the action is pure fiction and the country of the setting is pure fiction. So readers should create their own country and place those actions in the country of their choice." And then he says, "So one is supposed to choose their own time. If you want to place it yesterday or last year or many years ago, you are free to do so." In other words, the reader is invited to choose a time, a place. So there is a collective protagonist who is not really bound by time or space.

**R.D.:** And then the reader is invited to relate that back to his or her experience.

**Ngũgĩ:** To whatever is relevant to what you know. In this case, of course, the Kenyan reader identifies with Matigari. Matigari is asking awkward questions about truth and justice in his country, the kinds of questions which must be on the minds of many Kenyans.

**R.D.:** So the Kenyan government in banning it did something similar to what you were saying they wouldn't want to do with *Devil on the Cross*: they pointed a finger at themselves. They said, "Yes, we recognize this portrait." In banning the book, aren't they recognizing the relevance?

**Ngũgĩ:** Oh, yes, definitely, they supply their own country, time, character, setting, and so on.

**R.D.:** You said, "Do what you want," and they said, "This is about us."

**Ngũgĩ:** Yes. In a sense, the regime's seizure of the book was the first critical reception of the book—no, not the first, the second critical reception. The first one was by the people because they were reading it and talking about it, and they were appropriating it into the oral tradition just like they had earlier done with *Devil on the Cross*. They were reading it in buses once again, were reading in their own homes, in groups, and so on. There was a wide reception of the novel, of the character Matigari. The second reception was that of the government in banning it.

**R.D.:** Do you think they'll ban it when it's published in English?

**Ngũgĩ:** I don't think Heinemann will publish it in Kenya. I think they're publishing only an international edition in English.

**F.J.:** There's been a good deal of attention paid recently to the colonial period in Kenya, through the film of *Out of Africa*. *The River Between* is a direct parallel to *Out of Africa*, in a sense a rewriting of it. What do you think is the cause of the new nostalgia for things colonial that is pervading all our media?

**Ngũgĩ:** I don't see it really as nostalgia. I see this playing a very important role as part and parcel of the ideology of neo-colonialism. Every political and economic system has its own ideology, and I believe the economic system of neo-colonialism also has its ideology. And this ideology is being passed on through works like *Out of Africa*. Karen Blixen was not very different from other settlers. She didn't say, "I hate the African people!" She said, "I love African people." But she loved them the same way that people love their animals, their house, and goods and so on. And the sentiment that's expressed in her work as part of the relationship between, let's say, the settler and the Kenyan people, was one of charity, aid, benevolence, which are in fact some of the sentiments which now tend to govern the neo-colonial relationship between the Third World and Western countries. That's why she becomes much more acceptable, and in some ways, much more relevant today, because she makes this form of neo-colonialism acceptable. For example, Reagan vetoed Congress' call for comprehensive sanctions against South Africa and proclaimed before the entire world that he was doing this to prevent the African people from suffering more. This was despite the fact that these African people themselves were calling for the very same sanctions. A work like *Out of Africa* expresses the ideology that went with Reaganism and Thatcherism.

F.J.: The tradition of imperialist or neo-colonialist writing is something you've set yourself very firmly against. What literary tradition do you see yourself a part of? What kind of literary tradition did you grow up in as a writer, and what kind of literary tradition do you want to be identified with?

Ngũgĩ: Obviously, I'm part of several traditions. One, of course is the peasants, the tradition of storytelling around the fireside and so on.

F.J.: An oral tradition.

Ngũgĩ: Yes, oral tradition, or orature as we call it. Then of course, there's a Western literary tradition, that is a written tradition: Dickens, Balzac, Tolstoy, Dostoevsky, and Faulkner, and others. Of course, one can talk now about a literary tradition that includes Third World writers, like George Lamming, Narayan, and others. So I'm part of that also, but in my recent work, particularly *Matigari Ma Njirũũngi*, I found myself leaning more and more heavily on traditions of orature.

F.J.: I suppose we have all read some Dostoevsky and Tolstoy in translation, and now you want us to read you in translation. Will we lose something there?

Ngũgĩ: Yes, of course, translations always lose something. But I think what is gained is much more than what is lost. In a sense, I could not wait to learn French, and Russian, and German for me to be acquainted with Balzac, to be acquainted with Tolstoy, with Brecht, and with other people who are important to me.

**F.J.**: Do you feel a relationship to Afro-American traditions? Do you draw on the works of Afro-American writers? Do you think they're drawing on yours?

**Ngũgĩ**: Yes, I think they are. But so are we. There's a very vibrant connection between Afro-American traditions in literature and those from many parts of the third world. I know that African literature as a whole has borrowed quite heavily from the Afro-American literary tradition, and I hope vice-versa. Writers like Langston Hughes, Richard Wright, Amiri Baraka and Alice Walker are quite popular in Africa.

**F.J.**: Just to conclude now, can you say what the role of criticism is in the development of Third World literature? What should the critics be doing?

**Ngũgĩ**: The critical and the creative traditions feed on each other. First of all criticism is an integral component of literature. But the critic who contributes to the writers' evaluations, to the assessment of gains and losses, who asks questions—all this contributes to the overall development of literature in any community.

**F.J.**: Now, you're living here in Britain. What do you see as the future of the multicultural British-born generation, West Indian, African, Asian, that we are faced with?

**Ngũgĩ**: I'm sure that they are having, and they're going to have, a very big impact on this society. They've already had a big impact. Their struggles and economic assertion, cultural assertion, political assertion, is definitely part of the overall democratic struggle in this country. The democratic struggle in this country, the struggle of the working people in this country, will never be the same again. So the black presence here can only accelerate, I think, the movement of social revolution.

# Nuruddin Farah

We were fortunate to be able to interview Nuruddin Farah for this book, not just because he is one of Africa's finest writers but also because he is one of the most peripatetic. But this voyaging has not all been self-imposed: Farah has lived in exile for many years, threatened with death if he were to return to his native Somalia by the recently overthrown dictator of Somalia, Siyad Barre. Exile is unfortunately a fact of life for many African writers, but one of the things that distinguishes Farah from other exiled African writers is that he prefers to live in Africa as much as possible, not London, Paris or New York. Yet he is also to be distinguished because his work does not demonstrate the explicit Africanist commitments of language or style of writers such as Ngũgĩ or Achebe, as we discuss in the interview that follows. And this serves well to demonstrate the complexity of the work of Nuruddin Farah, one of the greatest—and most underappreciated—of contemporary African writers.

Born in 1945, Farah has published a half-dozen novels in English. An attempt to write a novel in Somali was quashed by the regime in Somalia; and though Farah has written plays and some essays, he is primarily a writer of full-length works of fiction. Several themes marked his fiction from the very beginning. First, a considerable sympathy towards women and feminist themes. His first novel, *From a Crooked Rib* (1972), is the story of an illiterate woman from the countryside experiencing oppression and sexism but finding her own ways to fight back; *Sardines*, the middle novel of Farah's trilogy, *Variations on the Theme of an African Dictatorship*, is also told from a woman's and feminist point of view. Second, as the title of the trilogy— Farah's major achievement to date—shows, Farah's work has been deeply engaged with political themes from the start. His second novel, *A Naked Needle* (1976), the trilogy that followed, comprising *Sweet and Sour Milk* (1979), *Sardines* (1981) and *Close Sesame* (1983), and his most recent novel, *Maps* (1986), are all deeply engaged with the history and politics of recent Somali history, in particular with attempts to resist the rule of Siyad Barre, the dictator who ruled Somalia from 1969 until last year, sometimes with Soviet support, sometimes with American support, but always with an iron hand. Our interview with Farah was conducted while Barre was still in power, but we have resisted the temptation to try to update it in response to the changing political situation, both because it has importance as a record of Farah's position at that point and also because what will take shape in Somalia after Barre is still unclear.

In any case, Farah's fiction is never parochial or of interest solely because of its content. He is a writer with a broad international culture, who was educated in India, has taught in Nigeria, West Germany, and the United States, has lived in a number of other African and European countries, and whose characters seem as familiar with John Coltrane and Wilhelm Reich as with Somali oral poetry or politics. This makes his work hard to place in the categories of geography and nationality with which we tend to approach the "new literatures," and as Farah himself admits, he probably has more in common with writers from South Asia with Islamic backgrounds such as Salman Rushdie—who has praised Farah's work highly—and Zulfikar Ghose than with other African writers such as Ngũgĩ and Achebe. But this is in a sense in keeping with cultural geography on a deeper level, for the Somali culture in which Farah was raised is part of an African littoral with close contacts with the Arabian and Indian subcontinents in terms of religion, trade, culture, and language. And this is simply one more instance where to understand these writers, we cannot rest content with the familiar categories of Asia, Africa, etc., but must understand the particularities of each writer's situation and be able to place these writers in broad comparative categories appropriate to them.

**Reed Dasenbrock:** I would like to start with the issue Ngũgĩ has made so prominent lately, the question of writing in English or African languages and the political implications of that choice. Your published novels are all in English, but I remember reading once that you started writing a novel in Somali once; is that true?

**Nuruddin Farah:** Yes, it is true that I published three-quarters of a novel in Somali in 1973. It was serialized in the local newspapers in Somalia, until one day the censorship people did not like a given chapter and publication was stopped forthwith.

**R.D.:** They were reading it in advance?

**Farah:** The censors telephoned the newspapers and publication was discontinued, that's all I know. Unfortunately, I couldn't defend the passages which made them nervous because I was out of the country at the time. I was in the Soviet Union, I think, and when I got back, I discovered that none of the chapters which I had left behind had been run.

**Feroza Jussawalla:** This is the note on which my interview with Ngũgĩ ended. He wanted very much to turn back to Gĩkũyũ and to write in Gĩkũyũ, because he felt that he could reach more of his own people through his mother tongue, but that caused his work to be banned.

**Farah:** Yes, but the question always is, "Who are our people? Are our people those who speak the same languages as we do? Or are our people all the Africans, all the Third World people?" Personally, I think of all Africans and Third World people as my people, and I will use any languages that I choose to write in. I don't think that Ngũgĩ is banned because he's writing in Gĩkũyũ. It's what he writes that makes him a banned writer. I am a banned writer, even for my works in English. The reason why I have problems with Ngũgĩ's stand especially is because when I come to define who my people are, and I ask myself, really and truly, who I feel closest to, I find that not only are Somalis my people, but the whole of the continent of Africa; India, where I grew up intellectually, and where I wrote my first novel; the Arab world, which has also influenced me culturally; all these are my people. My people are the people in any part of the world who have been colonized and have been deprived of their own self pride. If you take the question of Ngũgĩ insisting that he's going to be writing in a Kenyan language, my problem also stems from the unavoidable thought that Kenya, as an entity, as a nation, is a colonial creation. And so when Ngũgĩ says he's writing in a Kenyan language, is he not conscious of the fact that Kenya does not exist other than in the colonial formation which it has been given by the colonists?

**R.D.:** And they're colonializing a few Somalis there as well.

**Farah:** The Somalis in Kenya are a minority, if you want to look at it that way. Now, in Somalia, for example, the Somaliness of the language coincides with the Somaliness of nationality. And therefore, I could say that I am writing in Somali, the language of the country, Somalia being the only country in Africa with a sizeable population where people speak one language. But I cannot write in Somali because, as I explained earlier, the censors discontinued publication of one of my novels, and all the others are banned. A single telephone call would make one cease to exist as a writer.

**R.D.**: And then it would be impossible to get your novel in Somali published as a book.

**Farah**: Exactly. As a matter of fact, not only are my books banned, but there is no mention of my name in any of the bibliographies that mention Somali writers. And as a practicing novelist who is a Somali, I have produced far more than any other in any language, for that matter.

**R.D.**: So you are a non-person for the government.

**Farah**: I am a non-person for the government, but an honored person for the people, who revere my political stand against the dictatorial regime. It is curious how when Somalis read *Sweet and Sour Milk* they write the names of the characters on the left-hand side of a white piece of paper, and on the right-hand side put down the names of the people on whom they believe my characters are based. I've not been able to convince them that I did not base my fictitious personages on real ones.

**R.D.**: But readers find these correlations?

**Farah**: Readers find names of people, and they tell me that this is who this person is. And then I say, "I do not know that person."

**R.D.**: So your response to Ngũgĩ's claim that one must write in an African language to reach the people would be twofold. One is, "What people do you want to reach?" but second, what's more important is what you say as opposed to the language in which you say it?

**Farah**: Precisely.

**R.D.**: So if your sense is that the choice of a language isn't as politically important as Ngũgĩ thinks it is, what led to your writing in English?

**Farah**: I started writing in English in 1965, at a point in the Somali nation's history when Somali had no orthography. Somali had no script until 1972. So no one could actually have accused me of evading or avoiding that phony issue of language and writing in neo-colonial or colonial languages.

**F.J.**: Is it the same situation in Somalia as in India, where English is the language of business?

**Farah**: It depends on the region you come from. In the North it used to be English. In the South, Italian is the language in use; it still is, as a matter of fact.

**R.D.**: You've also done some writing in Italian, haven't you?

**Farah**: I did write a few pieces, now and again, when I lived in Italy for three or four years, yes. Fiction and a couple of essays as well, but I don't feel as comfortable as I do in English. Languages are like knives, you see; if you don't sharpen them often enough, they get rusty, and like blunt instruments, they don't serve you well.

**R.D.:** Were you brought up in what was originally British Somaliland, in the part of Somalia in which English was spoken?

**Farah:** I was born in the once-upon-a-time Italian part of Somalia, in the south. I was born, actually, at a time when the whole of the Somali-speaking area, with the exception of Djibouti, was under the British administration, following Italy's loss of its colonies in Africa, namely Somalia, Libya, and Eritrea.

**R.D.:** Because of the war.

**Farah:** Yes, I was born at the end of 1945. Then my father was transferred to what is nowadays called the Ogaden, because he was the interpreter to the British Governor of the Ogaden. When the Ogaden, or that part of the Ogaden where my father had worked, was handed over to Ethiopia, my father decided to stay on, and therefore we did not go back to where I was born. Eventually I grew up in the Ogaden, virtually an Ethiopian citizen, at least in name. I went to school in Kallafo. Not until 1963 did I set foot in Somalia again, when the family fled the skirmishes in the border area in the 1963–64 war.

**R.D.:** Then there's some overlap between your own childhood, growing up in the Ogaden, as opposed to Somalia, and the story of *Maps*.

**Farah:** Yes, but I can assure you *Maps* is not autobiographical in so far as I am aware of it.

**R.D.:** But your education was in the Ogaden, not in Somalia itself.

**Farah:** Yes, speaking English and Arabic. And the official Ethiopian language, Amharic. Somali was spoken orally, though not written. Since Somali had no orthography when I was growing up, at some point I actually expected, or it was expected of me, to write in Arabic. It was the first foreign language I received my formal written tradition-based education in. For some reason, I started writing—well, toying with the idea, so to speak, of doing some writing—in English, not Arabic, at the early age of about sixteen.

**R.D.:** Why English, as opposed to Arabic, if you can remember back to when you were sixteen?

**Farah:** Because I could find a typewriter in English, as you can see a practical thing that has nothing to do with the politics of language. To me, to this day it doesn't really matter what language I write in. If what I write is important to people, what I write will be translated back into Somali or perhaps into all other languages. Mind you, I'm not being translated into other languages simply because I write in English. I believe my writing has been translated or read because I'm making literary contributions that are worthy of being rendered into another experience, into another language.

F.J.: How many years did you live in India?

Farah: Three, four years. But they were very important years. I was at Punjab University, Chandigarh. And that's where I say I grew into maturity intellectually, because I was twenty, twenty-one, and had by then written two novels, which are still unpublished.

R.D.: In English?

Farah: In English.

F.J.: Did English become for you a language of your own consciousness? It's not until I was in the States that I realized—when people asked me, "How can you speak English so well?"—that English was not supposed to be my language.

Farah: As you will know, there are millions of people in various parts of the world who really have no language as such, in the sense they have never put any effort in highlighting their experiences by writing. Most of these people are inarticulate. What I mean is there are some people who are native speakers of English but who don't make any articulate use of the language. One becomes conscious of using a language, and one may give it a status of a first language, although one may have learned such a tongue later. It depends on the effort one has put in. Conrad's is a known case.

F.J.: Did you learn any Indian languages well enough to write in them?

Farah: I learned Punjabi, but not well enough to write in it.

F.J.: Did you speak any Urdu at all? Did you find that you could move easily from Arabic to Urdu?

Farah: No, I guess for the same reason that I found learning Spanish difficult. It's so close to Italian that there was interference. And in any event, there came a point when I had to decide what I was going to be, a polyglot or a novelist. For some reason, you see, I have kept picking up languages fast enough, and then, somehow, their burden on my memory assumed such a weight that I became obsessed with acquiring more and more of them, acquiring more and more words in different languages, until one day I tried to write a play in as many languages as five, which I did. Alas, the play made no sense. Not even to me when I was doing it. Result: rubbish bin.

**R.D.**: What were the five languages of the play?

**Farah**: Arabic, Italian, Somali, and English, some Punjabi, but as I said, none of that made sense.

**R.D.**: But would you say that knowing all these languages has been an advantage for you as a writer?

**Farah**: Not really, no. In my subconscious memory, when I'm sitting at the typewriter and working on something, I often ask myself how many new ideas can come in how many different languages? You can concentrate on something to the detriment of all other things. And then you might find that these languages have become interferences, obstacles. If you're communicating in a language, every now and again you may be able to find a very, very poetic metaphor that's in another language. But to render everything in English would take ages; you would become a translator, not a writer. You could avoid clichés by employing a poetic phrase in another language, sure. But that remains just another cliché when your passage is re-translated into the language from which the original has come.

**R.D.**: So to be the kind of writer like, say, Raja Rao in India or Chinua Achebe, who is trying to give a very strong flavor of another language in English, doesn't really work for you.

**Farah**: No, it doesn't. And the reason why it doesn't work is that my writing is metaphor and leitmotiv-based, not proverb-based. Even in terms of the day-to-day living and analysis, some of my novels could with little change be set somewhere else if you wanted, because of the metaphoric nature of the writing. Unlike Achebe, for whose writing I have immense respect, I am not proverb-dependent, in a manner of speaking. My subconscious level has a great storage of Somali proverbs and poetry. But my conscious memory is terrible, and when I run out of new ideas or I can't remember something or can't quote the original, since I belong to the written tradition, I go to an encyclopedia or look it up. But in the oral tradition you don't do that. You go ask someone else, in the hope they will remember it. Unfortunately, I live away from home, in total isolation most of the time, writing, working on my texts. I can't find Somalis at times; I would have to travel, sometimes, a hundred kilometers to be able to find another Somali who might remember a proverb my memory has mislaid or who might not.

I have problems with oral narration, in any case, not just because my memory is defective, but also because you can't run a metropolis efficiently using the oral tradition. I am a city person. I write, I am cosmopolitan; oral tradition, when you've put aside its ancient or current histories, is defective. Can you imagine a society going the industrial twentieth-century way without it adopting the methods of a written tradition? How could you memorize all those sophisticated mathematical formulas? Let us not be romantic about the oral tradition.

**R.D.**: But isn't the style in which Achebe gives a strong sense of Igbo culture and language partly a function of his closeness to that oral culture?

**Farah**: No, it's part of his conscious effort to bring to the fore some of the things I am incapable of making my readers see. I am conscious of my being Somali, my novels are basically Somali—all Somalis can see it, I can see it, everyone can see it—but I don't bring it to the fore as much as, let's say, Achebe does. I also think that similarities are to be looked for and are likely to be found, for example, between mine and North African writing. And not, say, between Achebe, Soyinka and me.

**R.D.**: Because of the Islamic frame of reference?

**Farah**: Because of that, and also because we all seem to have been brought up in the narrative richness of *The Thousand and One Nights*. The storytelling is different. The culture from which we all hail and upon which we base our thoughts is not dual, that is to say, not just European and African, but it's African, Islamic, with influences from Europe and America thrown in as well. Take somebody like me, who speaks Italian, who has lived in Germany, in the States, in all these places: all these also form my culture. Additionally, a large number of these African authors are also Christian—Achebe, Soyinka, Armah. They quote from the Bible consciously. I don't.

**F.J.**: So you would see yourself more in line with Khatibi and Tayeb Salih and others?

**Farah**: Yes, with Tayeb Salih and Taher Ben Jelloun. Or even Salman Rushdie. There are more similarities, for example, between Salman Rushdie's and my work than between my writing and that of some African writers I can think of.

**R.D.**: Because of your focus on narrative as opposed to proverbs?

**Farah:** Yes, and the metaphor-based, leitmotiv-based writing, which is also Islamic, because Islam is a very symbol-conscious culture. Suppose you camp somewhere in the desert for a few days. You spread your prayer rug out and you point it in the right direction. And then you start a small mosque and also you build a small, little semicircular structure representing the mihrab. And that mosque will have technically the same shape as any other masjid within firm foundations and serving a large, settled community in a city.

**R.D.:** I must admit that I don't see your work as that symbolic. We may not worry about the anthropological details, but we are invited to take it as a fairly realistic account of some actual situations.

**Farah:** Yes. Except in *Maps*. The dream sequences in *Maps* are not realistic sequences.

**R.D.:** But they're framed. We know they are dreams, I think. You don't blur the line between the real and the fantastic.

**Farah:** No, I don't do that. I'm tempted now and again to do it, but I don't.

**F.J.:** Because you have the reader in mind?

**Farah:** No, because sometimes in Africa the real is more fantastic than the fantastic.

**R.D.:** It seems to me that in terms of what we were talking about in terms of an international background or trying to address a wide spectrum of readers—

**Farah:** I am not conscious of a wide spectrum of readers. The irony of this is that I'm very ambiguous about my own writing and my place in the hierarchies of the canonical writing, i.e., among writers who are in the canon, say, of African literature. The reason is, I work on a novel for two years at a stretch, and I am shut to the world. Once I'm done with it, and other people have acquired it, or let's assume read it, I'm finished with it, and remain indifferent to it, in order that I can concentrate on the work at hand. I also think that every book is an experience, and certain experiences appeal to some people. What makes, for example, *Close Sesame* appeal to a reader, is something that I've never quite worked out. And to be honest, I don't believe it worthwhile to reflect on this.

**R.D.:** You don't really worry about it?

**Farah:** No. The one thing I am aware of is that there is a certain type of reader the novels will appeal to. In other words, the person need not nec-essarily be Somali or African or Muslim, but then again I can't be more specific, I've encountered all manner of people who love my writing—how vain! Could it be that my books contain a heavier dose of intellectual con-tent which appeals to some of these readers? I have no idea.

F.J.: Is this a matter of there being some universal themes, or now, as you are calling it, intellectual content?

Farah: Let me make my point clear. I said earlier that every book is an experience. Every passage, actually, is an experience. You enter into a dia-logue with that experience. Does that experience talk to you? It does not matter who has written it, so long as you understand the language.

F.J.: And it does not matter where you come from?

Farah: It does not matter where you come from.

R.D.: That's certainly true of my own experience of your work, because I am not Somali, I am not Muslim, and I have not been to Somalia, and yet, when I started reading *Sweet and Sour Milk*, after the very first pages, I said, "This book is wonderful." Something spoke to me very directly across what for someone else might seem to be an enormous gap; it did not seem to me to be a gap at all.

Farah: Yes. I also am of the belief that when I read a book, if I don't understand something I don't give it much of a bother. The reason is I, myself, the author of, say, *Sweet and Sour Milk*, if I go back to it years after it was first published and read a passage, I may not be able to remember what this passage was meant to say, or to specify the particular experience it was meant to point out. That experience may not be immediate when I read it after many, many years. Yet certain experiences are so immediate that their urgency speaks to you. This is the importance, I think, of writing: there are shades of experiences which are nebulous, ambiguous, meaning-ful.

R.D.: Rather than worrying about this reader or that reader, you aim to create an experience that works—

Farah: Exactly. For me the essential thing is to have this dialogue with the spirit of the experience, with the thing that makes that experience im-mediate, appealing, something I can express and others are touched by. When I read a poem by, say, Iqbal, it's so beautiful, I say, "I wish I had written it." It is of such an appropriating experience that I speak.

**F.J.**: What contains the spirit of the experience? The theme of Iqbal, love, or love of God—is it that, or is it just the vocabulary, the words—

**Farah**: Yes. The tension between words, between ideas, between, actually, his Islamic upbringing and his lack of faith as we understand it. Sometimes he's so mystical, a Sufi of some kind. And if you read the same passages of Iqbal to some Muslim fanatics and if Iqbal was sitting there, they would perhaps kill him, burn him, on the spot, and feel unburdened by the act.

**R.D.**: So there are some writers who are very concerned about what language they think writers should write in, and there are others who are very worried about who they should be writing to, but your concern is more with the integrity or the intensity of the experience you create for any reader.

**Farah**: Yes. Some writers bother too much with the politics of language and not with the experiential content of what they pen.

**F.J.**: Let's talk about your work, then, about "the experiential content of your pen." Do you see it just in a chronological order, or do you see it falling in certain categories, something written before belonging with something written later?

**Farah**: I confess I haven't read my works in ages. *(Laughter)* If I pick up a book of mine, in fact, I can see one of them right there, *Close Sesame*, it would read as if it were written by someone else.

**R.D.**: Now you are working on a second trilogy. *Maps* is followed by—

**Farah**: *Gifts*. Which will be published when I'm pleased with it, to be followed by *Letters*, on which I am working now.

**R.D.**: How does that trilogy vary from the first one, from *Variations of the Theme of an African Dictatorship*? They seem very different to me, based on *Maps*.

**Farah**: They should. The intensity of the experience in the first trilogy was actually informed by the urgency of the politics and the social happenings that were unfolding at the time I was writing the books. What runs through the first five books, if you include *From a Crooked Rib* and *A Naked Needle*, is dictatorship of different kinds. In *Crooked Rib*, there is societal dictatorship. Society, and in particular, that segment of society called men, becomes a dictator. The community of men become dictators subjugating a community of women. There may be some women who are much more dictatorial towards other women than some of the men, but I'm speaking in a general sense about a community of men and a community of women, since there is this segregation of the sexes in Islam.

**R.D.:** That's very important in *Sardines*, also.

**Farah:** Yes. Often, I write a novel whose central consciousness is female, to be followed by one whose central consciousness is male. *Maps* is followed by *Gifts*, whose central consciousness is a woman, to be followed by *Letters*, whose central consciousness is male. In the same way as *Sweet and Sour Milk* was followed by *Sardines*, followed by *Close Sesame*.

**F.J.:** Do you have trouble doing that?

**Farah:** No. I don't.

**F.J.:** Do you feel you can get into a female consciousness?

**Farah:** Well, I haven't felt uncomfortable so far. Now and again, sometimes you may have a situation in which you could not actually determine whether the central consciousness is male or female, as in the case of *Maps*. For example, who is the central consciousness of *Maps*? Is it the young boy, Askar, or Misra? Because he assumes her to be much more important than she is, in the long term. Because she informs every thought he entertains, every movement, every gesture.

**R.D.:** So in the early books, the theme was, in a sense, male dictatorship or patriarchy. *A Naked Needle* is an interesting book in this context in the sense that the protagonist, Koschin, seems very supportive of the "revolution," as he calls it, but other people in the book are much more skeptical and much more cynical. As I read it, I wondered what your perspective was when you were writing that book. I came to it after *Sweet and Sour Milk*, where your stance towards the general's regime is very clear.

**Farah:** I may have been very cynical at the time I was writing it. The reason why *Naked Needle* was not published earlier—it came out actually in 1976—was because my editor at Heinemann, James Currey, was worried for my safety. He felt that my life would be endangered. This was why he withheld the book from publication for four years, not releasing it until after I came out of Somalia.

But in *A Naked Needle*, the experience I was trying to address myself to was male chauvinism in a socialist society. Or male chauvinism in a newly independent country. During the years people were fighting for independence against colonialism, women sacrificed their lives as much as men did. But when independence was gained, then the men began to push aside or to dominate women, just as before, if not worse. The dual curse, you may describe the gender domination as such.

**F.J.:** I'm interested in knowing about your feminist consciousness, because you also say that there is an Islamic consciousness in your work. That's a contradiction in terms, is it not?

**Farah:** Can a man have a feminist consciousness?

**F.J.:** That's what I come back to when you say you have a female consciousness that's the center of a novel. Can you get into a female character's mind?

**Farah:** Could it be that I am actually merely the medium?

**F.J.:** What do you mean by the medium?

**Farah:** The person through whom that experience is communicated.

**R.D.:** The Nigerian critic Juliet Okonkwo has written in praise of your work, saying that you're the only African male writer who has given female characters female readers can identify with. I don't know if you know her article, but she goes on to give Achebe and Soyinka a very hard time for their sexist attitudes, and praises your work against theirs. So at least one woman agrees with you on this point.

**Farah:** She's extremely kind and generous, that's all I can say. I've actually been given, generally, a hard time, in the sense that the same question comes up again and again. For whatever this is worth, let me mention that when I submitted *From a Crooked Rib*, as a second-year student studying in India, to Heinemann, the editor James Currey wrote a letter, asking whether I was a man or a woman. Someone sent him a photograph to answer his question. *(Laughter)*

Something similar happened ages ago, when I lived in Mogadiscio. A woman bearing the name of Ebla came and told me that the story as told in *From a Crooked Rib* was her real tale. Not only that, but that I should share with her my royalties. *(Laughter)* I said I didn't know her, I had never met her before. And then she said I must have written it when we were living in the same area or in the same city, or something like that. To which I responded that I wrote the novel when I was in India, when I was a second-year student at Punjab University, Chandigarh.

There was another incident when *Crooked Rib* was translated into Slovenian, I think. A woman reader wrote to me saying, among other things, "that between us women, since men will not understand," assuming that I was a woman. Now what was I supposed to say to this woman? Some of my friends suggested: "Maybe you should not disappoint her, because she'll be very unhappy if she learns that you are not a woman." That was politics, you see, gender, writer-reader politics.

**F.J.:** You didn't send her a photograph?

**Farah:** No.

**F.J.:** But there is something about Islam that is distinctly anti-woman, isn't there?

**Farah:** Not more than other faiths. For Islam, Christianity and Judaism, the book religions, as we call them, take the same sort of hostile, male-oriented position vis-à-vis women. All of them. The reason why Islam appears to be more relentless is twofold. One is that for everything Muslims do, they tend to resort to the holy book, from which they seek divine approval. The second is that Islamic societies have not been secularized in the same way as Christian societies have been, wherein it appears as though there is more space in which to maneuver and to live your own personal life outside of the dictates of the scriptures. But if you had Pope John Paul II as the head of a state, I assure you he would behave in the same manner as Khomeini.

**R.D.:** So Christianity is really no more feminist than Islam, but our societies have been more de-Christianized than Islamic societies have been de-Islamicized.

**Farah:** Also, you see, your societies, North American and Western European societies, have been individuated, if I may put it thus. That is to say, every individual is dealt with as an entity. In Third World countries, one is more a community of persons than one is an individual.

**F.J.:** Yes, but in that setup, it's what you say, the dictatorship of the society.

**Farah:** My first trilogy, *Variations on the Theme of an African Dictatorship*, is a study of why dictatorships survive in Africa, what makes them work. Because we are dictatorial as societies, it follows that we produce grand patriarchs, dictators par excellence.

**F.J.:** Yes. That's true.

**R.D.:** So dictatorship begins at home.

**Farah:** Exactly.

**F.J.:** It's interesting that you're saying this, because Achebe's *Anthills of* *the Savannah* and even *A Man of the People* talk about why it is that neo-colonialist post-colonial governments are giving birth to so many dictatorships. My answer to that is always that in India, it's not been so, at least up to now. Even Mrs. Gandhi we have dealt with. So it's not just an effect of colonialism.

**Farah:** No, no, it's not the effect of colonialism, it is the stage at which a society is, and whether that society is a dictatorial society. I grew up in a household which was dictatorially run by one voice, my father's. It didn't matter what happened. Now, it worried me immensely when I was growing up whether or not I too would be a dictator. And as a matter of fact, I have become some kind of a dictator in my own small, little cubicle, which I call my life. I am extremely rigid, extremely dictatorial, and do not accept anyone else telling me what to do. But I do not run other people's lives.

**R.D.:** So you're not the grand patriarch.

**Farah:** Thank God I am not.

**R.D.:** So how do you get away from this? Everything you're describing fits in with the themes of the trilogy about dictatorship. How in a Somalia or in a Nigeria or wherever could one avoid dictatorship? Is there any hope?

**Farah:** We have to change. It's not the system. You could have any system you like, our societies will remain dictatorial, and will breed their own kind. The three books of the trilogy on dictatorship attempt in different ways to tackle the core of the problem, which is dictatorship. The young enthusiasts in *Sweet and Sour Milk*—I'm simplifying—argue that you must give everybody information. Once you give people information, that solves the problem. Medina in *Sardines* keeps on saying it is male chauvinism. But pray, who is the chauvinist, the one who gives her the hardest time?

**R.D.:** It's her mother-in-law, Idil.

**Farah:** Yes. Mothers-in-law can also be dictators, because they continue to perpetuate that kind of tyrannical rule, inherited as a result of being widowed, tyrannical as a patriarch.

**R.D.:** But in the trilogy, it seems to me there are spots of hope that you delineate. You portray families which are authoritarian, and obviously that's an image of the authoritarian society as a whole. Yet in *Close Sesame*, there is the old man, Deeriye, who is my favorite character of all of yours. He has somehow gotten beyond all that. He's not ruling anymore.

**Farah:** No. Because he is fortunate in being born into the ruling position, a sultan. Also he abdicates, or is not willing to give any importance to his status at birth. Whereas it is small midgets, like Siyad Barre, who, believing to be God's chosen luminaries, try to force mortals to accept them for what they are not. Result: psychosis; madness; dictatorship; economic underdevelopment; corruption.

**R.D.:** I suppose that's why *Close Sesame* works well as a last novel, because in the first two, in a sense you have children trying to overthrow their parents and not succeeding. And then in the last novel, you have a father who is willing to be overthrown, and therefore he doesn't need to be. I presume that's your image of how one would want things in a larger world to operate.

**Farah:** I think it is important to note that even if Siyad Barre were overthrown tomorrow, the people who come after him will be as dictatorially wicked as he. And the reason is because society has remained unchanged, with patriarchies and matriarchies at the helm of power. Until a change occurs in our societies—

**F.J.:** In what sense?

**Farah:** Society has not become tolerant of individuals living their lives, a man or a woman running his or her life the way they see fit. A woman living alone may be considered a terrible thing in some countries. In some societies women are discouraged from living alone, a man reaching the age of 20 must marry—you see how traditional societies become dictatorial in imposing a value system on its individuals. In the majority of cases these laws are enforced through tyrants.

**F.J.:** So traditions are dictatorial.

**Farah:** You will notice that the more traditional societies become urbanized, the more it is demanded that its members become tolerant. Because the new situations demand tolerance. So you find nowadays women not only living alone, but living alone in cities that are as far away as a thousand kilometers away from their villages in Pakistan where they were born. And the reason is because the economic situation has become so difficult that the families will allow their daughters to go away and work, or elderly parents with no pension to fall back on encourage their children to earn money. These let tradition be damned. So do the dowry extricators. No parental love, only the money goddess.

We can have hope in society, if societies are urbanized, educated, and if these changes in our way of life teach us something. At times I pray for more and more droughts in Africa, because then people would start working harder, or would they? I have an idea there has to be a confrontation of a kind. When there is a confrontation, people will start thinking. People have not been angry, not sufficiently enraged. The dictatorships have not been really wicked, not to the extent where people rose up in rage, united in their effort to regain their sense of human dignity. Wherever dictatorships have been extremely wicked, people have overthrown them. Numeiri was overthrown by the Sudanese people. The Sudanese people are no more intelligent, no more hard-working, than the Somalis or the Zairois or anyone else suffering under a tyrannical dictatorship, but Numeiri put his foot on their heads and their necks, strangled them, and then they had nothing to do but to overthrow him.

In the Sudan, they're moving towards another dictatorship, again because society hasn't changed. Elsewhere the Shah was overthrown; you have Khomeini; Haile Selassie has been replaced by Mengistu. Sadly it is the same bloody society. Dictatorial.

R.D.: Is this what your new trilogy is about? What you're saying leads into *Maps*, it seems to me—of course, there is the voyage to the city, the depopulation of the Ogaden, more from war than drought. Is this a depiction of things getting so bad that there won't—

Farah: The central theme of the second trilogy, if there is something like a central theme, has to do with the lives of Africans in the past five, six, seven years. The war situation, for example, which has produced *Maps*, is unique. But the central theme of the three books is that in all of them a baby boy is either found or lost. Now, imagine: an African Islamic society in which babies are abandoned. Horrors of horrors. And can Satan be said to remain idle? Who are the parents of the abandoned baby?

F.J.: But it cannot be, can it?

Farah: Well, it is apocalyptic. The whole thing is apocalyptic. Something has happened to this little boy. What has happened? Society is an orphaned baby, parentless, with no wise elder to guide it.

R.D.: So it's that family structure collapsing under the pressure?

Farah: Exactly. And then the one I'm working on, *Letters*, is how literacy or the notion or concept of reading or writing has affected the lives of people in Somalia, say, or Islamic Africa—

**F.J.**: It's interesting. Because *Maps*, *Gifts*, *Letters*, sounds in some ways very colonial. The British mapped, and they thought they were bringing gifts, and then they brought writing—

**Farah**: Well, this is perhaps what it will sound like when I'm finished with it.

**R.D.**: So these family structures which have been so powerful, so claustrophobic, in the earlier works, are breaking down under crisis now, and you're saying there might be—

**Farah**: Hope in that.

**R.D.**: —rather than simply catastrophe. Because out of that will perhaps create a new kind of individualism.

**Farah**: Sure. With people standing up for themselves against dictatorships. I am hoping to write another book to crown the two trilogies and with which to link them together. But we'll have to wait a few years to see what happens or what thoughts come to me.

**R.D.**: Do you go back to Somalia at all?

**Farah**: No. I can't go back, because I have been threatened with death. Besides, I am enjoying myself living, writing, travelling, why should I go back to a place where it is certain I'll face a death squad.

**R.D.**: I ask because it seems to me in some way *Maps* is a more nationalistic work that your earlier work. "Nationalistic" is not a word that I particularly want to use positively, but one of the things that comes across very strongly in *Maps* is a very strong sense of the Somali people and the—

**Farah**: I oppose Siyad Barre's dictatorship, not the Somali people as such.

**R.D.**: But that comes across more strongly in *Maps* than in some of your earlier books, where, it seems to me, your protagonists tend to be disaffected from nationalism and looking more toward Italy or toward—

**Farah**: In my reading of the works, when I have read them, that is, this is not what I get. Of course they're disaffected with the regime, and are rather pessimistic, in a general sense, about most things. At least they articulate a form of resistance.

**R.D.**: Let me try to rephrase my question. It seems to me that the cultural ambience of the earlier works was more cosmopolitan, self-consciously so, with references to John Coltrane and Wilhelm Reich, whereas *Maps* seems within a more purely Somali frame of reference.

**Farah**: Yes. Well, in the second part, *Gifts*, the main character is a midwife, and this in itself is a break with my previous tradition of choosing articulate characters who always said the right things.

**R.D.:** I'm wondering if that's a response to being away from Somalia?

**Farah:** If I returned to Somalia today, I would be living exactly the same sort of life that I lead here, or in Khartoum. I will write. But the question, as a matter of fact, is charged with meanings: Can Nuruddin Farah, although having not set foot in Somalia all these years, can he continue writing novels about Somalia? As it happens, Somalia survives better in my mind when I write about it than it would when I speak about it.

It's in response to this that I have written a novel called *Gifts*, which is the most Somali of my novels. Just to show that in spite of my not visiting Somalia for fourteen years, I can do it as well as anyone who lives there. I live in Africa, I live in the Sudan, I have lived in the Gambia, I lived in Nigeria, countries that are as economically underdeveloped as Somalia. The universals about these African countries supply me, so to speak, with Somalia's particulars. I am a novelist, not an anthropologist.

**R.D.:** Well, the Sudan would of course be close to Somalia.

**Farah:** The Gambia, too. People there are poor. When people are poor, undereducated, illiterate, and are being ruled by a dictator, benevolent or no, they behave and think alike. It is conceivable that the anthropological grid of the city of Mogadiscio is different from Banjul or Khartoum. I may not have the grid in front of me or in my memory. But to set that right, all I have to do is ask for a map.

I promise you that people behave exactly the same way in the Gambia and the Sudan as they do in Somalia. And remember: I am not an anthropologist. I am a novelist, and novelists deal with higher themes, not anthropological datae or tribal sense of Pudore. Take another pertinent example. The Soviets are out of Somalia. And yet when you read *Sweet and Sour Milk* today, it should read as if the Soviets are still there, the Soviets being simply a symbol of an outside tyranny imposing itself on the Somali mind.

**R.D.:** So, for a novelist, the level of detail that you would pick up from being in Somalia really doesn't matter.

**Farah:** It doesn't matter, and these are things that change. If you describe a street in Mogadiscio, a bulldozer can drive up to it to demolish it in fewer minutes that it took a novelist to describe it. But then you still have it in your novel. And two or three years later, some anthropologist critic will be walking in the streets looking for the novel there, searching for the faithful description. This is just very, very naive.

**F.J.:** What makes up your literary consciousness? What is it you grew up reading and then said, well, now, I'm going to start writing this first novel?

**Farah:** It probably goes back to the time when I was four and read *The Thousand and One Nights* and stumbled on someone bearing the same name as myself, Nuruddin, and I cut the name out and pasted it on my exercise book, to say, "See? See? My name is in print." *(Laughter)* It probably goes back to that early age in which the world and everything that is in it belongs to you. The universe was mine and I thought I would write to describe what was mine, and this is what I've been doing ever since.

**F.J.:** And then do you continue to read, to be conscious of literary traditions?

**Farah:** No. Half-an-hour before you came, I was in front of the typewriter and was totally engrossed in what I was doing and not thinking about the world outside my head. This has always been my way of being. I have always paid very great detailed attention to what I'm working on and live in total isolation from the world and its worries.

**R.D.:** But you prefer living in Africa to being here in London and in the States?

**Farah:** Yes. I'm going to the Sudan next week, to Khartoum, yes, then on to Uganda, my new home base.

**F.J.:** You have greater freedom in the Sudan?

**Farah:** I have greater freedom in the Sudan, and I also feel much more comfortable living in Africa than I do in Europe or anywhere else, for that matter.

**R.D.:** Do you teach there?

**Farah:** No, I don't. I write full time. I teach sometimes, because the university is now and then short of teaching staff, although I don't get paid for my teaching, anyway, the university support system supplies me with permits and such-like. In Africa you must be a member of a family, a tribe or a clan; mine is the university.

# Chinua Achebe

If someone has read just one work of African literature, indeed just one work of non-Western literature in English, that is most likely to be *Things Fall Apart*, Chinua Achebe's first novel. Achebe was born in 1930, *Things Fall Apart* was published in 1958, and it quickly became a modern classic. Three other fine novels followed in quick succession, *No Longer at Ease* (1960), *Arrow of God* (1964), and *A Man of the People* (1966), and these four novels remain among the most widely read, studied, written about, and imitated works of contemporary world literature. In these same years, he also wrote a work of children's literature, *Chike and the River* (1966), and a number of widely influential essays of criticism, subsequently collected in *Morning Yet on Creation Day* (1975) and *Hopes and Impediments* (1988). Achebe's influence has been everywhere, seen even in reactions against him.

But there have been impediments as well as hopes in Achebe's subsequent career. *A Man of the People* is a less than flattering portrait of life in Nigeria (or a country much like it) after independence, and shortly after the publication of his fourth novel, Achebe's own Igbo people tried to secede from Nigeria and form the independent nation of Biafra. Achebe was a prominent spokesman for the Biafran cause, protesting the genocidal policies implemented by the Nigerian regime with the support of the West, and in the interview that follows, he traces his long silence as a novelist after *A Man of the People* to the turmoil of Nigerian history. A collection of short stories, *Girls at War* (1972), reflected his experience of the Biafran War, but aside from that essays, poems, and a busy public life occupied Achebe for the next twenty years. But in 1987 Achebe made a triumphant return as a novelist with *Anthills of the Savannah*, which was nominated for the Booker Prize and is a complex intervention into the ongoing dialogue concerning African literature and aesthetics. Feroza Jussawalla was able to interview Achebe on a visit to New York while he was a visiting professor at City University of New York.

**Feroza Jussawalla:** Your most recent novel, *Anthills of the Savannah*, was published in 1987, twenty-one years after *A Man of the People*. Can you say why it was so long in the making? Did you just have a long period of silence?

**Chinua Achebe:** Well, it was a long period, but it was not a period of silence. The novel is not the only form of expression I have; I was expressing myself in other ways, in other activities, in those years. But what happened in terms of novels was that this novel refused to make itself available. As to why that should happen, anybody's guess is as good as mine. I think it probably had to do with the very traumatic history that we have had in Nigeria. I'm thinking here, of course, of the Biafran war as well as before and after. It seemed as if all our hopes and beliefs had been misplaced, and we just had to begin again to deal with the situation of the Nigerian nation and what one's place in it was to be.

F.J.: What went wrong, do you think? Is your disappointment focused specifically on issues related to the Igbos or is it part of a larger disappointment with post-colonial governments? The same disappointment is obviously very strongly there in Ngũgĩ's work also.

Achebe: I don't think that separation is possible. It's not simply a matter of Igbo issues either. It's a question of what does citizenship mean? What rights do citizens have in a nation they call their own? The question of safety, for instance. It is all part of the post-colonial question. It takes different forms in different places. When you mention Ngũgĩ, I think he's also preoccupied with post-colonial questions. He seems to have worked out some very clear answers to his problems, and I haven't, so there is a difference there.

F.J.: Am I right to notice a certain ambivalence in *Anthills of the Savannah* about the heritage of colonialism? I'm thinking about the scene near the beginning when Chris and Ikem are talking about Sam, the dictator. There's a sense at that point that they think he's somehow gentlemanly or good because of his British ways—he's smoking his pipe and listening to *Eine Kleine Nachtmusik* and reading the Sunday newspapers.

Achebe: Is there some intrinsic value in the fact that Sam had these British tendencies? Would we be better off if we were to recall the British? No, I think what they're saying initially about Sam is that he is a gentleman the way the word is defined, "thoroughly decent," the British would have said, but then something was missing in his character.

F.J.: But later, after the coup, somebody says, "What should we do, ask the white man to come back?"

Achebe: The question of whether we should bring back the colonial power, is, of course, a joke. But people do get so frustrated and disappointed that they might say that. In the scene just before Chris is murdered, somebody proposes a plan, "send me to England to invite the IMF." That jolts you, and it shows the degree of disenchantment with the post-colonial government when people are ready to say, "Well, let's bring the slave master back." What is the answer? Is the answer then to bring back the old masters? This doesn't really require any discussion because it's totally unacceptable. It's really no solution. The colonial situation does not prepare people for independence, and therefore, there's no question of prolonging it, of calling it back in order to solve the problem.

F.J.: I was listening to an interview with you on National Public Radio in which you said that the Westminster model of government did not prepare us to run our own countries. How do you mean that?

Achebe: No, no, no, that's not what I said. No, I said we did not experience the Westminster model. That's the real point. It was not the intention of the British to practice their system in the colonies. They practiced a colonial system, a totalitarian system, whether in Africa or India or wherever. So, to expect the colonial subject to have imbibed the Westminster model during the colonial period is farcical. Because there was no Westminster model practiced in the colonies; there was no training. No matter how long the system continued, you would not get that training. The Portuguese were in Angola for five hundred years. They did not train the Angolans, because it's a colonial system, a system of servitude. So you have to wrestle with independence—that's really the issue. You don't deal with it by running back to servitude.

F.J.: What can be done to get away from this embittered history?

Achebe: Well, that question is open. This is something that we all should be addressing our minds to. Obviously something very serious needs to be addressed. In my traditional society, the way they would have put it is, we must go and ask. In other words, go and do some divination. When there is something very serious, which you cannot explain, or a recurrent disaster, then they say you must go and ask. There is nothing within the immediate vicinity to explain this, so we must now go and find out. We must go and ask, "Why are we in this bind? Why are we imprisoned in this situation?" Obviously something has a grievance against us. We must find what we did wrong. We must look in all directions to see whether we can discover the source of this unhappiness, of this distress. I think one can speculate, one can suggest some of the areas where this search should be done, but I don't think that's really for the novelist to do. It's not really for the novelist to say, "This is what you must do to be saved."

F.J.: What is the writer's role in this situation then?

Achebe: I think our job is to agitate all our minds so that we can all start worrying about it together. I have a few suggestions, but it does not constitute *the* answer, *the* solution. I'm very hesitant when people push for one answer, a simple answer, "What shall I do to be saved?"

F.J.: I was very interested in this quotation from *Anthills of the Savannah*: "He promised to be brief. He was raising these issues as a sociologist of literature in the context of the writer's ideological development and clarity. . . . Secondly, on a general note he must state once again his well-known contention that writers in the Third World context must not stop at the stage of documenting social problems, but must move to a higher responsibility of proffering prescriptions." (*Laughter*) Is that satire?

Achebe: Well, it's up to you. (*Laughter*) My friends talk like that so I can't call it satire! (*Laughter*)

F.J.: Can a writer proffer prescriptions?

Achebe: He can if he wants to, but I think his real job is to give headaches. You can't really say, "this is what a writer must do." I am so democratic that I will fight to the death to let my opponent have his say. In other words, if the writer feels he has a prescription to give, let him do so. I don't feel that's my responsibility. I don't think that's in the nature of my work. I think what is in the nature of my work is to expose a condition to a reader and get people agitated and bring in as many people as you can into the process.

F.J.: But when a writer does that, as Ngũgĩ has, then he ends up with the kind of situation that Ngũgĩ is in—his voice is being stamped out.

Achebe: Who is stamping him out?

F.J.: Well, Moi essentially, in the sense that his books are banned—*Matigari* is banned again.

Achebe: I really don't want to spend too much time on Ngũgĩ now because he speaks for himself. I think he comes from a country where there is now a very strong tradition of extremism. He is *almost* as extremist as Moi. (*Laughter*) And it seems to me that's the nature of the Kenyan society. I find it most unattractive. I'm against a one-party state. Ngũgĩ is probably not against a one-party state, depending upon the kind of party. So there's a fundamental difference there. I am opposed to any one-party state, right or left! I spent ten days in Kenya last December watching this one-party state, and I find what's going on there quite unattractive—the news in the evening shows people marching against the dissidents burning their effigies or burning their coffins, including Ngũgĩ's. Now that's a right-wing government, but it's not less frightening to me if it's done by a left-wing government.

So that's why I believe there should be openness; there should be possibility for dissent, for disagreement. Even if that means slowing us down, that's worth it. For that reason, I'm worried about what's about to happen in Zimbabwe. It seems to me one of the brightest spots in Africa. Mugabe is brilliant, and things have gone remarkably well there considering all the problems. But there is this obsession with getting rid of opposition. There'll be all kinds of theorists and dogmatic people telling you that "We'll have dissent within the party." And it seems to me to be just an obsession that we must all be in one group. It's neater that way; it's tidier; but that's not the way life is.

F.J.: Is there a way to get beyond that period for a country like South Africa? Can they go into a new government and skip the neo-colonial disappointment period that we have all had—India has had, Nigeria has had, Kenya has had.

Achebe: I don't know. I'm not that kind of prophet. I don't pretend to be able to see into the future in that way. There's always the element of surprise. The future is made up of so many imponderables. This is why history is as interesting as it is. In addition, there are also certain things, certain experiences, that people seem to go through before they can arrive at a certain point. One hopes that by study, by the application of reason and common sense, one might avoid mistakes made by others. We don't all have to be run over by a car before we know that it is dangerous to stand in the middle of the road. So there are certain experiences we wisely avoid, but it seems that there are some that we can't. When you have such a complex situation as that of South Africa, one can only hope that they don't make all the mistakes that other people have made. But I think they have been through too much to expect that they would emerge without any scars. I think they are likely to make some mistakes, perhaps new ones even! If we have learnt anything from the post-colonial experience, it is the fact that you make one step forward and take two back, and perhaps stop, catch your breath and then move again. It seems to be that way. It's going to be slow and painful and expensive. But we can work to limit the expense and the delay and the waste.

**F.J.:** Obviously one of the problems in the immediate post-colonial situation is the kind of leader who gains power, but I have to say my all time favorite character of yours is Chief Nanga in *A Man of the People*, primarily because of the language that he uses. He's a great rhetor in terms of persuasion and argumentation. I realize that at the end we're saying this man's a thoroughly corrupt person, but the way in which he can use a straightforward English in conversations with Americans, and then switch to a proverbial and an African style when he's talking with Odili, and then again into pidgin and out when he's talking with "the people" is very complex and intriguing.

**Achebe:** He's very important. He's the only character who has the title of the book named for him. *A Man of the People* is him in a way that no other character—maybe Ezeulu in *Arrow of God*, but not the same way—is in the title. So, yes, he's a very important character. He knows what he wants to do. He's prepared to do it and has the training, the historical preparation for it. This is perhaps the tragedy of our situation. He's very proficient, and yet he's applying it all to destroy the society. He's applying it in a very narrow, selfish way. He's not applying it as Ezeulu is to save the system.

I think that disjuncture, that separation of the leader from those he leads—that a leader like him is utterly alienated from his community—is perhaps the greatest evil, the worst consequence of colonization. The leader is not a leader of his people. He's something totally outlandish in terms of the interests, the concerns, the comfort of his people. One can see how the creation of a ruler who had no responsibility to his people came about as a consequence of the colonial system. The colonialists wanted somebody who can run this foreign, alien institution for the advantage of the colonial power.

**F.J.:** In *Anthills of the Savannah*, you talk about how the British trained people to go out to the outposts and be potentates as it were.

**Achebe:** And hold the empire together for the benefit and comfort of the metropolis.

**F.J.:** But not to be friends like Chris and Ikem and Sam who were college classmates in a British college, Lord Lugard College, and who begin to be rivals as they work together. There is a line in the novel, "Lord Lugard College trained her boys to be lonely leaders in separate remote places."

**Achebe:** No, no, well, that's why they are in trouble. They're not supposed to be friends. If they were sent one to India, one to West Africa, they'll never get into any trouble.

**F.J.:** One of the things that interests me most about *Anthills of the Savannah* is the way it is a kind of distillation of all your work. We've just been talking about how it reflects the whole colonial and post-colonial situation as depicted in your earlier novels. Something similar seems to happen on the level of style. The beginning seems to come right out of *A Man of the People* and *No Longer at Ease*, as it has the less poetic, more straightforward style of those books. Then towards the end it gets to be more and more like *Things Fall Apart* with a poetic and proverbial style which comes through quite differently. I was wondering if you were consciously doing this, if it implied a metaphor for going back to a kind of Africanness?

**Achebe:** I don't know. I wasn't consciously patterning the work that way. But that's not to deny that, whether or not I was consciously patterning the work that way, the work did end up that way. There are things in any work or any novel which the novelist does not put in deliberately. So you may be right. As for this book bringing together some of the thoughts in the earlier books, that's true. I had not realized, for instance, how close in many ways to *A Man of the People* the book is, because I've never read *A Man of the People*. *(Laughter)* It is a book that I never read, for instance, at readings. It's only in the last one month that for some reason I picked it up and began to leaf through it and saw in fact that some of the characters there are prototypes for characters in the new book.

**F.J.:** In that sense I see a development or progression in your work. *Things Fall Apart* is a work about the landscape, the ethos, the area, the culture. But from there on, *No Longer at Ease* or *A Man of the People* are largely character portraits, and *Anthills of the Savannah* has character portraits of the sons and daughters of a country. So you seem to be moving more from an interest in the environment to the individuals who shape that environment.

**Achebe:** Well, I suppose you are right. That's one way, certainly, of looking at it. I hesitate a bit, though, because don't the environment and the character balance each other all the way? Certain historical moments, of course, seem to favor individual action more than social action, but other moments do the opposite. I think there's always a balance, really, between the two. I think what makes the ethos, climate, atmosphere in *Things Fall Apart* appear more is that we are not familiar with it. As one would say, "It strikes us." The atmosphere in which we live doesn't strike us quite so strongly, but I think it is, nonetheless, playing the same kind of role. Also, I think that when the individual and the climate seem to have the same view, when the individual is working within the parameters set by the culture, then the result of the cooperation is bound to be stronger than when people are at odds—with themselves and with the environment.

**F.J.:** One of the new aspects of your work emerging in *Anthills of the Savannah* is that there's a lot of "feminism" in *Anthills of the Savannah*. But I was disappointed that Beatrice doesn't emerge as a leader at the end.

**Achebe:** Doesn't she? *(Laughter)*

**F.J.:** Well? What would you say?

**Achebe:** I think she does. Leader in the sense—

**F.J.:** She's the last surviving one.

**Achebe:** Surviving is part of it. You have to survive in order to lead. She suddenly has the group around her acknowledge her leadership; I would call it leadership. If you mean that she's not going to take over the state of Kangan, no, no, no, there's no need for her take over the state of Kangan. That's not the kind of leadership that is available or necessary. It may in fact be that leadership at that level is doomed. Perhaps someone ought to be working out some other way. I'm not an authority on feminism, so I'm not sure what the agenda is. If it sees leadership only in the terms of the conventional, the kind of leadership that man created for himself, then there's going to be a lot of trouble because that's precisely the definition of leadership that's wrong, I think. Although I do not myself describe what the new leadership or what the new role is going to be because we are waiting for it, I do not think it should be necessarily the same as one that has just been failing.

**F.J.:** Is the leadership then just going to come from her maternal "woman sense," where she would take the backseat and not take over the government?

**Achebe:** That's entirely up to her. I really don't know how it's going to be. But I simply suggest that when the system fails, you don't take over and start to revive it. You look for something else. Women have got a maternal sense. That's in the nature of things. I don't think that can be suppressed. How Beatrice manages that with the other things will be entirely up to her, I think. I don't know whether I'm making sense.

**F.J.:** I like the ending because it's a nice affirmation of faith in women, in women's power and women's instinct and women being able to come together in a way in which men are not able to come together. Chris and Ikem never came together, but Beatrice is able to come together with Elewa, Ikem's girlfriend, after he has disappeared and Chris is killed. Elewa's mother comes in, and they are able to get something going and start getting the people together. In that sense, it's nice, but where I was disappointed was that I wanted another chapter in which Beatrice somehow became a leader. *(Laughter)*

**Achebe:** That's not my style at all. In fact, I was in considerable doubt whether I should have gone on to the present ending or end it a little before. The ending was originally not the whole chapter you now have. No, I think the ending is where it should be. It does not rule out women in political positions. We've had such women, but what this story is concerned about is really not that. It's something more about the essence of the problem than simply who is running the State. Beatrice has the capacity to be an Indira Gandhi, she has. I don't think that is the issue, whether you can have a Margaret Thatcher instead of a Kinnock.

**F.J.:** But that's not quite a parallel thing. *(Laughter)*

**Achebe:** I think what women need to bring into human civilization has to be different from what men have so far been able to bring. Otherwise, there would be no reason for a change, you see what I mean? *(Laughter)* We feel that things have come to such a pass that we are looking for something different. While not able to define what this difference is, I know it must be different. There are suggestions about what this could be from our tradition. Women came in in critical moments, you see, in the past. This century alone, Igbo women have stopped the government three times. They've not become Prime Minister yet. Maybe they don't want to be. Maybe it's not necessary. Maybe it is. I don't know if they want to be Prime Minister. So, I think here again like everywhere else, I'm quite open and I want to leave things open because all the facts are not in.

F.J.: It's very different from *Girls at War*, with the banner—

Achebe: "We are Impregnable."

F.J.: Yes. There's kind of a double edge to that, and there you seem more to be satirizing. Here you are much more sympathetic and concerned about the role women can play in making the world better.

Achebe: You think I was not sympathetic before? *(Laughter)* I've always been very sympathetic. But you know, the sharp edge doesn't really damage my fundamental beliefs. I think even when I'm satirical, it's that impish fact of "perhaps" which is useful. People shouldn't become too grandiloquent about things, or too serious, too obsessed, too self-righteous. There's always that possibility of things having a funny side. Maybe the impish side doesn't come out enough in *Anthills of the Savannah* because things are now going to such a pass that there's less and less room for humor, but I think there should always be the possibility to laugh at yourself, to make fun, to ridicule in a sense, not to put down but to point at things that don't quite fit even in the best of conceptions. I think it's always useful to keep the eye open for that. It saves us from self-righteousness. I'm so certain that self-righteousness is the worst possible thing that could happen to us. Once people become sure that they've got the answer, there's nothing else but to go downhill, that's my belief.

F.J.: Can I go into the issue of language? John Updike did a review of *Anthills of the Savannah* in *The New Yorker*, in which he expresses irritation at your use of pidgin. There are also some people in Africa who feel that pidgin should not be in African literature at all because it's not a relevant language. How do you feel about this?

Achebe: I think again we're dealing with these people who are irritating in their "this cannot be; this must not be; this will not be." Why, why, why are people so frightened of letting things that happen in real life happen in literature? Pidgin exists. Pidgin English is there. On the other extreme, there are others who say everything must be written in pidgin; this is our language. That's just as absurd.

F.J.: Is pidgin the right term for it? Is it Nigerian English, should we say?

Achebe: No, it's not Nigerian English because it's just one form of Nigerian English. There's no such thing yet as Nigerian English. It's evolving, and Nigerian English will be some kind of Standard English approved in the schools but taking into account the environment of Nigeria. I don't like the word pidgin; I don't know how it started. If somebody comes up with a better name for it, I'll be quite happy to adopt it. But this is what it's called, what it's called in Nigeria. We say, "they talk pidgin." It's used in Nigerian society in the same way as I reflect in my modern novels. It's there, and it's a valid language with its uses. There are things which it cannot do very well. There are things which it can do very well. People think it's rather inefficient, but there are even moments when it is more concise and far more efficient than Standard English. At Stony Brook, I was reading the scene between Ikem and the Superintendant of Police. That's why this particular example comes to mind—where the Superintendant says—

**F.J.:** "Do you know this man's face? Do you remember this man's face?"

**Achebe:** No, not that. Something like "You think na so we do am come reach superintendant." Now if you were to say that in Standard English, it would be much longer, something like, "Do you think this is how I have worked all these years and succeeded in becoming Superintendant?" In pidgin it's very, very short—"Na so we do am come reach superintendant." If you understand pidgin and you're from Nigeria, that's an excellent way of putting that. So, pidgin English, or whatever name we shall invent for it, lives in Nigeria and it's used. Even the most educated will use it when the need for it arises, and the need for it does arise from time to time. So I really don't see any other argument that one can put forward for or against pidgin. It is one of the varieties of speech available in Nigeria. It is no more Nigerian English than Amos Tutuola's English, which is not pidgin, by the way, as many people think. Tutuola does not write pidgin, he writes what he imagines to be standard English.

**F.J.:** What would you call Tutuola's English?

**Achebe:** It is very personal. It's personal to him. Tutuola's kind of English exists. It's a minority kind of English, an eccentric kind of English. It is Tutuola's own because of the level of education he has and the kind of mind he has.

**F.J.:** It's not Yoruba English?

**Achebe:** No, I wouldn't call it that, though there are some things you read in Tutuola which are distinctly Yoruba.

**F.J.:** Are there any people in Nigeria for whom Igbo or Hausa or Yoruba is the only language, or does everyone have at least a little pidgin and at least a little English?

**Achebe:** There are people who only speak one language. You will find such people. But the linguistic picture is so dynamic and so vital that I think such people—the people who only speak one language or who've never heard and never used a few words of English—are getting fewer and fewer. Nigerians are quite competent with languages, and they have to be. In the kind of society we have, it's quite common to find people who speak three or four languages or more.

**F.J.:** The Nigerian situation is therefore more like the Indian situation in that respect. As you said in *Morning Yet on Creation Day*, English provided us a language with which to talk to one another. "If it failed to give them a song, it at least gave them a tongue for sighing." So it brings everybody together and is a kind of connector. In that, is it then different from Kenya with its Gĩkũyũ-speaking majority?

**Achebe:** There isn't a predominant Gĩkũyũ-speaking majority in Kenya. Certainly the Luo would not say that. Gĩkũyũ is bigger than the others, but it is a minority if you put the others together. The Kenyan situation is not very different from the Nigerian situation, it's just smaller. Instead of two hundred languages, they perhaps have twenty. So there's no question at all that the linguistic complexity is there and will remain, unless of course we are to decide that we don't really want to keep bothering ourselves about these new nations called Kenya and Nigeria and so on. If the old nationalities, what all these people were before, should go their separate ways, it'd be a different matter. Then the argument would not really arise.

**F.J.:** If we did that, then we would go back to the older model, which is we would become tribal nations or separate people. Do you think that's suited to modern Nigeria or modern Kenya?

**Achebe:** It's not going to happen. Nobody's going to let that happen. It's not really a question of whether I like it or not. I've said quite a number of times that strictly speaking, I don't really mind one way or the other, but everybody else seems to mind, and I know that we cannot eat our cake and have it. We already fought one bloody civil war in Nigeria over the question of whether somebody can decide to leave the Nigerian federation. And the whole world seemed to say, "No, you can't," and allowed a million young people to shed their blood over that. So it seems to me, really, a foregone conclusion. The OAU has gone further, purely as a result of the Biafran experience, to pronounce that they will not tolerate tampering with the

European boundaries. So it's not really a matter of, do we want this or not? We've got these nations; we begin from there. So, what do you do in the event of a decision that they are going to abolish the language with which these units are administered, English? In my view, I don't think this will happen. And those who insist that unless this happens everything we've done is wasted can go on thinking so; they can go on saying what they are saying. I don't think it's going to affect the situation at all. If you say it long enough, I think you will simply be shown to be irrelevant to the real issues of modern Africa.

It's interesting that the people who are saying this in Kenya and elsewhere are those who see themselves as radicals, as Marxists. It doesn't occur to them that the only nations in Africa who have ruled out the discussion completely are the Marxist states. I remember the shock we had in Germany some years ago when the people from Mozambique came as a group. They were not talking about languages. They simply said, "It's Portuguese for us." We were shocked. The Angolans would say the same. Burkina Faso has said the same.

So what we are seeing here is people who are politicking with language. They are really mixing their political ambition with literature, that's all. That's not really what I'm talking about. I am talking about the situation which will go on because that's where history has placed us now. I'm not saying it's this or nothing else, it must be this and not that. And when those radical nations are saying it's Portuguese for us, I think that's outrageous too! I'm saying that it's got to be both. We must do that; we must insist. But again, you see, we are dealing with people who must have their answers clear and straightforward and simple because that way life would be easier. But life will never be easy. Life is not intended to be easy. Life is very complex. And even when we look for parallels with Europe, like saying the Russians write in Russian; the Japanese write in Japanese; the Finnish write in Finnish, somebody said that Africans should therefore write in Afrikaans! So even at that point, with that joke, we realize immediately that it's not the same thing. History has not treated the whole world the same way, and we would be foolish not to realize how we are in a peculiar situation as Africans. Our history has not been the history of England.

F.J.: So if history hasn't treated Africa the same way it has treated Europe, what are the implications of that fact for African writers? How does this affect those who are actually creating a literature?

**Achebe:** Well, I think the debate must go on. I think we need to dispose of the language question, the banning of certain languages, and accept that what we need is to ensure the development of this multiplicity of languages. I'm not suggesting that two hundred languages will survive in Nigeria. It's impossible; it's unlikely, but some of them will survive. Nigerians will see to that. Now that our government says we have four national languages— English, Hausa, Igbo, Yoruba—the minorities whose languages are not mentioned are up in arms just for the reason that we say "good night" at the end of the news in English, Hausa, Igbo, Yoruba. Many people are ready to fight over it. *(Laughter)* These are issues which you cannot ignore. So we have a problem on our hands and the theory about how we take all this into account is not my business. It's for those whose business it is to work out theories to do that. The critical canons will be evolving.

**F.J.:** I'm surprised to hear you say that it isn't your business, since for a long time in our literatures, both African writers like yourself and Indian writers like Raja Rao and Nissim Ezekiel were both writers and critics.

**Achebe:** Well, I know some people would say to me, "Why are you doing both?" My answer is, "Well, if you do it better than I do, I will stop, *(laughter)*, but until you come up . . ." The thing to bear in mind is the historical sequence. Criticism does not exist before what is criticized. What is criticized comes first, and when it comes there are no critics. That's why we had some of the most amazing—amusing too—criticisms of our work in the first few years. Everybody who felt like it had a go at it, so you had some very extraordinary things. Meanwhile, the critics were training themselves on the work, on the literature, and today the situation is better. There are better critics now, I think, by and large, than we had in the sixties. So that's the way it's happened. That's the way it's bound to be. Meanwhile, before the "professionals" arrived, we the writers—people like Raja Rao, like me— were having to cope with these adventurist—I almost called them interlopers—critics who saw this thing and so began writing about it. Sometimes they'd got it totally wrong, so wrong that you simply had to say, "Look, that's not what I meant."

So we were not satisfied with the criticism that was available, and that explains our presence as critics. Beyond that, also, we must recognize that we are not alone in this. Some writers elsewhere have also doubled up as critics. Some of the best criticism has been done, in fact, by those who write; sometimes the most significant statements at various points are made by writers. So there's no real conflict between writers and critics. Here again, both can work, and I'm sure as soon as the work of analyzing and expressing is done adequately by competent critics, writers will feel the need less and less. There is so much to do, and really I would be quite happy to feel that I don't have to bother about one particular area, like children's writing or some other area. Why am I saying to people, "You must write one children's book"? This is, in fact, a recognition of a disaster looming. Someone has to do something. So in that same line of argument, I will say that criticism is our business for now.

F.J.: But you write beautiful children's literature.

Achebe: Well, that just happens to be. *(Laughter)* It happens to be the case.

F.J.: But you didn't write children's literature out of a concern just to educate children, but you just wrote it and it came out.

Achebe: No, no, no, I did it out of a concern for children. I wrote children's literature out of concern for children because I would have been quite happy doing the adult things. As a matter of fact, it was Christopher Okigbo who said, "You must do one children's book for us." And that led to *Chike and the River*. As it happened, I was already also noticing some dangerous trends in my little daughter of four years reading all the poison that was wrapped up in European children's books that she was reading. So there definitely was what I call a missionary drive to go and save the children.

F.J.: To create for them stories out of their own myths and—

Achebe: Yes, and stories that would not damage them as people, stories that would not be full of racist imagery. I'd never read children's stories myself; my wife never did, you see, and so we had no idea what we were buying for our daughter. But when we noticed notions—

F. J: What specifically?

Achebe: She was talking about color, "I'm not Black; I'm Brown," and other things. So we began to worry because these things were not coming from our home. They might have been coming from her school. But I ultimately discovered that some of it was coming from the books she was reading, and some of them were really bad! I actually discovered some terrible stuff. It was things we went out and bought on her birthday. As the saying goes, we are like a fire brigade. Where there is a fire, we run there. If there were many people taking care of different things, we would probably not have to be trudging around the whole field of criticism to novels to children's books. But I'm not complaining. I just happen to enjoy it too. But I would want, also, to see a solid body of criticism emerge from our own critics who make a job of that.

F.J.: What would an indigenous African perspective be if one were developed in criticism? This is what Chinweizu has been calling for, but I find a dichotomy in Chinweizu's book. On the one hand, he says we should go back to searching for our African roots and writing from an African tradition, which of course you did very well in *Things Fall Apart*, and he criticizes Soyinka for being so European in his tradition. But Chinweizu doesn't argue for a return to African languages.

Achebe: What Chinweizu is saying, I think, is useful and valid, but like all people who are preoccupied with one thing, there would be exaggerations. I don't think that does, in the end, too much harm. I don't agree with everything he says about things that are admissible and things that are not. For instance, he would rule out most of Christopher Okigbo as being modernist European. Now I find Christopher Okigbo absolutely admirable, you see? So I think what we are feeling is a kind of ferment which I expect should be happening at this stage. It shouldn't discourage us, but it's in line with my own beliefs and preferences that there should be a multiplicity of positions and arguments and ideas and the result would be a rich literature rather than a sterile one.

F.J.: I'm struggling with this also for India, to develop a real Indian criticism. We may have gone from Matthew Arnold to Lacan, but we live under the same kind of hegemonic domination of Western critical criteria.

Achebe: Yes, well, I think we know what we don't want quite clearly. We don't want just an imitation of somebody else. I think we are still wrestling with the definition of African or Indian. I think once we know that—what is it that makes something Indian or what is it that makes something African—if we are sure of that then we will simply add that to criticism, and we would have what we need, but that's not settled. That's part of our growing up, part of our problem today, part of the predicament. There's no one tradition that we are talking about. We do have several traditions. We have the indigenous tradition, the oral tradition, the vernaculars, the ancient traditions of literature before, but we also have today. You can't disappear back into the past, so we need to create a synthesis out of these two. That is the issue.

F.J.: This is very interesting to me because one of the developments that has disturbed me is the way African literature is increasingly approached through the rather mechanical application of a number of Western ideas. I was recently visiting another university doing a seminar, and a student came to me because her teacher had given her an assignment saying she should take the theories of Marx and look for the Marxist elements of *Things Fall Apart*. I'm not talking about any very sophisticated Marxism here, just some very crude ideological labelling. And she had this assignment, and she had *Things Fall Apart* in her hand, and I said, "No, I don't think there's anything consciously Marxist in *Things Fall Apart* at all; I've read it a dozen times." (*Laughter*) I'm amazed at the tunnel vision with which people approach some works.

Achebe: Oh yes, that is not me. My whole life and my fundamental culture is open and is insistent again and again, over and over again. Where one thing stands, another thing must stand beside it. I don't make any bones about it. This saying "There is only one way" is something which is new to my people, and I'm not going to die in defense of it. They tell you where there are two heads, there are four eyes. You multiply the possibility to see around things. That's what my culture teaches, and I think it is more civilized, more sensible, than the fanatical view that "I've got the truth; I've got the righteousness." This is what is in fact probably going to destroy the world. Now I think that's terrible.

F.J.: *Anthills of the Savannah* ends with a reference to Mazisi Kunene's *Shaka*. Are you expressing a belief there in the strength of orature, or the stories of orature?

Achebe: Orature is a word I don't like. I have a strong belief in the story, and that is of course stated much more comprehensively by the old man from the North in *Anthills*, when he's addressing the young people in the capital. He goes into considerable detail to explain why the story is the most important thing in the human condition. The story decides the other elements of the war—the struggle, the preparation for the struggle, the struggle itself. The recounting of it, the story itself, crosses the breach between the generations. We can't witness the struggle of our fathers, unless this is conveyed to us through stories. This is why it has continued to be very important. Now when we begin to write, the same thing remains; the form changes from the story which is told to the story which is written. The story of Shaka as told by Kunene combines both, because here is an event that belongs to oral tradition but has now been written down. It is our story. Our future depends on this constant putting together of the past and the present through the story. That's something we cannot ever neglect. The storyteller is so important. What he does is so important, and the struggle and the conflict between him and the ruler, the emperor, is also something we mustn't take lightly. It is important that the storyteller tells the story the way he sees it, not the way the emperor wants it to be told.

# Buchi Emecheta

Nigeria has the largest population of any English-speaking country in Africa, indeed of any country in Africa. And Nigerian writers have been preeminent in African writing in English, beginning with Amos Tutuola and Cyprian Ekwensi in the early 1950s and Chinua Achebe and Wole Soyinka in the late 1950s and 1960s. But Nigeria has had a very troubled history since its independence in 1960, with coup after coup starting in 1966 and with the internecine communal strife that led, most tragically, to the Biafran War. Some of the flavor of its political life can also be found in its literary life, which is unusually pugnacious and combative. For instance, most countries would be honored when one of their writers won the Nobel Prize, but there was a firestorm of controversy over the awarding of the Nobel Prize in 1988 to the Nigerian dramatist and poet, Wole Soyinka. Soyinka has long been attacked by critics such as Chinweizu for his "eurocentrism" and "euromodernism"; Soyinka has retaliated, calling Chinweizu's kind of criticism "neo-Tarzanism."

Achebe, as the previous interview should have shown, has tended to stay above the fray, even though he has been praised by his fellow Igbo Chinweizu as the exemplary African writer. But some of the climate of Nigerian literary life and its effect on writers can be seen in the following interview with Buchi Emecheta. Buchi Emecheta, from the publication of her first book, In The Ditch, in 1972, has won worldwide recognition as a chronicler of women's experience both in England and in Africa and particularly as a chronicler of the diaspora's woman's experience. Emecheta feels quite strongly that the Nigerian literary scene is not a productive environment for writers, and she herself, though born in Nigeria in 1944, has as much if not more claim to be a British as a Nigerian writer, as she has lived in London since 1962 and has written powerfully about the situation of black women in Britain in In the Ditch, Second Class Citizen and elsewhere.

Emecheta is the first of several such black British writers we interviewed, and given their reliance on national categories to organize literature, critics have had a hard time placing her work (and that of Roy Heath and others). But readers have had no such trouble, as Emecheta's ten novels have been widely translated and read all over the world. The community she places herself in as a writer, however, is less with "black British" or Nigerian writers than with black American women writers such as Toni Morrison and Gloria Naylor. This is a perfect example of how literary affiliations in contemporary literature in English do not respect national frontiers and of how American literature has a closer relation to world literature written in English than many readers know or would like to admit.

We interviewed Buchi Emecheta at her home in one of the suburbs of north London. She had just moved into a new house with a lovely garden in back, and she was obviously and justifiably proud of her new home and of her hard-earned success as a writer. But she was even more proud of her children, several of whom were in and out as we talked most of an afternoon over successive pots of tea.

**Reed Dasenbrock:** I want to start by asking you about the direction of your work. Your first book was *In the Ditch*, which was set in London, and then your more recent books, such as *Destination Biafra* and *The Rape of Shavi*, are set in Africa, in Nigeria. Is there a pattern there?

**Emecheta:** When I first lived here, even after my books began to be published, I couldn't afford to go home. It was too expensive. But as soon as I was able, I started visiting home. When I'm not busy here, I'm in Africa. That way I also keep my children in the culture—that's what I have tried to do.

**R.D.:** So one of the reasons why your more recent books have been set in Nigeria, after your first books were set in England, is simply that you've been able to spend more time in Nigeria lately?

**Emecheta:** Yes, I think that's fair. The book that should have been my first book, *The Bride Price*, is set in Nigeria. But I had to rewrite that later, after my ex-husband burned it, as I've told in my books.

**Feroza Jussawalla:** How did you reconstruct it after he had burned it? You just had it all in your head?

**Emecheta:** You have the story in your head anyway before you start a book. The sentences may not be the same but—

**F.J.:** Did you keep the same plot line?

**Emecheta:** Yes, I kept the same plot line, though in the first version I had written, the girl didn't die. There they live happily ever after. But toward the end, when I was rewriting it, I think I'd just gone through so much I was fed up with everything, so I made the girl die. *(Laughter)* And by the time I'd published it, my marriage was over anyway. There were five years between the two versions.

**F.J.:** And then *In the Ditch* came next.

**Emecheta:** Yes, *In the Ditch* originally was carried as articles by *The New Statesman*. And then it was published as a book, and to explain the way *In the Ditch* happened was why I had to write *Second Class Citizen*.

**R.D.:** So in terms of publication, you started writing about England and then went back to Nigeria. But in actual writing, you've always gone back and forth.

**Emecheta:** Yes, when I began to recreate my first book, I was wanting to write about what I remembered of Africa. After I went back the first time, I found I was out of touch. Africa was ten years behind me—the Africa I remembered was definitely not the Africa of ten years later. So I started going back more often and writing more about Africa. By now I think my writing isn't English or African as much as more international, more universal.

**R.D.:** So as you're becoming more of an international person, your books are too.

**Emecheta:** Yes, even in the children's books, even if these are set in Nigeria. The themes are universal. That's so for *Second Class Citizen*, too, I think.

**R.D.:** When you say you are writing universal themes, do you have an eye on a particular kind of reader? Do you think your works are understandable by everyone, or do you think in writing about Nigeria, there are things that an English reader wouldn't understand, or an American reader wouldn't understand?

**Emecheta:** No, I try to write for the world.

**R.D.:** But if you're writing something set in Nigeria, do you think, well, here I have to write about this in certain ways so that it's understandable, or do you think the theme just carries across those kinds of national boundaries? Do you find your writing gets changed in that way?

**Emecheta:** The theme carries across, but it can be difficult for a reader. The difficulty I have as a writer is one of translation. I just try to keep my English language as simple as possible. It is not my emotional language. Most of my readers do not know my emotional language, Igbo, and it can get quite complicated translating yourself. At the beginning, when I was translating a song, sometimes I just let the Igbo language take over. Now when I have to express something from my emotional language, I use the exact words. I try to translate literally, not to make rhythm or poetry. When it is translated it becomes flat, we don't get the same rhythm, but I try. But otherwise, I write it from my own point of view, the way I see it. I don't try to make it particularly poetic or literary because of British or other readers. Nigerian critics say that the language in my books is very simple, too simple, in fact.

**R.D.**: So the critics in Nigeria would like you to be more experimental in your use of language?

**Emecheta**: Nigerian critics feel that the language I use in *Destination Biafra* is not appropriate. They would like me to use big military words, because I'm writing about what happened at Biafra. So I say to them, "If you know what I should do, then write it yourself. Write your own truth!"

**F.J.**: Language and style seem to have been the central focus of criticism of Nigerian literature. There has been a lot of praise of Achebe for the way he varies the language and tries to give it the flavor of Igbo proverbs and the oral tradition.

**Emecheta**: Well, Achebe is a great writer. He is the father of our English literature. You can't take that away from him. His work is highly original. When I was doing my degree here, I used *Arrow of God*, which I think is his best work. But the critics seem to think everything should be like *Things Fall Apart*. Everytime you want to read Achebe, you feel you want to study it as literature. You don't pick it up as though you want to enjoy the literature. That is why for a very, very long time, if you went to the African Writers Series, you had the feeling that this is not for the common people. But I refused to go into that when I started writing.

**F.J.**: And that's why critics such as Chinweizu think Achebe is so much better?

**Emecheta**: Chinweizu is the kind of Nigerian critic I was thinking of. When I launched *Destination Biafra*, Chinweizu came to the Africa Centre here in London. And he said, "Buchi, I am going to ruin you." I said, "Why? What did I do?" "Why should you be writing about what men are doing? Did you go to the warfield?" I didn't believe what he said. When I was teaching at Yale, students came to me and said, "Oh, Buchi, we didn't believe what you were writing about Nigerian men until we read Chinweizu's review of you in the *Times Literary Supplement*. What did you do to him?" He did not review the book and simply started attacking my personality. It's not the work that's the issue, it's who the writer is. Chinweizu wants the world to believe that Wole Soyinka committed a sin by winning the Nobel Prize. Why this obsession?

Well, it's natural. You see, Wole is Yoruba. Everybody thought Achebe would win it first, even I thought so. But he didn't. So that's as simple as that. To them, in the heart of Igboland, Achebe is the god. But this is not healthy in literary circles. There are good women writers from Nigeria who don't even get mentioned in Nigeria.

**R.D.:** So as opposed to any kind of evaluation of whether a book is good or not, you think there's a lot of artificial boosting, according to who you are.

**Emecheta:** According to who you are, your people, and the people you know. And I've been guilty of this too. I was reading the reviews of *Anthills of the Savannah*, and the reviews were full of adulation. So when it came to vote for the Booker Prize, I voted for it. Then when I was going to Chico, I took the book and started reading it. And I became ashamed of what I had done. People do that. Here is an Igbo man or a Nigerian or a friend you have to promote.

**R.D.:** Is this particularly true in Nigeria, do you think?

**Emecheta:** No. Look at what everyone has done to Alice Walker's *The Color Purple*. When *Color Purple* came to me first, I did not like the book. But, as I heard everyone say that it is a good book, so I thought that my own judgment might have been too harsh. And I read the book again.

**R.D.:** And?

**Emecheta:** It is not a bad book. This has happened to Flora Nwapa too, to her first two books. Now she is coming back to writing and doing her own publishing. It can happen here in England, too. People will just artificially boost a black person. I find that a most hurtful attitude—more patronizing than supportive.

**R.D.:** So what should a critic do?

**Emecheta:** I like a writer like Ngũgĩ, who lashes out, because he knows what is good and bad in writing. And I think this is true of Wole Soyinka, too.

**R.D.:** You don't feel that Soyinka is someone who has been artificially boosted.

**Emecheta:** No. I admire Soyinka because I think he's continuous, much more continuous, as a writer. He didn't have that long break Achebe had. Achebe was not artificially boosted. As I said, he is the father of all our literature. But Wole Soyinka deserves the Nobel Prize.

**R.D.:** Why do you think Achebe had that long break?

**Emecheta:** It's easy in Africa to do other things, to move away from writing. And that's what's happened. That was what happened to Flora too. Even Ama Ata Aidoo. She became the Minister of Information in Ghana. Then she fell out with the Government and now she's starting to write again. Like me, she is very outspoken.

**F.J.:** What do you think happened with Tutuola? There was the first big buildup about how good his language was, and then there were people in Nigeria saying, "Well, his writing is not that good, his English is not proper." Was that an artificial boost of the kind you're talking about?

**Emecheta:** No, not at all. Tutuola was writing in the ethnic English, which we call pidgin. But we admire Tutuola, because if you read him, you get the flavor of Nigeria. Critics say it is bad English, but people understand it. It's like Zora Neale Hurston's work. Do you know her work? When I was teaching at Yale, I got to know Gloria Naylor's *Mama Day*. If she had been writing in Nigeria, the critics would have rejected her. They would have said her English is not the Queen's. In Nigeria, because people don't go out of the country, they feel the real English is the English that the colonials spoke twenty years ago. That is how you find English spoken in Nigeria by people who didn't leave Nigeria. But English is a language that grows, like any other language.

The African writer who stays in Nigeria and uses the English language is being left behind. He's using this old English language to write. He thinks people are still speaking like that. So when he comes to the West, people make fun of him without his knowing.

**R.D.:** So what they like is a certain kind of more stilted, more officially "English" English—

**Emecheta:** Yes, the old official English language. As somebody said, if you really want to hear the old English, the way of speaking of twenty years ago, get a letter written by these old colonials from Nigeria. Because they write, "I have written to you thrice. And your letter of the 18th instant," and so on, you know, full of things you have in the Bible.

**R.D.:** So they look down on Tutuola—

**Emecheta:** They look down on Tutuola or on writers, like me, who try to write the way we speak now. They look down on the modern English of today. They say that the English, the language you're writing in, should be such that you're going to have to open your dictionary on every line. When people don't understand a work, they think it is a great work. I met one man from Heinemann about five years ago. We were having breakfast, and he said, "I've just done something great. I've just finished reading Wole Soyinka's *The Interpreters*." I said, "But you published it." He said, "Oh, yes, I never read it, I just published it." It's like the emperor's new clothes. People will say, "you didn't understand." So people are afraid. I said, "Well, I didn't understand that book." And he said, "Well, everybody said, 'What a great writer so I published it.' " So that's another instance of artificial boosting.

**F.J.:** You admire writers who use the kind of Nigerian English that's being generated today?

**Emecheta:** That was what Amos Tutuola was doing. The man who tried to champion it, Cyprian Ekwensi, says, you shouldn't write in formal English, because we are writing about our common people. His work is not very appreciated and writers like him are neglected. The Americans like him, but the Nigerians don't take him seriously. So everything that comes from Nigeria must be backed right.

**F.J.:** So you feel Nigerian literature in English, or Nigerian literature per se, has been dominated by a kind of Western-educated, male establishment, and they have not let either the women writers or those writers who would do something different get ahead.

**Emecheta:** Exactly. It's hard for the outsider to know what is going on in Nigerian literature; they don't know any literature beyond Achebe and now Wole Soyinka, because of the Nobel Prize. They don't know any other writers. And it's not just women—there are many ordinary writers who would have done well if they had some encouragement. But they just take these two men as tokens, even though it's a country of one hundred and ten million people. When I taught in Calabar, I was in the creative writing department. I taught four or five students whose work was almost finished and quite good, but unfortunately there were no local publishers to encourage them. Their writing was never published. But that was definitely what they came to university for. So some of them will become administrators, not writers.

**R.D.:** There is a lot of talent that's blocked?

**Emecheta:** Yes. There's a lot of talent that's wasted, and there's a lack of encouragement. These are some things I said in Nigeria, and I have done so up here. At home, some people would say, "Why should you say anything against Wole Soyinka or against Achebe?" It's not that at all. I like Wole, I was very proud when he won the Nobel Prize. I kept saying, "It's about time." And I always respect Achebe.

**R.D.:** So it's not their work but the use of it that you're objecting to?

**Emecheta:** No, not objecting. I'm just saying that it's unfair for the Westerners just to pick out these two writers when there are other good writers. There is a patronizing attitude at work here. And sometimes a Nigerian has to come here to be recognized. And that is where our situation is different.

**R.D.:** And that distorts.

**Emecheta:** Of course it does, yes. It comes down to a "recruit the noble savage" syndrome. Which, again, is stilted.

**R.D.:** How could that be changed, do you think?

**Emecheta:** How could that be changed? If we would have our own publishing houses, like Americans have their own publishing houses.

**F.J.:** As Flora Nwapa does.

**Emecheta:** Yes, but she can't publish too much. She only publishes her own books. And I tried to do that too, with my own publishing company. But they have to come here to do the printing, so by the time a book goes to Nigeria to be sold, it's awfully expensive. Flora is still working very hard at this.

**F.J.:** So the making of literature is tied up with the politics of publication.

**Emecheta:** It is, the politics of publication and the economics.

**F.J.:** So how do we know what is literature nowadays?

**Emecheta:** That's what I'm saying, that it's very artificial. In England here, you can know what is literature, or when something is taken out and translated, you know what is literature. In America, you know what is literature. But in the African situation, you have to know somebody to be able to push and stand up. And on top of that, we can't publish or print inside the country, even though we have so many people. The printing that is done inside the country depends on who you know or on someone pulling out his money to print his own book. To publish in Nigeria is difficult. And one pound is about twenty naira in our money. It used to be almost one-to-one.

A book, say, like my *Head above Water*, is twelve ninety-five. It's somebody's income for a month. It's that bad now.

**F.J.:** How can a woman writer break through this kind of publishing establishment to make a name for herself?

**Emecheta:** That's what I get asked all the time by women from Nigeria. *(Laughter)* They come here and say, "How do you make it? How do you manage to get ahead?" But they forget I'm in the West. I didn't "make it" first in Nigeria. I wouldn't have been able to do it in Nigeria. If I had stayed in Nigeria, maybe the best I could have done was just to print a few children's books and seen if anybody would read them. I probably wouldn't have done even that because they criticize so much. You have to belong to a certain class to break through. Flora came from the colonial class, so she could break through. And Achebe and the other writers are very middle class. His father was a preacher, something high in Nigeria in those days. My father was only a moulder on the railways. On top of that, I'm an Igbo person from the West. They are from the East, and therefore they think "We're the real Igbo." Someone like me could not have broken through in Nigeria.

**F.J.:** Was it a great surprise to the Nigerian establishment when you started to get serialized in *The New Statesman*?

**Emecheta:** Oh, yes, a great surprise. I'm still not forgiven. I think I won't be forgiven for that.

**R.D.:** And that's partly because you're a woman, and partly because you come from the wrong class, and partly because you're not from the Igbo heartland?

**Emecheta:** Yes, all of that. And on top of that, I'm not writing in the accepted mode of telling how great the country is.

**R.D.:** What about your *Destination Biafra*?

**Emecheta:** That was the one that Chinweizu really couldn't handle, because I came into what he felt is a masculine domain. Why should I write about politics? I should go on writing about women.

**R.D.:** You also worked for the Igbo side?

**Emecheta:** Because we were here in England, we were here as students, we saw the faults of both sides. I didn't go for Ojukwu, the Igbo leader, at all, but then Nigeria was attacking all Igbos.

**F.J.**: So in a sense, you have the same kind of disillusionment with post-colonial government there in Nigeria as Ngũgĩ does with Kenya?

**Emecheta**: Yes, I think so. You know, Ngũgĩ was really unlucky, because when he was there, he was put in prison.

**F.J.**: How can the situation in Third World countries change?

**Emecheta**: I've tried to change the publishing situation. I have my own publishing company. The bank here was very sympathetic; they gave me a loan. But by the time I finished printing, by the time we got the books, it got so expensive that I hardly made any money. So what I do is—and this is my new charity—that I sell the hardback here. With whatever profits I make, I give those books free to libraries in my country and then sell the paperback to Fontana which is my income now. But in hardback, which I started in order to help others, I can't make money. So you can see the difficulties—although I am only one person. Maybe if there were two or three, maybe it would work better. It's working very slowly because people can't afford to buy these books.

**R.D.**: And so you started your publishing company here, but you're finding the economics are very difficult.

**Emecheta**: Yes, indeed. Even if I furnish all the printing. It's just a matter of photocopying and binding. We ought to be able to do that in Nigeria. But we can't find the paper. Even if I've done all the printing and everything here, we still can't break even.

**R.D.**: So you can't break out of the cycle.

**Emecheta**: No. In Nigeria when they find a book they want to read, they photocopy it. People will even sit down and type it out. When that happens, I don't get anything but I don't mind, because I want them to read my books. I've seen them in black markets. What can you do? You're just relieved that they're reading them. What is the point of writing about people who can't read what is written about them? A woman came here yesterday, from the government, wanting to put my books on tapes. I said, "That's a very good idea." Because then more people in Nigeria can access my books. So she is trying to do that. She came to buy the rights for four of my books so she can do that.

**R.D.**: Of course, the tapes may be expensive too.

**Emecheta**: You can use them as community property, in libraries.

**F.J.**: Have your books been translated into Nigerian languages?

**Emecheta:** No. Because English is our lingua franca, there is no real need in Nigeria to translate books from English.

**R.D.:** I think it's fair to say that you're not very enthusiastic about the Nigerian literary scene. *(Laughter)* What are you enthusiastic about? Who are the writers who you think are doing important work?

**Emecheta:** To me, the great writers who come from ethnic minorities writing in English come from America. I think the deep, the real deep thinkers now writing in the English language are the black women, such as Toni Morrison, Gloria Naylor, Alice Walker, etc.

**F.J.:** Where they are using black English in a certain kind of way to signify their difference?

**Emecheta:** Exactly. You must read Naylor's *Mama Day*, because she's a modern Zora Neale Hurston. She uses language when it comes to conversation that is not like anything else. So there's an amalgam of the old and the new, and it's beautifully written, the way she's written it. She's a child of today, so she knows what she's talking about. Or Maya Angelou—she's another good writer, isn't she? You can understand what she is saying.

**R.D.:** So you feel more kinship with the black American women writers than with the Nigerians?

**Emecheta:** Yes.

**F.J.:** Much of the work written about you now is concerned with feminism and your attitudes towards what women can do to change their lives. You must have gone through a very difficult time, trying to do your college work and your writing and bringing up the children.

**Emecheta:** Yes, I had them to mother, anyway.

**F.J.:** Now, you are one example of someone who has made being a working mother a success, because you are now a success, and an established writer. And there is always the question, still, among feminists, is it possible for women to work and have children? Should they work and should they have children?

**Emecheta:** I feel that for the average intelligent woman, raising a child is not enough. You need something else. I think I covered this subject in *The Joys of Motherhood*. If you don't keep something for yourself, you just become entangled with that child. And that is not very nice. You'll be cheating yourself and cheating the child. And there is no other time that is better for you to be yourself than when you are raising the child because there you are growing together. I find that then children will value you. When they are older, they look after you and they look up to you. And if you are in a position to buy houses for them and are able to support yourself and them too when they are in their twenties and late teens, they appreciate this. But if you are giving everything up just to wash their clothes and make sure of clean windows, then you are allowing your house to rule you, so as to keep it tidy, perfect. At the end of the day you have nothing to show. So I feel that for the average intelligent woman, children can be very emotionally demanding, but after a time you get fed up with just meeting their needs.

F.J.: You know, we think of America as being mostly liberated and feminist. But in my son's preschool class, for instance, I'm the only working mother. And the other mothers will raise questions with him, "Why does your mother work? Why doesn't she stay home and take care of you?" He has trouble understanding this. It's interesting that most of middle-class white America is still reinforcing the stereotype that the mother should stay home and take care of the children. It's very interesting to me that that break hasn't come through.

Emecheta: This time two weeks ago, I spoke at a women's school in Bristol, and I spoke of the special pleasure of the woman who goes out and works. The reason why we Africans have difficulty identifying with feminism is because we have always worked. So it's no use telling us that feminism is something new. Even when you are going to your husband's house in the village, your mother will not just pack your beautiful clothes. She will give you utensils and tools for your work, or what she thinks you will need for you to go on working. Women bring their arts and their industry to their husband's house. So for us, it is never ever that childbearing is a full-time occupation. It is easier in our own area because we find the older women can help in raising the younger children so the mother can work in the fields or go out and teach or do the industrial work in the factories. So to me, it's not really different. A woman is always outside working for her keep. Had I just been living in Nigeria, I wouldn't have known that a middle-class woman is just living at home with her children. And I didn't work so hard for my education in Nigeria just to come here to be a middle-class woman who just made tea. No, I wouldn't have done that. I needed that extra.

F.J.: You're right about the fact that Western society does not have that support structure of women suporting women, like in the extended family.

Emecheta: They don't have that supportive culture. But don't they have nurses and nannies? Yes, they do. Then why don't they use them? And this is just what I say. It's entirely up to you. So they do have support systems here. I went to Chico, California, in November 1988, where I saw women bringing their children to the conference in the morning. They had play groups. People were hired especially to look after the children.

There are a lot of people from my town in Nigeria here. They are not all highly educated. And even with the little education they have, they will go to work. Some of them still wash clothes and clean offices. In the morning, at 5 o'clock, you see them go out and wash things, clean something, just to have that extra cash in their own pocket, to say, "It's mine." Some of these women have husbands who are lawyers, in positions of great influence. And people used to ask them, "Why do you do this?" And some of them say, "I just wanted that extra freedom." If your mother is sick, you don't have to ask your husband for money. You know you have your own money; it gives you some dignity. And if your son or daughter is suffering, you just want to give something extra as a mother. You don't ask anyone because you have your own money. All these things do matter. They do make you a person. It gives dignity.

F.J.: Is women supporting women really possible in Western society as you see it?

Emecheta: I think Africa is ahead of the West here. If women in our area are oppressed, we have a kind of freedom most Western women haven't. You don't have to live up to any rule. No African woman will criticize another one for going out to work. Besides, for that society, if after marriage you are still at home, they see you as a lazy person. You must have something to do even if it is a tiny piece of labor, just as many women own their own business in Africa. So that is the way we are. We always work. But that doesn't mean, as it can in the West, not having children.

I remember before I met Alice Walker, she made the statement several times that most women writers just can have one child. And then she interviewed me when we met at Yale. The children were younger, they were at home. In the piece she wrote about me, she said, "She wrote not despite the children, but for the children." What she had in mind is that I had to work,

I had to get some income. I was not being supported. And the more children you have, the harder you may have to work at whatever your occupation.

I have this image of people telling me, "you can't do this," and there you are doing it. But what if my mother had told me that? Then you have the "alabaster woman" going to break if she does anything. What of the Jewish people who work in the kibbutz? They have arranged the community, again, so that older people and others are looking after the children. There is always someone looking after the children, and that's that person's work.

F.J.: Now, interestingly, most of your work has come out of this experience in working with children, and most of your fiction and imagination have been triggered by that, so most of your themes, then, are themes about the kinds of things you have gone through in your own life, being a single mother raising children.

Emecheta: Yes, because most writers' imaginations are triggered by their lives' experiences unless you separate your life and work. I try to limit myself to the subject I know I've experienced, that I am certain of.

F.J.: How has that changed over the years in London?

Emecheta: I'm beginning to notice that my friends are not just friends from Africa anymore. My friends are those who are going through the same experience. They don't have to be African, and they don't have to be black. I've found that as I get older and I stay longer, I have something in common with you, maybe, if you are here, than with my sister in Nigeria.

F.J.: I've been hearing the term black British a lot here in London, as an umbrella term for the Asians, Africans, and West Indians here. Is there that kind of solidarity among these groups here?

Emecheta: Yes and no. There's discrimination here too. When you come here, the Westerner will say, "You are black." Okay. And that, again, is bad. And the West Indian will say, "You're African." The Asian will say, "You are African." And so when they say "black writer," the Asians find that it suits them to be black when it pays. But when it's not, it suits them to be white. They are "black" when they know there is something to gain and "white" at other times. They are still on that borderline. There are always these factions. I think it's human. And writers explore these themes, always, because they are there. Many write from the totality of their lived experience.

F.J.: In your twenty-five years in London, now, you've become a multicultural person, a person who embodies both a kind of English consciousness and, at the same time, a Nigerian consciousness and a certain kind of Igbo consciousness. Do you still maintain all of that, or do you think you're becoming a more cosmopolitan person?

Emecheta: I think I've become more international, because for the last ten years or more, I've spent about two or three months every year in America, for example. And then in Nigeria. And of course I have travelled to a lot of places, Germany, Holland, France, and elsewhere in Europe. You can't have all these experiences without changing. They make you what you are. So much that when I get to Ibuza, the village which is still my home, I've seen so many things that make me different. For example, I don't want to spend all my money on clothes like women at home. If I have a clean pair, that's enough. People at home will ask me, "Are these the only pair you have?" I say, "Yes." "But," they say, "you have money." I answer, "Yes, but I don't spend my money on unnecessary clothes." They say, "But you wore this last year. This is not the latest of fashion." I do that because I stay in England where you look for comfort and warmth as long as the stuff lasts. So you go with something that's reasonably clean. That makes me un-African in a sense, because the African woman is bathing and dressing, dressing, and showing everything. That's one difference. So that's why I say I'm just a citizen of the world. My own immediate family and all are here, particularly my children, and they are growing now.

R.D.: How does their frame of reference differ from yours? They were all born here or grew up here, right? Do they see themselves as English?

Emecheta: They are just like myself. Because when I go home during holidays, I always take them with me. I brought plans for a house from California and am building it in Ibuza. That, I hope, is a place that will be calm and relaxed. So when we come here to London, we know it's work. I find that for my children there is no boundary. We have connections here in London, we have connections in Nigeria, we have American connections. I think it is safer that way.

R.D.: What about their languages? Do they speak Igbo?

Emecheta: They speak English and understand Igbo. But for them, English is their emotional language. My son is a writer now, but English is his language too. You know that he is somebody whose English is his first language. His style is completely different from mine. And he explores and plays with the language more than I do.

**F.J.**: So you don't experiment so much with language, you feel, because your first language or your emotional language is Igbo?

**Emecheta**: Yes, my emotional language is Igbo. I also speak Yoruba. As this is the first language I spoke as a child, it will always be my emotional language.

**F.J.**: I notice in your works, for instance, when you are angry or cursing someone or expressing some joy or thinking of a song, it's written like a poem.

**Emecheta**: Yes.

**F.J.**: And it's a translation.

**Emecheta**: These are always a translation of my emotional language. My children don't have that. They can understand the city's Igbo language. When it comes to the idiomatic, the curses, they can't understand them. They don't know that. So when they speak Igbo, they have the social city style. African languages are spoken at a certain level in the city. In the villages, there is an idiomatic language, so you can say, "this is an Igbo person from this village." But you have this in the English language also. You know someone is from Texas from the accent.

**R.D.**: I'm wondering about what you just said, because there are writers who would say that they do a great deal of playing around with the English language precisely because it isn't their own language. Because they come to it from the outside, they feel in a sense more playful.

**Emecheta**: The way I play with the English language, I translate my thoughts from my own emotional language into English, and try to adjust as much as possible. An example of that kind is I don't say the child says "thank you," I will say "she dances her thanks." That is because it belongs to my culture. If I say thank you, I say "thank you and good." I show a feeling, "She cried her sorrow," or "she cried her woes." And so she mourned, or something like that. The verb shows exactly what you are going through. You say in English, "that man is very sad." We say, "that man is walking his sadness." In *The Slave Girl*, for instance, I translated almost word for word like that. Why I did that was that when I was writing the book, I was told it was not too long. So I started experimenting in English to put in more words. *(Laughter)* And it came out gradually. That's the only way I can play with words. But I feel that I cannot reach the writing from the generation of my son who, for instance, is experimenting a lot with style.

**R.D.:** Maybe in a sense they're in between. They have the best of two worlds: they certainly haven't assimilated into being completely English, but they know the language inside out because they grew up here.

**Emecheta:** I think so, because the English students I teach, the British English students, don't seem to have that. There is a freshness in their work, which is lacking in the stereotypical English student. But it's also different from my own prose because I started speaking the English language when I was fourteen. So I can never really fill those fourteen years in which I had another mode of expressing myself.

**F.J.:** Is there a new, central black consciousness coming out of this new generation like that of your son, where the African and the West Indian and the black American are all seeing themselves as black—

**Emecheta:** The black writers in the States see this in a different way. They express their own consciousness. Toni Morrison, for example. This is being done by women, black American women, not us from England. Not yet.

**F.J.:** So you see the future of literature, or a literary tradition lying now in the hands of black American women writers, essentially. And they are expressing this new black consciousness.

**Emecheta:** Yes, because they, as modern women, are combining the slave tongue which they gave us with an African consciousness. They've put everything together. It's women who are doing it. And that is my tradition. Women are carriers of culture in whatever language.

# Sam Selvon

The island of Trinidad in the Caribbean must have the highest concentration of good writers in English of any place since Ireland at the height of the Irish Literary Revival at the beginning of the century. V. S. Naipaul is of course the best known of these writers, though he is not overly fond of his native land, and his fellow Trinidadians have tended to repay the compliment. Other important writers from Trinidad include the late Harold Sonny Ladoo, Michael Anthony, Earl Lovelace, and though Trinidad—again, like Ireland—has exported many of its writers, primarily to England and Canada, it has also been a magnet for other writers, as the leading West Indian poet and dramatist, Derek Walcott, lived and worked in Trinidad for many years. But the first major writer from Trinidad was Sam Selvon. Born in 1923, Selvon was with George Lamming the first West Indian writer to make a name for himself in English literary life, with *A Brighter Sun* (1952), a sequel to that novel, *Turn Again Tiger* (1958), and most famously, *The Lonely Londoners* (1956).

*The Lonely Londoners* is a literary landmark in at least two different respects: first, and most obviously, it is the first West Indian novel to rely extensively and successfully on West Indian English—not standard English English—as the medium of narration, and this is the aspect of Selvon's work most influential for later West Indian novelists. Second, Selvon's novel—as the title shows—is not about the country left behind but about the new reality of life in Britain for the new immigrants from the non-Western world. In this sense, Selvon's novel is the first work of what is now called black British writing, a forerunner of later work by Emecheta, Farrukh Dhondy, Hanif Kureishi, and others. This is a path followed less by subsequent West Indian writers than by writers from Africa and Asia. But the tension between representing the old, the exotic, the attractively different and the new, the urban, the often less than attractive settings of contemporary life is one that runs throughout the writing of all these writers. Selvon was the leader then for an important development in world writing in English towards the rendering of contemporary life, and though *The Lonely Londoners* and its two sequels, *Moses Ascending* (1975) and *Moses Migrating* (1983), won broad acclaim, they have not received the recognition they deserve for anticipating this important development in contemporary literature.

We interviewed Selvon in London, at the offices of his publisher, Longman's. He was visiting from Canada, giving some readings and meeting with his publishers, and was gracious enough to give us some of his busy time.

**Reed Dasenbrock:** You've been living in Canada now for some years.

**Sam Selvon:** Yes, I moved in 1978, and I've been in Canada now about ten years.

**R.D.:** Why Canada?

**Selvon:** I came to England in 1950, and I spent twenty-eight years of my life here which I consider to be a good slice of my life. I suddenly felt that I had had enough of English tradition and European culture. I wanted to get back to the West before it was too late. Everyone asks about why I selected Canada. Some of my wife's relatives who had settled there some years ago were doing pretty well for themselves, so she said, "let's go to Canada," and that's how I ended up there.

**R.D.:** Did you think at all of going back to Trinidad instead of moving to Canada? I'm thinking of *Moses Migrating* in which Moses thinks about returning to Trinidad but finally returns only for a holiday. Were those your sentiments as well?

**Selvon:** Well, I go back from time to time. In fact, I've just been down there for three months at the beginning of this year. But I feel that I do as much for the island and for the people by living abroad, as I would be able to accomplish if I went back. I don't see that there is going to be any useful purpose being served by my returning for good. I go back from time to time and teach, but the way I see it is that I would just feel myself to be somewhat retired and off the scene if I went back to live in Trinidad.

**Feroza Jussawalla:** You are among the first wave of world authors writing in English. You are in the first generation together with many Indian writers like R. K. Narayan and Raja Rao and with Wilson Harris.

**Selvon:** I suppose I am one of the first writers in that period of time shortly after the war when so many writers moved towards London. I don't know specifically how that happened but we did have quite a convergence of literary talent here in London around the early fifties. Writers from all the other islands in the Caribbean seemed to come up to London.

**F.J.:** How did you come to writing? Did you move to England to do something else and then started writing out of your experiences, or did you move in order to do your writing?

Selvon: No, I started writing in Trinidad. I worked with the Trinidad *Guardian* just after the war. I started to write poems and short stories, and I was successful with the BBC program in those days. There was a program beamed from London called "Caribbean Voices," and they used poems and short stories from Caribbean writers. I was fortunate; I had quite a few pieces accepted, and that encouraged me a great deal. I must say that when I came to England I was prepared to do anything. I didn't have any dreams that I would get into professional writing; and in fact, it was some time before I really got established. In the meantime, I couldn't even get a job as a journalist because I was told that I had to belong to the English Journalist Union, and to be a member of that I had to be working for an English newspaper, so it was one of those catch–22 things. But I did a fair amount of free-lancing, up to the time when my first novel, *A Brighter Sun*, was published three years later in 1952.

R.D.: You're part of a group of West Indian writers who are roughly contemporary, George Lamming, V. S. Naipaul and others, all of whom began writing in the 1950s and quickly became well known. In 1960, West Indian writing was certainly much better known than African writing in English or Indian writing in English because of these writers. Yet today, I think, one would have to say the opposite was true. Soyinka has won the Nobel Prize, one reads a great deal about Achebe and Rushdie, etc. What's the difference?

Selvon: I don't know. I think that there has really been a lull in literary activity, if you like, in the Caribbean since that surge, since that time of which you speak. Certainly I don't think that there have been very many new writers since that time. Perhaps there ought to be more.

R.D.: Is there a missing next generation?

Selvon: I think so. There are some writers, for instance, who are about to reestablish themselves and have gone back and stayed in their island. In Trinidad, there's Michael Anthony and there's Earl Lovelace who both reside there. My feeling is that the new writing will have to come from the new generation rather than from the older ones like myself. That is where the surge will have to come from. It isn't that I haven't got more to write, but I just feel that is the direction from which this new movement will come.

F.J.: And yet you're very avant-garde in your own writing style. You use a kind of nativized English or local English, West Indian English, in a way no one did before you. Can you comment on the ways in which you use English?

**Selvon:** It's what is called "nation language" in the Caribbean. I started it out as an experiment really in the first novel, *The Lonely Londoners*, and it worked very successfully there. It got a wonderful reception. I was wondering what reaction I would get, but certainly my using that kind of language, a kind of dialect of English, caused no difficulty at all in understanding. In fact, it was highly praised, both in England and in America, and people talked about injecting new blood into the English language. The language, in particular, got a kind reception. If it were not for the language, the book would not have come about. I think that the language was the right vehicle to bring out the essences of what I tried to do with standard English and just couldn't succeed. This is why I turned to the dialect.

**F.J.:** How realistic is it? How much of the style is made up of realistic cadences you're catching and how much of it is creative variance?

**Selvon:** I think it's a bit of both. I really try to keep the essence, the music of the dialect. I've tried very hard to keep that. I don't do any phonetic spelling, and I try to avoid some words or phrases which I feel would be very difficult for an audience outside of the Caribbean to follow. Or if I do use it, I would try to make it clear in the text.

**R.D.:** Can you give an example of something you might avoid?

**Selvon:** Well, for instance, there's a phrase that I use that has been criticized as not coming from the true dialect. The phrase is "monkey smoke your pipe." That's a phrase that I use; in fact, the Trinidadian phrase is, "Crapu smoke your pipe." Now you're going to ask me what a crapu is, I'm sure. Do you know what it is? It's a kind of frog; it's a toad. It's in the dictionary, but that's a Trinidad word. Now, I think that "monkey smoke your pipe" has a much more universal appeal and brings a good visual image to the reader much more than "Crapu smoke your pipe." That is definitely going to throw off the reader, immediately. However, it wouldn't throw a Trinidadian, who would say, "ah, yes, that's the real thing."

**R.D.:** So there you would need a footnote or something like that to make it clear.

**Selvon:** Exactly, and I don't like using footnotes. I like it to be all in the text of the writing. So that's a small example. Even when I began to use the word "lime," to go "liming about," I try to make it clear in the text that it just meant passing time away standing at a corner and watching the girls go by.

**R.D.:** So on the one hand you try to be as accurate as possible, but on the other hand you keep at least one eye on the reader who would not understand.

**Selvon:** Exactly, on the reader who might have difficulty in understanding fully. And as I say, I think that is responsible for the success that has happened. In fact, a great many other writers are now seeing that this is a form that could be used well.

**R.D.:** Do you see your work as an influence, let's say, on Earl Lovelace in *The Dragon Can't Dance* or on other younger writers using dialect?

**Selvon:** I think so. I think that children of the new generation in the schools in particular, when they are trying to write dialect now, follow that pattern by avoiding, for one thing, phonetic spelling. What I have also done with the dialect is that I have kept to standard English where I felt that it just wasn't necessary to change even the spelling of a word or anything like that. I didn't use d-e for t-h-e; I feel that t-h-e is fine with me. When I open a book, I look at a sentence, I look at the writing of it, and I say that's ok if the rhythm of dialect is still there. I feel that writing in phonetics jars the reader. I've heard many people say that reading different dialects with phonetic spelling is a bit irritating, having to analyze it all in your mind.

**F.J.:** One thing Wilson Harris has said to us about your work is that you've made the dialect part of the consciousness of the narrator which he doesn't do. He admires you for that. He moves from standard English to dialect only in dialogue, as opposed to having it be the consciousness of the narrator.

**Selvon:** I think that those are the parts that have really shown the extent to which one can use that kind of language. If it were relegated only to dialogue, then I don't think you would see the potential. But with the narrator using dialect you can see it a little more.

**R.D.:** It seems that the novels with Moses as the protagonist all are written almost entirely in what we've been discussing—dialect. But some of your other novels go back and forth a little bit more. In *A Brighter Sun*, or—

**Selvon:** Oh yes, that wasn't my style with all my work. When I started to write, at that stage it wasn't my aim to try and do something with the dialect language at all. In fact, from my earlier work up to *The Lonely Londoners* and even after *The Lonely Londoners*, I have written works like *The Plains of Caroni* using both standard English and the dialect form. I started out like most of the other writers, using the dialect form in the dialogue only. Maybe there was even a slight bit of dialect in the narrative with the first novel, but I wasn't quite conscious of it there. Some people have pointed that out to me and said: "But look, even in your first novel you were using that dialect form in some of the narration itself." When I looked at it, I had to agree, but that must have been really something unconscious that happened during the process of creation, because I wasn't aware of it then.

**R.D.:** You were in a sense working towards the later works?

**Selvon:** I don't know, I think I would have continued to write in both standard English and using the dialect form mainly with dialogue. It was only that when I started to write that particular novel, *The Lonely Londoners*, I just could not do it with standard English. Suddenly when I started to use "nation language," the Trinidad form of English, I just got on the right vehicle. It shot along and in six months the whole book was finished. It just wrote itself. It just seemed as if one was waiting for the other, as it were, and as soon as they matched, it took off.

**F.J.:** So you were not consciously trying to create a style or consciously trying to create a language, but writing in what was out of your consciousness.

**Selvon:** That's quite true, though it's developed into something else now, in the sense that having had that earlier success, I went on to push it even more in *Moses Ascending*, where I used that same dialect form together with a kind of an English dialect of its time. I merged them and used them, I think, to great effect in that particular novel. Again, the reception of the novel was mainly about the language, what has happened with the language.

**R.D.:** *Moses Ascending* seems a little different in the sense that Moses himself uses a broad range of English. He moves from dialect to a very almost literary, almost Shakespearean kind of language. So his linguistic range seems enormous and then you follow him where he goes linguistically.

**Selvon:** But this was the aspect I wanted to show with the Trinidad dialect. That one would work with the other. Moses's flowery language is a great deal of his pretension. The book is a satire but a lot of people are still making mistakes and not interpreting my character quite properly. Moses is a very strange, ambivalent figure, and he can't be pinned down at all. He's almost an Anansi spider character. I used him very much as I wanted to, sometimes expressing my own feelings, but sometimes he himself would take over in the process of writing the novel. There are actually sections of the book that some people feel offended by for no reason at all, because the whole thing as I say is a satire.

R.D.: They identify you with Moses.

Selvon: Yes. That may be true in some instances; I don't suppose any writer could deny that part of himself gets expressed. But not always. Sometimes Moses is there, sometimes I get into Moses, so it's a two-way thing that's going on there all the time.

F.J.: When you started to experiment with style, were you conscious of a tradition before you? Were you thinking, "I'm working in the tradition of James Joyce" or someone else who had been experimenting with style, or you just did this on your own as an expression of the consciousness that you were trying to depict?

Selvon: I did this on my own. I admit to being what one would perhaps call a primitive writer, as you talk about a primitive painter, someone who does something out of some natural instinct. I've never studied the novel or studied the short story. I did a great deal of reading. I read everything I could bring my hands on from the time I was able to read, and when I started to write, I just started to write short stories. When I moved on to novels, most of my novels began as short stories and then they developed further along.

F.J.: So you didn't see yourself as coming out of a certain literary tradition?

Selvon: No, not really. I paid very little respect to the rules, purely because I'm ignorant of them. Intuitively I found that if I was succeeding by my primitive way, I would continue to use it. That way, I also feel that I do maintain some kind of individuality in my work. For me the best pleasure I get out of writing is for someone to be able to say that that's a Selvon novel or that's a Selvon short story. I've always felt that if I probed too deeply and started to become knowledgeable about what the novel is, I would lose that individuality. Whether it is good or bad—that's something else. Should I sit down and define the novel and define the short story and write to certain accepted principles of the art of the novel or of the short story? I've decided, because I have succeeded, that I'm going to just stay the way I am—I'll be ignorant of all these things. So I really don't think of form. I don't start without any idea, I don't sit down and wait for the muse to come to me. I do have a concept, and I do try, of course, to tie up loose ends or to round off my concept and so on, but most of the writing happens during the actual process of creation.

R.D.: Do you think that other writers can get too conscious of the rules or a certain tradition, which makes their writing overly intellectual?

Selvon: I don't know. Sometimes I feel I am the freak because I work so differently from other people. I really do. I don't conform to those things, and this is why I feel that to keep my individuality, I have to maintain a certain amount of deliberate unattachment to too many literary things. I actually teach creative writing, but I do it in my own way, with things I like. I tell my students that you can't teach writing. There are hundreds and hundreds of books that they can read that might help them, but I'm not going to help them that way. I'm just going to assist them—I can do that. I know what is good writing and what is bad writing. I've been writing long enough to know that.

F.J.: Do you think the reception of your books has somehow been conditioned by that literary environment? Do you think that you were seen as just another step, maybe, in this innovative writing technique style, or do you think it's the characters that go out and grab the reader? I know that for my own point of view, it's the characters, because you bring the characters so much alive. I find myself at some points very sympathetic, at some points laughing out loud responding to the characters. But I wonder if you think the English reception of the books may be conditioned because it's another step in stylistic experimentation?

Selvon: I don't know. I suppose it could partly be that too. Also, of course, there was the whole feeling that this was an exotic literature that had sprung up in the early fifties, and that it would not last. But it has not only lasted, because of the spate of books written during that time, it is actually been part of building the whole Caribbean literary tradition. I feel that I still have novels to write. I still feel I haven't written my best novel, my best book, and what I'm working on now I hope will be better than all the rest.

R.D.: Can you say a little about that, or would you rather not talk about it?

Selvon: I keep talking about it so much, and it's been delayed because I write slowly, but certainly it's a very ambitious book. I want to explore the psyche of the Caribbean mind, and to find out if in fact the West Indians have not accomplished very much and are not capable of accomplishing much, as some people say. I want to explore why that is so, if in fact it is so.

R.D.: You're responding to Naipaul's famous remark, "Nothing was created in the West Indies."

Selvon: Naipaul is pretty outright about it, but there are a lot of people who feel that we are not creative enough, we are indolent, and we just don't seem to care as much about literature and the fine arts. We're just happy-go-lucky kind of people, and I want to get to the psyche behind all this. I want to really explore why, if it's because of the mixture of races there or what. It's a very ambitious novel, and I know what I want to do, but it isn't easy to sit and do it.

F.J.: But you reinforce some of those stereotypes a little bit. I always remember Moses criticizing Cap in *The Lonely Londoners,* so that might even be you criticizing the West Indian consciousness. What is the consciousness of the West Indian man? What would you say?

Selvon: Well, I don't know. This is what I'm really going into. I think it's a creative one. I have hopes for it. This is what I'm going to try to find out in this novel that I'm working on.

R.D.: You mention the mixture of races in the West Indies. Certainly one of the things one notices about the Moses books is that, of course, Moses is black, and you are of East Indian descent. Have you been criticized for that?

Selvon: No, not at all. In fact, I think that I am representative of what I always say is a third race in Trinidad. We talk about the blacks and the Indians being the two races there. But there is a third race who are people from my generation who grew up Westernized, who still remain what they are because you can't change yourself, but who have adopted a way of life which tries to work and operate between the two races and who are Creolized, as it were, and who see themselves more as West Indians than as perhaps belonging to people who originally came from India.

F.J.: And they also see themselves as more Westernized.

Selvon: They are more Westernized and they are creating a nation out of this mixture. I'm not the only one. Very few people talk about that third race, but that is a race that exists. I know that it exists, and that is the race that I am putting my hopes on for any future for Trinidad.

R.D.: So as opposed to those people who would see themselves first as black or first as Indian, there are other people who would see themselves first as West Indian or Trinidadian. How does your work express that?

Selvon: I think I've always tried to keep an element of that in my work. I've always tried to give voice to this publicly in many ways, whenever I talk, wherever I go. Even from the first novel, from *A Brighter Sun*, I've been concerned with the existence of these races that could live in some kind of workable harmony.

R.D.: Like the friendship between Tiger and Joe.

Selvon: Yes. It's something that people know about. If that never existed, a lot of people would have criticized the book to hell. But people of my generation know that kind of living together happened, actually existed and still exists to some extent in Trinidad.

F.J.: That's similar to the whole generation here now both in England and maybe even in America of the children of immigrants from Asia and the West Indies. So, for instance, there's the Asian writer here, Hanif Kureishi, who really should be British because he's part British and Pakistani, yet that generation seems to be less accepted by the white establishment than the purer West Indian or the purer East Asian generation. It's an interesting comment to me that this generation which is by birthright British or American is less accepted than the immigrant generation.

Selvon: I imagine that there are very, very interesting aspects about that new generation that you talk about that I am hoping will come out. I would hope very much that the new writing will come out of that generation already. I know that there's been a considerable amount of short story writing and poetry and so on. I am hoping that there will be one or two big novels coming out from that new generation that will depict their times and experiences as *The Lonely Londoners* did for the fifties and sixties.

F.J.: I wonder what happens to the consciousness of this generation. I've been thinking about this a lot just because I just finished reading V. S. Naipaul's *Enigma of Arrival*. It's interesting in the way in which that book is both Hindu—gives expression to his Hindu consciousness—and yet wants not to be. I wonder if this forthcoming generation will then also be like a Naipaul consciousness that says, "No, we're not really what we came from; we don't want to be associated with it; we want to be white, mainstreamed."

Selvon: I don't know. That would be very interesting to see. I think that this is a kind of dilemma that doesn't face just one individual. I think it's a dilemma that faces any number of people who move out of one culture into another, particularly people from Third World countries because of their color, who move into white societies to settle. And I think that they have this problem of how they are going to identify themselves. Are they going to keep their original identity or keep their roots, or are they going to allow themselves to be assimilated completely into their new culture?

R.D.: Is it different in Canada? Is the dynamic different in Canada and Britain?

Selvon: No, there is no difference in this particular point that I was just making. The difference that does exist is that West Indians who are westernized get along much easier, I think, in a place like Canada than they do when they come to England. English culture is so much more stiff upperlip and closed which they're not quite accustomed to. There has always been a fairly easy going relationship between the Americas and the Caribbean—we are part of the same area. We practically come under American politics, so we are already somewhat Americanized in the Caribbean.

F.J.: Should these people make some effort to retain either their Caribbean selves or Indian selves or African selves, or should they seek to mainstream themselves rather than to retain their identity? If they did this, would it just generate a kind of a robotic culture, a culture without culture, as it were?

Selvon: I don't know. It could evolve a new culture for that matter. If you say a culture without a culture, that is a kind of culture. (*Laughter*) However the dilemma would be resolved, I would certainly feel that they should not forget their past, their background, where they come from. I have always remained Trinidadian myself. I know where I come from, and I know that by race I am mixed. I am predominately East Indian, I know that, but that doesn't stop me from formulating my own philosophy or my own psychological approach as to how I'm going to assimilate myself into the culture. I don't know which is best, but I would certainly hope that they would not forget their past or turn a blind eye to the origins of the whole thing. I don't think that you can build a future without using the past, and I don't think that they should try to forget their origins at all. But certainly I think they should make some effort to assimilate into the society in which they have to live day by day. Are we going to have just ghettos of people who are living completely apart?

R.D.: Of course, if the East Indians had done that in Trinidad, you wouldn't have the third race that you're talking about.

Selvon: Exactly, you see, so that's not integrating at all.

F.J.: What is the reception of the East Indians in the West Indies? Have they integrated themselves within the fabric of society or are they, as I see here in London, in almost separate townships, as it were.

Selvon: I think that it's about half and half. There are people, like myself, my generation, who have been Westernized. Then there are others who have remained more Indian.

R.D.: Is that true of the writers too do you think?

Selvon: I've never studied the writings of the writers to that extent, but I am pretty sure that probably you would get elements of that existing in the writers as well.

R.D.: George Lamming many years ago in *The Pleasures of Exile* praised you at the expense of Naipaul because he said that you were exceptional among West Indian writers for being willing to deal with the multi-racial situation.

Selvon: Well, it's true; what else have I got to deal with? That is the problem that we have. So, you know, I can't turn blind eyes to it. In fact, the thing with me is that I am so much Westernized, so much Creolized, that it's the only element that I think that I am really strongest in. In some of my books, I've had to avoid going into too much description of Indian ritual and custom purely because I don't know them myself.

F.J.: Could I ask, are you from a Tamil background? The name Selvon sounds Tamil.

Selvon: I think so, I think perhaps it could be from a Tamil background. I've never really tried tracing it back, but I have a feeling that it might well be from the south of India.

F.J.: How many generations does that go back?

Selvon: I would be third; I guess about two generations back.

R.D.: Your grandfather came from India? And you were brought up in a completely English-speaking environment?

Selvon: Yes. That's right, yes, from the time I was small. My mother could speak Hindi very well.

F.J.: Your mother was half Indian?

Selvon: Yes, my mother's father was Scottish, and her mother was Indian.

R.D.: So then you were probably brought up in a more Creolized society than Naipaul.

Selvon: I would definitely say so. From the time I was small, it's what I knew. And yet, as I say, you can't forget who you are. I had aunts and uncles living in the country districts who were really what's called the orthodox Indians. I would go there and they would wear saris and cook roti, and so on, so I think I had a good taste of both.

F.J.: So you yourself are a kind of a multicultural consciousness. You grew up with that kind of multicultural consciousness.

Selvon: Exactly, you see. A lot of my friends in my neighborhood and in my school in the town that I grew up in were mixed blacks and Indians.

R.D.: You grew up in Port of Spain?

Selvon: In San Fernando. It's the second largest city in Trinidad after Port of Spain.

R.D.: Therefore what you're talking about in terms of this third race is very much what was being created when you were growing up.

Selvon: Yes, and as I say, I know this from people of my generation. I have to admit my Indian blood, what I am, but certainly I think of myself more as a West Indian. Perhaps I even want to go further than that and create a Caribbean mind, one who comes out of that particular part of the world.

R.D.: What's the difference there between West Indian and Caribbean?

Selvon: I was going to say Trinidadian, but even with West Indian there would be a difference. I prefer the word Caribbean. I like it; it's a nicer word. I think that people tend to make mistakes about what is a West Indian. People here in England hear the term West Indian and they say, "You're from West India?" They don't know.

R.D.: Let me go on a little bit with this Trinidad question. You're saying that you prefer to move beyond a kind of a local island consciousness to a larger area.

**Selvon:** Yes.

**R.D.:** But of course the Caribbean is not just English speaking; it is also French speaking and Spanish speaking. Does this change as you move from an English-speaking milieu?

**Selvon:** Yes, I think it will change, but we will just have to say the English-speaking Caribbean in that sense. We would have to move first to, say, an English-speaking Caribbean consciousness, and then extend it to incorporate the French and the Dutch and the Spanish and so on. The Spanish do that. They're incorporating the English-speaking Caribbean with their arts festivals and things like that in Cuba and drawing them in. So I think we also should be doing some of that sort of thing. But we should bring them to us rather than we go to them.

**R.D.:** What are the advantages of that? What if someone said: "I'm from Trinidad, I don't know what the Caribbean is," what would you say to that?

**Selvon:** Well, I think it's more likely that they'll know where the Caribbean is, but they don't know where Trinidad is. I think it'll work that way. I think that the concept is a bigger one. People in England all know where the Caribbean area is, but they can't identify what island is in it. They don't know where Trinidad is. It is also a much more ambitious concept to try and get a national feeling among the English-speaking Caribbean writers. This is not just my dream because they've tried it already with the Federation in the late forties. I myself was very disappointed when that fell through.

**R.D.:** Why do you think it broke down?

**Selvon:** Well, I think it's just because we couldn't agree among ourselves. There was all this bickering. Trinidad feels that it's a better island than Jamaica, and Jamaica feels it's the biggest English-speaking island. They want everything to happen over there, and Barbados doesn't want to have anything to do with it. That sort of petty rivalry that goes on has been keeping us apart for years and years. I think we are slowly growing out of that now, and we are able, at least, to get together and talk more about what will be done for the area as a whole. In fact, it is already, in a way, in practice with trade agreements going on between the islands and so on.

**R.D.:** But you're saying there's a cultural component?

**Selvon:** The cultural thing is what has to follow now. It should really be going side by side, but culture, of course, is the last thing in the budget of any Caribbean government.

**R.D.:** It may be, in a sense, easier for you in Canada or a writer in England to have that regional sense that you're talking about than someone in the area, because they may have more of a sense of the differences between the islands.

**Selvon:** I quite agree with you. Most Caribbean people who have moved out of the islands and settled abroad have really established themselves well, not only as writers, not only in the field of art and so on, but in other professions and in medicine and social work. Any part of the English-speaking world you go to you can see these West Indians in very responsible seats, you know, very high administrative levels they're working in all over. I feel that this is a very good thing for the Caribbean. I think that this is why the rest of the world has become interested in the Caribbean.

**F.J.:** Because it breaks the stereotypes?

**Selvon:** Yes. Who are these people? They've got these writers—what's it like down there? This is why people become interested. So I think they do a good job; I think we do a good job. We're not really exiles in that sense.

**R.D.:** Ambassadors perhaps.

**Selvon:** Yes.

**R.D.:** Therefore, maybe this broader consciousness will come largely from this community abroad.

**Selvon:** I think so. When I talk to West Indians who are living abroad about it, they sense it much more than back home. When I first came to England in the fifties, for the first time I met people from all the other islands that I had never met before in Trinidad. For the first time in my life, I was meeting Grenadians, Jamaicans, Barbadians—four thousand miles away from the Caribbean, here in the heart of London meeting these people from the other islands that I'd never seen in my life before.

**F.J.:** So your new Caribbean consciousness, the man with the new Caribbean consciousness, would blend all these as well as the immigrant consciousness?

**Selvon:** I would hope so. What I would like to see being done further is I would like to see writers writing about movement from one island to the other. I don't really want a novel about Trinidad. I want the characters to move and go up to UWI [University of the West Indies] in Jamaica and spend a week in Barbados—have friends in Barbados, have friends in Cuba. This is what I'm hoping to do in the new novel.

**F.J.:** That's a good note to end on, and we'll await your book then, in a couple of years or a year you think?

**Selvon:** I hope it'll be a year. It's a very ambitious project, as I'm sure you appreciate, but I hope it will be a year.

# Roy Heath

As Sam Selvon noted in our interview with him, if West Indian or Caribbean literature in English has had a "Golden Age," it was surely the 1950s and early 1960s, when a group of talented young writers gathered in London made the English-speaking world aware of a new literature. These pioneers include V. S. Naipaul, Andrew Salkey, Wilson Harris, and George Lamming as well as Selvon. In 1960 West Indian literature was doubtless the most prominent of the new literatures in English, much better known than African or Indian or Pacific writing in English. That no longer seems to be true, and one of the reasons is, again as Selvon noted, because this "first generation" has not been followed by others in the way successive generations have emerged in other new literatures. One of the most exciting "new writers" from the Caribbean is Roy Heath, whose first novel, *A Man Come Home*, was published in 1974, and the seven novels he has published since then, including most recently *The Shadow Bride* (1988), have established him as an important voice in Caribbean fiction. Yet Heath was born in 1928 and began to publish fiction comparatively late, so he isn't part of a younger generation as much as one more fine writer from the earlier one.

Heath is from Guyana, the one English-speaking country in South America. But for Heath Guyana is to be distinguished from the rest of the English-speaking West Indies less by this geographical fact than by its demography. After slavery was abolished in the British West Indies in 1834, the former slaves almost uniformly refused to work on the sugar plantations where they had worked as slaves; in response to this, the British brought large numbers of workers from India. The net result is that today most of Guyana's population is of Indian origin, though there is a large black population as well as Amerindian, Chinese and Portuguese minorities. The resulting multicultural population is a more complex mixture than anywhere else in the English-speaking Caribbean, though Trinidad—the other place in the West Indies to which large numbers of Indians were brought—approaches Guyana in this respect. Guyana and Trinidad are also the parts of the West Indies with the richest literature, and this seems no coincidence, as the complex interaction of cultures manifested there is probably the central subject of writers from Guyana and Trinidad.

This is certainly true for Roy Heath, and one reason is that though he has lived in Britain for nearly forty years, the same historical processes he portrays in Guyanese society are being replayed in contemporary Britain. There is both a mixing of cultures and a resistance to such mixing, a blending of the best of both worlds and a blending of the worst of both worlds. The resemblance between the Guyana of his youth and Britain today has not escaped as shrewd an observer as Heath, and his careful depiction of the creation of a Guyanese identity out of the mixture of different peoples in Guyana is therefore utterly timely today.

**Reed Dasenbrock:** When we were talking before the interview, you flinched when I used the term Commonwealth literature. Perhaps a good place to start would be to ask why.

**Roy Heath:** I think there are certain people here in Britain who are fond of labeling us Commonwealth Writers. And certainly we—my fellow writers, those I know, and I—object to this term, strenuously, because it seems to us that it is an attempt to perpetuate the psychological relationship between ourselves and people born in the imperial country.

**R.D.:** A relationship of dominance.

**Heath:** Absolutely. It is a way of denying us our nationality. What is the Commonwealth? It's a vague club which has very little political clout, in fact, none. It seems to do very little. We would rather not hear the term applied to us, as it encapsulates all the snobbishness and all the tensions in our relationships with England.

**Feroza Jussawalla:** So you would rather be known as a West Indian writer or a Third World writer, or a black writer?

**Heath:** First of all, I want to be known for what I am, a Guyanese writer. And in a larger way, a West Indian writer or Caribbean writer, and in a yet larger way, a South American writer. For instance, there is British culture, but then there is a wider European culture. And there's no doubt that there are elements which connect them. But first of all, an English writer is an English writer; a French writer is a French writer.

**R.D.:** When we talked to Sam Selvon last week, he said that he didn't like the term "West Indian." He preferred the term "Caribbean." I got the sense that "West Indian" bothered him in much the same way the term "Commonwealth" bothers you, as too British-oriented a term.

**Heath:** Yes, I would agree with him about shunning the term, "West Indian." The trouble is that it is a term which is consecrated by usage, but I sympathize with those who object to that term as well. I'd rather be known as a Guyanese writer, then a Caribbean writer, and then a South American writer, in that order.

**R.D.:** Guyana is, of course, the one English-speaking country in South America. How much do you think that affects your work? Is South America a part of your imaginative consciousness, in the way that it may not be for a writer from Barbados or Trinidad?

**Heath:** The fact is that everybody's conditioned by his history, by her history. We always had a lot of contact with Venezuela. There was a consciousness about Venezuela, because many people worked, and still do work, in the oil fields in Venezuela, hired by the Americans who owned most of them for a long time. But it was only after independence that we discovered South America in a big way. The second language in secondary school is no longer French, because education is no longer based on the British pattern; it is Spanish and Portuguese, as it should be.

Since the explosion of South American writing and Central American writing, I am certainly very conscious of its happening. I'm very conscious of many things, like the fact that we still roof our houses with material imported from England, when in fact we should be roofing them with clay tiles, as happens throughout South America. There was always a consciousness, especially about Brazil and Venezuela, but now there's an even larger, more distinct consciousness.

**R.D.:** So part of what Guyana needs to do to free itself from a colonial relationship to Britain is to become more aware of its South American, Latin American context.

**Heath:** That would help tremendously. In fact, it's essential. I think, of course, we first have to become aware of ourselves, because there is still the Old Guard, the older people in Guyana, who are hesitant about the implications of independence. But discounting the Old Guard, it is only a matter of time before we become fully aware of ourselves and our own very strong culture. These contacts with the rest of South America are not exactly facilitated by the enormous forests that separate us from Venezuela and Brazil. The communications between Guyana and the rest of South America are rather difficult.

**R.D.:** How does that affect your own work? Do you see yourself and your fiction as attempting to facilitate this kind of awareness?

**Heath:** Yes. In a small way, but decidedly so. There are things I have written about, the kind of sleeves that Colombian women wear when dressed up for an occasion, for instance, which would not have been mentioned in literature in the thirties or forties or fifties or even the sixties. Other Caribbean writers may have done this, but I'm not aware that anybody else has. But before it wouldn't have been thought necessary.

**R.D.:** I don't know whether "historical novels" is the right term for your novels, because they're not set that far back in time, but certainly most of your novels are set some distance from the present. What seems to fascinate you both in *The Shadow Bride* and the trilogy of novels about the Armstrong family [*From the Heat of the Day, One Generation,* and *Genetha*] is the process whereby two very separate communities in culture and habits and language begin to lose their separateness. And you seem particularly fascinated by the interaction between the black or Creole and the East Indian communities. On the one hand, a black man like Armstrong is attracted to Asian women, on the other hand, Dr. Singh in *The Shadow Bride* learns to become friends with the black pharmacist and his wife, and then his sick nurse, et cetera. I'm wondering what has happened to that process today.

**Heath:** Well, it is still going on. That is why the description of my work as historical novels is very accurate. I am trying to project the importance and the development, if you like, of this process. For instance, who has influenced whom? You can see in *The Shadow Bride* the personality of Sukrum, one of the first Guyanese Indians who describes himself as a Guyanese, rather than as an East Indian. That is something that still leads to argument. The fact is that the Creoles have been very little influenced by the East Indians, but the East Indians have taken on a considerable influence from the Creoles. And this can be seen in many ways, in cricket, for example, which must seem a peculiar and strange ritual to you, and probably one of the world's most boring games.

**R.D.:** Well, not to Feroza, because she's from India, but to me it seems a little strange.

**Heath:** Now, the fact is that I remember in the thirties the East Indian batsman was a very defensive batsman. He would hardly make an aggressive stroke. And now, in the history of the game, the most aggressive batsmen in the world have been from Guyana, and they have been East Indians. They have come out of the defensive role and have now become like the Creoles.

There have been influences the other way. For instance, we speak of the aubergine as ball-an-chay. Ball-an-chay is a corruption of a Hindi word, and I refuse to change the term for the understanding of people in Britain. And there are other examples from food. We don't speak of Indian food now. We speak of Guyanese food. That is curry, and so on. We no longer regard it as Indian food.

But the psychological influences have been almost entirely one way. We used to say, up to the fifties, that you could always tell when an Indian was speaking if you couldn't see the person. Though this is still so in many parts of the countryside, it isn't any longer in Georgetown. You can no longer tell because the women no longer speak in a high-pitched voice as they used to. Now there is a Guyanese person, very much so. And because the Indians came from this powerful culture, they were not destroyed. There was no attempt to destroy their culture as there was in the case of the Creole culture. Indians took a long time to change, because they had their culture. They brought pictures of Gandhi and colored photographs of their gods, and put them up in their stalls, and so on.

**R.D.:** So out of the two there has been a process of merging, but you think that there has been much more Creolization of the Indians than "Indianization" of the blacks.

**Heath:** There's no doubt about it.

**R.D.:** Is this process different in Trinidad?

**Heath:** I would say that it has been even more one-way in Trinidad, because in Guyana the Indians are destined to have political power because they are 58 percent of the population.

**R.D.:** So there are actually more Indians than blacks or Creoles in Guyana?

**Heath:** Decidedly more. In Trinidad the Indians are about 32 percent of the population, so the Trinidad Indians, I would say, are even more influenced by Creole culture. But here one has to be careful, because there would be differences depending on whether you're talking about the countryside or the town. The influence [of black culture] is very marked in the town. In the countryside there is a greater cohesion of this separate, original culture.

**R.D.:** Traditionally in both Trinidad and Guyana the city was mostly black or Creole and the countryside mostly Indian.

**Heath:** Very much so. But not anymore. Not in the seventies or the eighties.

**R.D.:** Were you brought up in Georgetown itself?

**Heath:** Yes.

**R.D.:** I have never been to Guyana, and yet from your work I have a very strong sense of the landscape, particularly the coast, of Demerara. This is not quite the sense you get from Wilson Harris of exploring the interior, but a sense of the districts along the coast. Where does that come from?

**Heath:** I worked in the country, and where I worked, I met many, many East Indians. The village I worked in was East Indian—the villages are usually East Indian villages or African or Creolese villages, you see. My best friend in the town was an East Indian boy, and that was my first introduction to Indian culture, as it were, because his mother ran a cook shop for beggars, nearly all of them East Indian beggars. And I always saw his grandfather, with his hookah pipe, smoking over the Sanskrit text, and so on. That gave me an emotional entree into the Indian world. But I couldn't write a great deal about it. It was when I went and worked over the river in Vreeden-Hoop that I saw this culture in all its vibrant forms, its music, etc. There used to be a special court for East Indian immigrants alone. It was an official court, official in the sense that it was run by a government department, but the East Indians who had recourse to these courts didn't have to pay. These were courts especially for immigrants because they were disadvantaged people. Many of them were illiterate; therefore, it was felt that they should have this first recourse instead of paying lawyers money. If they didn't like the decisions of the court, they could always apply to the official courts and pay a lot of money to the lawyers. The man who ran the court, Mr. Umar, to whom I've dedicated a novel, incidentally, was a Muslim, and he and I became very good friends. I used to tutor his son in French. He was that kind of man who played fourteen musical instruments, who was very well educated, who spoke Urdu; those were his qualifications for running these courts. It was a remarkable family. So I saw East Indian culture at many levels, and this was a revelation.

**F.J.:** And that first generation, like in V. S. Naipaul's novels set in Trinidad, retained its culture and its roots.

**Heath:** Oh, yes.

**F.J.:** Then it's from the next generation onwards that the increasing merging begins. For instance, Wilson Harris has a female character who is East Indian, but knows no language other than the Creolese that she has picked up. So was it time that led to the immigrants changing, or was it social stratification?

**Heath:** No, it was time. The East Indians learned their English from the Creoles when they came after slavery was abolished. A very common problem was the quarreling between husband and wife about whether the children should learn Hindi or not. And one of them would say, the mother would say, "What's the use of learning Hindi, because it's not going to do him any good. He must learn English; that's the way to success," and so on. And regretting it later, now, when there is a resurgence of interest in things like Hindi. But you see this here as well. In the seventies, you heard Indian children speaking Gujarati or another Indian language at school, but now you hardly hear any Indian children speaking an Indian language. They don't do it. That is a matter of only 15 years.

**F.J.:** So in Guyana you have already a generation that's partly assimilated and that is partly Indian, partly Guyanese, partly even, maybe, British; a whole generation as you're beginning to have now, born actually of immigrant parents, in England. I guess this must be the first experience in England of British-born colored people.

**Heath:** Yes. Well, not the first, but the first on a very significant scale. In the late 1500s, Queen Elizabeth issued an edict according to which black people had to go home. So, you see, this isn't the first time that has happened in England. But on a very large scale, yes, it is a new experience.

**R.D.:** One of the themes of your work has been describing this process of creation of a Guyanese identity from a number of different perspectives. You've been living in London for—

**Heath:** Thirty-seven years.

**R.D.:** It strikes me that living in London now, you're seeing in many ways a replay of the same historical process as in Guyana.

**Heath:** That's why it's so important. It's happening among the Turks in Germany, it's happening among the Italians in Switzerland, it's happening among the North Africans in France.

**R.D.:** My sense of your work is that someone reading it in London today would gain as much insight or more insight about what's happening in London in the 1980s and 1990s than they could by reading anything being written directly about it. I don't know of a writer delineating this multicultural fusion or "Creolization" taking place here in England nearly as perceptively or as carefully as you are of a very similar process. But that raises a question. Is this depiction of barriers breaking down in Guyana something that you see happening in Britain, or something that you would like to see happening in Britain?

**Heath:** First of all, when one speaks of barriers breaking down, there are two processes going on. There is a psychological process of barriers breaking down; there's a political process of barriers being maintained and even reinforced by leading politicians who see it to their advantage to maintain these barriers. Now, not only can't you discount the political influence, the political influence in fact might be destined to decide what happens, eventually. So it's a dialectical process. Just as in Northern Ireland there is a division between Catholics and Protestants, although they're the same people, we have divisions in Guyana, and you have politicians taking advantage of these differences and doing so successfully.

**R.D.:** So there's a cultural dimension and there's a political dimension, and there's been more fusion in culture than in politics.

**Heath:** Absolutely.

**F.J.:** Then there's a language dimension to it, too, I take it. What is the language situation, then, in Guyana? You were saying that now, after independence, Spanish and Portuguese are getting to be the second languages.

**Heath:** Well, not the second language; the second language taught in secondary schools, the foreign language taught in secondary schools. I mean that we are English speaking, although we speak Creolese amongst ourselves. The situation is like that in Switzerland, where you speak a Swiss-German dialect but you write German. Or, indeed, in Belgium, where they write Dutch, but speak Flemish dialects.

**F.J.:** What are all the different languages that generate the Creolese that emerges?

**Heath:** The dominant element is English. It's simply an English that has changed in crossing the sea and is spoken by people whose mother tongue was not English. There are developments which will have occurred necessarily. The past is not used in Creolese. They simply use present tense. By analogy, there is a reduction of tenses, a reduction of inflections. For instance, we don't say "the boy's head"; we would say, "the boy head." These are dialectal differences that have occurred in the development of the language among people who took on the language while having a mother tongue of their own. And it is now their own language, since the African languages were not only not encouraged, but there was a policy of having slaves from different cultures in Africa to reduce the possibility of revolt. So the dominant language is English, although many aboriginal Indian languages are spoken in the outlying areas.

**F.J.:** Is the dialect or Creolese in Guyana pretty standardized, or does it vary from the black community to the East Indian community?

**Heath:** It's very standard, standard in the sense that there's mutual comprehension wherever you go in Guyana. It is far more standardized than, say, the English spoken in England, for instance. Scottish dialect is incomprehensible, in fact, to most English people. Indeed, when I first came over here I had great difficulty in understanding Cockneys.

**F.J.:** Is there a standard English that one feels one must aspire towards or keep, or does the Creolese become the English of consciousness, the emotional language?

**Heath:** Creolese does not have to become the language of consciousness. It is and always has been the language of consciousness. The difficulty, then, from a linguistic point of view—not the difficulty, but the interest—would be in whether Creolese can become a language of literature. And everything seems to militate against that.

**R.D.:** What militates against it?

**Heath:** Well, it's like the Swiss, who do write poetry in German-Swiss dialect but, for reasons it would be difficult to go into here, without a large audience. Because there is a standard German, there is an implicit rejection of German dialect as a language of the novel.

**R.D.:** So there are two different issues: one is the question of how large an audience can you get, but there is also a question of what's the accepted medium.

**Heath:** This isn't necessarily psychological, it can be actually a question of the difficulty in reading it. I remember in Guyana in the thirties and forties there was a man called Uncle Stapey who wrote for a newspaper. He was extremely popular and was a very funny man. He wrote an article every Sunday in Creolese, and it was really one of the most popular things in the literature there. So that shows something, that gives you the possibilities of

Creolese. But if you wanted to set up a publishing firm in Guyana to publish Creolese, it isn't viable because for a start you don't have enough people who would read it. No publishing firm is viable there. All the publishing in Guyana, nearly all of it, is self-publishing. There isn't a large enough audience. But even in England, you find that very, very few novelists take the risk of writing even dialogue in dialect.

R.D.: In your work, you tend to write the narrative in something we could call standard English, and the dialogue in dialect. What do you think of the work of someone like Sam Selvon, who has written novels in—but I don't know—would you say his work is written in Creolese?

Heath: Yes. He's very successful in that. Now, he's an example to us all, because it is important to write in Creolese, and it can succeed. I think he succeeded because his novels in Creolese [*The Lonely Londoners*, *Moses Ascending*, and *Moses Migrating*] are comic novels. And comedy goes down very well in this country.

R.D.: Have you thought about writing novels where the narrative would be in Creolese? Is that something you've rejected, or is it something that you don't think would ever work for you?

Heath: Well, it might well work. This is why I said he's an example.

R.D.: But one you haven't chosen to follow.

Heath: Not yet. But in fact, I have just had a commission to write a novella in Creolese by a publishing firm. It was only yesterday, the day before yesterday, that we were discussing it. I had had a talk with the chap about it, and he claimed that since my dialogue in Creolese was so successful, I should try my hand at it. And I said yes. In fact, I would have loved to have done it before, but I had never been asked.

R.D.: You felt that writing for a London publisher, a novel in dialect simply wouldn't fly?

Heath: I would have thought the same for a Guyanese publisher as well. My thought was that the very broad range of ideas I tried to express demanded a vocabulary that was very wide, very broad. You have the same problem among the Latins, with classical Latin, if you like, and the popular Latin. Many Latin poets and writers wrote popular Latin, but when it came to writing pieces of length, they wrote classical Latin. Now, it might well be a matter of investigation by a psychologist to find out why that is done.

F.J.: You teach here in the London schools. Do you get now a generation of students with mixed language influences, and what do you do as a teacher? Do you get them to aspire more towards a standard English, or would you like to let them express a Creolese voice if they wrote for you in class? What do you think should be the educational perspective toward this kind of language use?

**Heath:** For a start, I teach French, not English. But you see, this isn't a simple subject. Where Creolese English is attempted to be taught here, it is usually a way of evading the responsibilities of the teacher; that is, they usually do it to children who are severely disadvantaged, and they tell them, "Look here, this is your mother tongue, this is the tongue of your parents, and we're teaching it to you." Now, that might sound fine, but they do not do it to the children who are not disadvantaged.

**R.D.:** So it's a kind of ghettoized language.

**Heath:** Absolutely. You are living in a world of examinations and the teacher's way of teaching is determined by the examinations that the children have to sit. I'm speaking of realities here. I do not see a contradiction between teaching standard English and writing in Creolese English. In fact, people like Uncle Stapey were not taught Creolese. You don't have to be taught Creolese. It has the advantage of coming straight from your consciousness, while it is standard English which you have to think about in terms of structure, punctuation, spelling. If you want to write in Creolese, you don't have to be taught it.

**R.D.:** So one doesn't need to try to teach Creole to keep it going, precisely because it would be ruined by that kind of formal training.

**Heath:** Oh, yes. Fractured and then ruined. Fracture it desperately and then you will ruin it. In fact, I think there are disadvantages in studying the language in which you write, because you become self-conscious in your use of it.

**R.D.:** Are you speaking from experience? Did you study English literature?

**Heath:** No, I took a degree in French. I had to do English as a subsidiary subject, but I have always said that the university education is a severe handicap. It is the kind of thing that I could do without. My literary education did not come from my university studies. The literature I admire most, the European literature I admire most, is nineteenth-century Russian literature, which to my mind has explored the human psyche more profoundly than any other European literature. And I read that before university. I went to university here because I couldn't get on without a university degree. But quite frankly, I have nothing but the most bitter contempt for university teaching in literature. If it's physics, that's something entirely different. But the study of literature chains you. It puts you into a straitjacket which you believe to be an advantage.

**F.J.:** Why is a university education in literature a handicap?

**Heath:** I'll give you an example of the serious handicap that can be produced by a university education. I wrote a novel called *Kwaku*, which is a comic novel, at least for the most part. It is a novel in the tradition of the trickster figure. Now, the trickster figure is one of the most important figures in the history of literature. You can write a history of literature in terms of this trickster figure, beginning with the Winnebago people of the East Coast of the United States, whose oral literature still preserves perhaps the most powerful trickster figure stories there are. You get the West African stories, which are far more diluted and not as powerful, and so on. The trickster figure, in the beginning, was both a positive and a negative figure. Today there has been a dichotomy between the two figures, and you have the bad trickster figure existing as the villain in the novel, while the good trickster is the hero. So there has been a division of labor, as it were. But it was clear from the reviews of *Kwaku* that there wasn't a single English critic who knew anything about the trickster figure. There was one man who went as far as to say he is Soldier Schweik from the Czechoslovakian novel, who is a trickster figure. But he could only see it in terms of *The Good Soldier Schweik*, not as *the* trickster figure.

**R.D.:** So the critics have had this English or European frame of mind which disables them from being able to read your work.

**Heath:** Absolutely. Now, nothing is wrong with that until you become a critic. If you become a critic and you are writing a review of an English novel, your limitations are practically unimportant. But your limitations become very severe when you are going out of your culture. Here people who have pretensions to be reviewers of foreign literature fall down terribly. Now, that is a handicap of university education.

**R.D.:** And one that particularly affects the reception of works like yours, which are written in English but draw on cultures outside of an English milieu.

**Heath:** Absolutely.

**F.J.:** Because the critics then want to take that work and fit it within the tradition of the English novel.

**Heath:** Yes. Which I understand, but I don't admire.

**F.J.:** What literary movements would you say have had an influence on your writing?

**Heath:** You have just put the question that I find very difficult to answer. You see, there are influences and influences. There are influences which appear to be influences but which in fact have touched something which is already within you and allows it to grow. There are other influences, like my own cultural influences, people like Uncle Stapey. I find myself using comic figurations, as it were, to coin a term, which he used. For instance, I would say to a boy in school, in one of the classes I teach there is a certain boy who doesn't do my homework. Now, I am not saying he is sitting in the third row, and I'm not saying that he's wearing glasses, and I'm not saying— and of course, everybody turns around and looks at the third row and looks at the boy wearing glasses, and they know who it is. That I got from Uncle Stapey. He always said that. "I'm not saying the person lives in Charlotte Street, and I'm not saying he lives in a two-story house," you see. And we thought it exceedingly funny. That sort of thing, the humor I heard in the barbershop, is a strong influence. So the primary influence, one of the strongest influences, is my own culture.

But the writer whom I admire most is Nikolai Gogol. I think he is the greatest European novelist. Practically everything you find in Dostoevsky you find in Gogol. The Russians say that we have all come out of the great-coat of Nikolai Gogol, but I think they didn't realize how true a saying that was. What I have seen to illustrate that statement doesn't come near to telling you in fact what *Dead Souls* was as a novel.

**R.D.:** Do you think there is a parallel between the situation of a Russian writer in the nineteenth century and a writer like you?

**Heath:** Very much so. This is one of the reasons I find it so comfortable to read nineteenth-century Russian literature. When I read of people painting the houses, when I read of the carriages, this is straight from the twenties in Guyana. There you can still find extravagant characters in the barbershops. Industrial society cuts you down to size, and you dare not be a larger-than-life character. In Russian literature I can read of the extravagant figures which you don't find here anymore, but which certainly were here in the eighteenth or the early nineteenth century.

R.D.: I was also thinking of the way that the debate in Russia was, "Do we adhere to a Western European cultural model, or do we go our own way?"

Heath: That is important, because this is one of the great debates taking place in the Caribbean now, and this was one of the great debates which was taking place in the early part of this century in South America. I have never seen it as a debate which it was necessary for me to take part in, because I have never had any difficulty in seeing what my aim was, what my goal was. I have always detested the idea of an English influence, which is probably more emotionally justified than justified in a literary sense.

R.D.: So just as many critics have misunderstood your work by trying to place it in an English frame of reference, your own work draws inspiration from non-English, Russian, or other models.

Heath: I don't think the critics have misunderstood my work. I think that they haven't been able to understand it. What they said was accurate enough, but it's that they were not knowledgeable enough to understand all the implications of the work. If I describe this room, I might impress my friends, but I might not impress you as an architect. To that extent, the critics by and large are no worse than critics anywhere. Most critics in most cultures are blinded of necessity. I think there are some very good critics here. But it is simply that having assumed the responsibility of being critics of world literature, their shortsightedness becomes more apparent.

F.J.: Does there need to be a different kind of a critical tradition developed? Should there be a native criticism, or is there a cross-cultural Guyanese individual who would be the most qualified critic?

Heath: Well, there are very good Guyanese critics. The trouble is that they all have been trained in Europe and America, and therefore they are European and American critics. Occasionally you do see sorties, sallies, that display an awareness of our peculiar cultural tradition. There was one lady who worked at the University of West Indies—her name was LaCosta—she is not only one of the most remarkable manipulators of the English language I have ever read, but she wrote a very, very long review in *Jamaica Journal*, of my very first novel, *A Man Come Home*, and it was the most stunning review I'm ever likely to get. I couldn't get anything like that again.

It astonished me, not only because of her uncompromising attitude of having been taken by this novel, but also of insights I did not think a Caribbean person would see. After all, the Caribbean middle class is very much an English class.

**R.D.**: So even when there have been Caribbean critics they've generally adopted English values.

**Heath**: I think so. I think it will take time. The most uncultured class is the middle class. They are an uncultured class. There is no doubt about that. I remember there was a man who won a competition at the time of our independence to do a sculpture of one of the slave heroes. If you saw his work, you would think he came straight from Africa. The most people could say about this man was that, "These are racial memories."

Well, there were no racial memories, it's simply that this chap lived in a part of Guyana where these things still happen, where they have not lost a great deal of the African influences. Now, a man like that is rare because he usually would not get beyond his village, either in influence or physically. Now, he was highly unusual in that he went beyond his village, he's articulate, and he's terribly impatient with anything middle-class people say or do; he thinks the critics should be placed in a dustbin and dropped in the sea. *(Laughter)* They hate this particular sculpture that won this prize, because it is very un-European.

**R.D.**: So one problem is that the cultural energies are really lower class or vernacular in inspiration, and the critics, the intellectuals, the university people, are, in a sense, taken away from those roots in a European direction.

**Heath**: They've never had direct contact with the culture. They don't even know who the aboriginal Indians are in Guyana. They couldn't name you three of the tribes. Now, the working class are ignorant to that extent, but they are still in touch with their culture; that's the vibrant part of their culture. They weren't ruined by attending university.

**F.J.**: So we have a problem with the criticism, if the English critics and the West Indian critics alike misread your work by applying English standards to it.

**Heath**: That's right. And curiously enough, this is the opinion of a friend who never pulls his punches. For instance, he didn't like *Kwaku*, which was the most successfully reviewed of all my novels; but he's a very blunt man. He and a friend of mine from South Africa think that *The Shadow Bride* is far and away my best work. Yet this work has been less reviewed than any of my other works, apart from the first one, when I was unknown. Where it has been reviewed, it has been very well reviewed, but it's been practically ignored.

**R.D.:** What's the difference?

**Heath:** I have no idea. To me it's a mystery. This friend is a very conservative man, Oxford graduate, went to the right public schools, and so on, so he doesn't like attacking his class. But he speaks of the Literary Mafia. He seems to think that it's time to get at me, that I'm becoming a dangerous person in some way, you see? Now I prefer to say nothing. I prefer to let other people say it for me. But I think the book is, on a purely sociological level, too important to ignore. On a dramatic level, it's the best of my books. I don't know what they're getting after.

**R.D.:** So you think there's a certain conspiracy of silence.

**Heath:** Oh, not I; my friend. *(Laughter)*

**F.J.:** How much does the critical response govern the direction you take a new work in?

**Heath:** Not at all, except to the extent that if an obsession of mine has been pointed out, then I look at it and see if it is an obsession. If it is an obsession, then I would say that this is something to watch. And this is why I've said there are good critics here. There are critics whose reviews one should pay attention to, simply because they're intelligent people. I react to good reviews, as any human being does. I like them, and I tend to feel that a bad review comes from a stupid person, which is just as foolish, but, again, it's very human.

**R.D.:** Your novels are often novels of decline. This is certainly true of *The Shadow Bride*, which has just been published, and of the trilogy of novels about the Armstrong family, *From the Heat of the Day* and *One Generation* and *Genetha*. Is there a title for those three novels taken together?

**Heath:** No. I'd like to call them the "Georgetown Trilogy," but the question hasn't arisen yet.

**R.D.:** Both of these, *The Shadow Bride* and the "Georgetown Trilogy," then, are narratives of family decline. I'm wondering if that's another one of the ways in which your work differs from English expectations? Let me make a gross generalization, if I may, which is that the English comedy of manners customarily moves towards a happy marriage. They are success stories, if you want, in a certain sense. But your novels all seem to me to go a different direction. Does that strike you as right?

**Heath:** As I said, my knowledge of English literature is not my knowledge of French or of Russian literature, and I couldn't speak authoritatively. But having said that, I'll accept it as an observation which is accurate. This has come out in some of the criticism—the critics speak of the novels as being bleak. Again, this is a cultural thing, they're of necessity judging from the standpoint of their culture, and they have been inculcated in believing that you must succeed. I didn't know that, and I don't care about it. All I know is, for instance, that if you were to take, say, Dostoevsky or Gogol, they are novels of decline. And it gives me great pleasure to know that my novels are different, because I am really speaking from my experience. We were brought up in a colonial society which was a kind of death. And of necessity, things decline. I think that in *The Shadow Bride* there is decline and hope at the same time.

**R.D.:** If you were writing a sequel to *The Shadow Bride (laughter),* one could imagine a novel about Dr. Singh's daughters, who are, as you mention very briefly at the beginning, practicing medicine in Canada and would seem, at least on English terms, to be a success story. Equally, Dr. Singh, himself, has obviously accomplished a great deal. And yet the ground you cover is—

**Heath:** Yes. The ground of decline.

**R.D.:** I find that very powerful, but I'm just wondering, is that a moment in your work, or do you think that those are the kinds of narratives you will always write?

**Heath:** It might be myself, you see. I think more that it is my culture, as expressed through myself, if you see what I mean. You see, in Guyana, up to the late forties, we died like flies from malaria. The Indians were the only successful immigrants after the African slaves. The rest all simply died out or they didn't take to the hard work on the sugar estates. Even the Indians from India who were successful afterwards at first died like flies, though many of their children began to acquire a partial immunity to malaria. Dr. Giglioli, who is a historical figure, studied the anopheles mosquito and its habits. They came up with spraying DDT, which was discovered in America. But you have to study the growth and the development of the mosquito— where they bred, and so on—in order to spray at the right time.

We did not realize that we were a people who were dancing with death continually. We thought it was normal because that was the only experience we knew. It might well be that there is a deep pessimism in Guyanese literature. I think in Mittelholzer, who is the most prolific writer from Guyana, there was this. There is also this profound interest in the unconscious which you find in Mittelholzer and Wilson Harris and in myself, which has to be a cultural thing, you know. Even when we are funny—I think I am probably the only Guyanese humorist writing in fiction terms—look how the humor ends; it always ends in tragedy. So that could not be an accident. It has been suggested that the forests in Guyana are a kind of physical hinterland which is a metaphor for a psychological hinterland. I think that's a good argument, but I think it could only enlarge on the idea of us being preoccupied with death.

R.D.: Because there was a lot of death.

Heath: Because there was, up until the late forties, a lot of death. Since malaria has been controlled, this isn't so; but you don't forget those experiences in one generation.

R.D.: I've learned a great deal about malaria reading *The Shadow Bride*.

Heath: Yes, I think that I made the mosquito the hero in that book, in one way. *(Laughter)*

R.D.: So you think that, for your writing, anyway, social facts are more important than the landscape.

Heath: Yes.

R.D.: I would have said that it was the landscape that was dominant in the work of Wilson Harris. But as you're talking about malaria and death, I'm thinking about the number of characters in his novels who are dead, or where it's a little difficult to figure out whether they're dead or alive.

Heath: But that's it: they may not die, but it's difficult to know whether they're dead or alive. There is a powerful vision of things in Wilson Harris which is very unusual. I don't think any modern novelist can do without reading Wilson Harris if he wants to be serious. At least, he would be missing out on something very important. There are ways of looking at things which can only come from a peculiar experience like that, a peculiar social experience. I don't think one person could have done that. Dostoevsky was not produced overnight. He came out of Gogol, and Gogol came out of

Pushkin, and so on. I don't believe that the individual is as all-powerful in things like that as people think.

R.D.: So though your work is very different in style from Wilson Harris's, you feel that you have a shared social, cultural consciousness.

Heath: Yes, I would say so.

F.J.: Something I've been wondering about is the curious doubling in the English attitude towards their former colonies. On the one hand, the English have trouble facing the fact of the emerging multicultural society. Yet, on the other hand, there's great interest in the Raj, interest in India and novels of the Raj. Even in detective novels, you go to Dillon's Bookstore and there's *Mystery of the Raga*, or something like that on sale. What do you think is causing this post-colonial colonialist phenomenon?

Heath: It is a hungering after a brilliant past. India has a special place in their affections. They don't love India; they love their past in India. The Indians fare worst of all among all the immigrants here, they attack them in the streets, yet the police will tell you, it's common knowledge, that the Indians are the most law-abiding of all the elements in this country, yet they're the most manhandled in the streets. You will not find an Indian lady in the streets in this country after dark. She simply won't go out. But there is a nostalgia for the Raj. Having lost the empire, they would like to retain its psychological goodies. It's understandable.

R.D.: I think the current craze for *The Jewel in the Crown* or *Out of Africa*, or whatever, is because the British can pat themselves on the back for the end of empire. They can say, "We did this great thing," but your narratives depict a very different world, where empire really hasn't ended. You depict the realities of the colonial situation in Guyana, and maybe that's why critics talk about bleakness. The critics may not like the bleakness because they would like to think that the empire was simply benevolence. But maybe there wasn't this great show of benevolence at the end.

Heath: Absolutely. In other words, to put it bluntly, I don't tell them what they want to hear.

R.D.: So faced with the reality of imperial decline, there is on the one hand a kind of heavy investment in a certain kind of imperial nostalgia, but on the other hand, a real desire not to hear the truth from writers from the former colonies.

Heath: One can't assume that writers from the former colonies are necessarily radical voices. I don't think that they always are. I would prefer to say that it's the really highly intelligent, articulate blacks which you do not hear.

R.D.: How do we get beyond that? We've been circling around this question from a number of directions, because we were talking earlier about the problems with the term "Commonwealth literature," and then about how critics misunderstand your work and perhaps the work of other writers, by judging it from an Anglocentric perspective, and now we're talking about the mass media equivalent of the same thing. You're suggesting that we need to move away from an exclusively English perspective towards a more multicultural view. But there's a tremendous amount of resistance to that, in the education system, in virtually every facet of society. I'm wondering how to break that impasse.

Heath: I have no idea. I have no idea at all. In a way, it can be to our advantage that this impasse has been reached because we will have to do our own work. And I am all for that. I think that we should say to ourselves, "We are in this position and it is up to us to do our own work." We need to move away from this dependence mentality that still exists and that is a leftover from slavery where we say, "We feel they should do this." To hell with it, and to hell with them, let us do it for ourselves, whatever little resources are at our disposal. It can lead into something positive. It's a desperate situation, but it can lead to something positive. There are dangers in having the establishment on your side.

R.D.: So perhaps that opposition could be a stimulus?

Heath: Absolutely.

R.D.: We've been moving from the Caribbean-Guyanese situation to the situation of being black in Britain. Certainly most black people here are from the West Indies. But one of the things that's been an issue in Caribbean writing is how much of a commonality is there with African writing. Everything we've talked about are issues also faced by African writers. Is that an important frame of reference for your thinking about these things, or not?

Heath: Yes. The African writer has the advantage of having publishing firms in Africa. He has problems that are very similar to our own. Ngũgĩ, for instance, insists on writing in Gĩkũyũ. That's a very strong point, because he's dispensing with a very large audience. But they have an African language which makes it easier in one sense to do this.

**F.J.:** So Creole doesn't really raise the same kind of issue, "Should I write in Gĩkũyũ or should I write in English or should I write in Hindi or should I be writing in"—

**Heath:** Oh, yes. It does raise these issues, because, as I say, many of the Kenyan writers write in English because they want a large audience; therefore, this man is to be admired. It's not only an honorable stand, it's a necessary stand. What is so special about the novel, after all? I mean, the novel is a historical phenomenon that came up at a certain time when capitalist society had reached a certain stage. It is an expression of the middle classes. The novel is special in the sense that it is long, it can include poetry, it can include politics, it can include everything. It's a marvelously all-inclusive art form. But speaking objectively, why should Guyana have novelists, in the first place? Is it really the most important literary art form for Guyana? One has to ask the question. It may be that my involvement in novel writing has something to do with my arrogance and my pride and my wishing to have a large audience. I don't know. But there's nothing remarkable in novels. At least those are questions that should be posed and discussed.

After all, we are a struggling little nation which has problems that are special to us. And these problems might actually be better expressed in a different art form. Let us suppose that you and I were to be in the government in Guyana and to be part of a cultural ministry. These are questions we would have to ask, because if you were given so many thousands of dollars to support literary art forms, whom do we support, do we support novelists? We have to ask some of these questions.

**R.D.:** And in your view the questions are being asked more sharply by people like Ngũgĩ than they are by anyone in the West Indies.

**Heath:** Yes. They are. They are being asked more sharply by Ngũgĩ than by myself, for instance. I live a fairly cloistered life. Ngũgĩ, in the nature of things, has not. He's been in prison, in politics, in lots of things.

**R.D.:** One final question. Guyana, this poor little nation on the edge of the English language community, on the edge of South America, has produced a very rich literature.

**Heath:** Well, yes it has.

**R.D.:** Why do you think this is?

**Heath:** That's a good question and a good final question, because I don't know and nobody really knows. But it's nice to be asked that because no one here in Britain seems to realize the richness of our literature. I tell people here I'm from Guyana and nobody knows what that is. There is a very rich Guyanese literature, and I'm glad someone recognizes this.

# Raja Rao

Indian writing in English is the oldest of the new literatures, as Indians began to write in English in the 1820s and a continuous tradition of Indian writing in English descends from that time. Much of this earlier work is derivative, but India was also the first colony (aside from Ireland and the United States) to begin to produce clearly major work in the colonizer's language. This was the result of a great generation of Indian novelists in English, all of whom were born in the first decade of this century and all of whom are still alive and writing in their eighties. Mulk Raj Anand, born in 1905, was the first of these writers to emerge with his social realist and politically committed novels starting with *The Untouchable* in 1935; R. K. Narayan, born in 1907, was the next, with his first novel, *Swami and Friends*, appearing in 1935; the last and the most unusual of this generation was G. V. Desani, born in 1909, whose *All About H. Hatterr* was published in 1948. But it is Raja Rao, also born in 1909, whose first novel *Kanthapura* was published in 1938 and most recent novel, *The Chessmaster and His Moves*, in 1988, who has had the greatest and most demonstrable influence on other Indian writers and intellectuals. He has also had a good deal of influence abroad, having for instance won the Neustadt Prize in 1988. This is not, however, because he has made his work readily accessible or because he has established a new set of conventions or norms. Narayan has always had the greater readership, and Rao has changed his mode of writing for virtually each of his successive novels. *Kanthapura* (1938) is the village epic of Gandhism, a re-creation of the oral tradition and of the rhythms of Rao's native Kannada language; *The Serpent and the Rope* (1960) is a densely philosophical novel rooted in the abstractions of the Sanskritic tradition; *Comrade Kirillov* (1976) is a re-creation of Dostoyevsky's *The Possessed*. And Rao's most recent work, the longest and most difficult of them all, *The Chessmaster and His Moves*, is impossible to encapsulate, as it seems a combination of all these modes, though it most closely resembles *The Serpent and the Rope*.

Part of the reason for Rao's influence is that, though he has lived much of his life abroad, in France and in the United States, he holds tenaciously to an Indian cultural identity and to Indian modes of thinking. This shapes not just the content but also the form of the following conversation. Though based on several conversations in Austin, Texas, where he is a professor emeritus of philosophy at the University of Texas, Rao did not permit us to use any recording equipment. So what follows is a reconstruction of several conversations based on extensive notes taken during the conversations. This means that the following is surely a less accurate mirroring of what was actually said among us than other conversations in the book, but that kind of mirroring, the mirroring of realism, is not a particular concern of Rao's. The traditional mode of instruction in India has been the guru speaking with the chela or pupil privately. In fact, many of the works of classical Indian philosophy are essentially collections of such sayings or sutras (literally meaning thread), memorized by students and later collected. Around such collections of oral sutras, written commentaries then emerge. So it was not the oral mode of transmission that was crucial but the combination of private communication and subsequent public interpretation. Rao's rejection of recording equipment has in a sense re-created this, casting us as his chelas, in the very modern form of the interview, and this is a nice image of his general approach to aesthetics.

**Feroza Jussawalla**: Here we are talking in Austin, Texas though we were both born in India, and this represents the increasingly international and multicultural nature of the world today. But many Asian and African writers feel suspicious of this internationalism. The Indian poet R. Parthasarathy believes that a writer must write out of his own native language. What is your sense of this? What is the role of the writer in today's multicultural society?

**Raja Rao**: I am not interested in the general picture but only in my own personal experience. I don't consider myself multicultural, I am totally a Brahmin and an Indian from India. And I believe that you remain basically faithful to your own self—to the genetic and psychological background of yourself, the bio-psycho-sociological existence. Apart from physics, biology is perhaps the most advanced science today. Genetics, for example, explains the killing by cancer generation after generation in the same family, which shows that genetic patterns repeat themselves. Mutation takes place by accident only and can't be changed.

**F.J.**: And this is true despite the increased contact between cultures around the world?

**Rao**: Yes, it only took living in Europe for a week, when I was nineteen, to realize that I was an Indian. Part of my Indianness is my honesty not to parade under a guise that I am not. Despite culture-contact, I am more and more an Indian. At the psychological level, there is the collective unconscious of history. Traditions are only the reprints of psychoanalytic patterns of human thinking and being. I don't think anyone can quarrel with this. Genetically, people don't change so much; sociological and political facts are not essential compared to these genetic realities.

**F.J.**: Is it hard to communicate this sense of Indianness you feel across cultures to readers of different cultures?

**Rao**: I am not interested in communicating across cultures. I am what I am. I am an arrogant Indian—some people have called me an Indian imperialist. India's greatness is its capacity to absorb.

**Reed Dasenbrock**: What then of communicating to a reader not from India, such as myself?

**Rao**: Writers do not communicate; that is a very misleading word. Writers have nothing to say; they experience.

**R.D.**: And provide the reader with that experience?

**Rao**: Yes, if the readers are interested. But writers are not so much interested in their audiences as you suggest, and as that word communication suggests. Writing is an aspect of living. I am first of all a human being. My writing comes out of my self, and it continues to mature.

**F.J.**: How does a writer mature?

**Rao**: How does a human being mature? By going deeper into himself. That is the Indian tradition. I am entirely Indian. I am more interested in what the Indian metaphysical and literary tradition says.

**R.D.**: Are there ways in which you would acknowledge an indebtedness to Western culture?

**Rao**: The most important contributions that the West has made are psychoanalysis, genetics, and quantum physics. But the university atmosphere in America is too concerned with books, not experience. It is encyclopaedic rather than interpretive. What is sad about the modern intellectual is that he is getting to be a generalist.

**R.D.**: Are there contemporary European writers you admire? Czeslaw Milosz, for example, has written that poem about you, "To Raja Rao," the one poem he's written in English, I think.

**Rao**: We met in Paris and then again in Austin. We had a discussion about how to address life. He and I differed, and he was honest enough to accept the differences.

**F.J.:** What differences?

**Rao:** He believes in evil and I don't. For a good Christian, evil is concrete. For a good Vedantist, there is no evil. In the Indian tradition, there is no evil.

**F.J.:** But what about differences in India? Indian culture is hardly one thing. Isn't it multicultural in a sense?

**Rao:** Why are you so interested in multiculturality?

**F.J.:** As a Parsi, it is natural for me to be interested in the expression of many cultures.

**Rao:** But India is essentially Hindu. I have been to Parsi marriages, and the background is similar to the Vedic.

**R.D.:** But if this is so, why write in English?

**Rao:** I would have liked to have written in Sanskrit. I have said this many times.

**R.D.:** Then you would have had a small audience.

**Rao:** Yes, but it would have been the right language to express my metaphysical and psychological experiences.

**R.D.:** Why didn't you write in Sanskrit?

**Rao:** I don't know it well enough. I have studied Sanskrit for many years, but I don't know the language well enough to write in it. I still think that I would have written much better in Sanskrit.

**F.J.:** What about your mother tongue, Kannada?

**Rao:** My Kannada was never adequate. Though I was born in a Kannada-speaking area, I was brought up in Hyderabad [where they primarily speak Urdu and Telugu, not Kannada]. Also, when I started writing, Kannada as a language needed to be modernized. I was too impatient then, but some of the writers have since gone back and modernized it.

If an Indian writer asks, and I am asked this question, "Why do you use English?" I say, "I am sorry. Historically, this is how I am placed. I'm not interested in being a European but in being me. But the whole of the Indian tradition, as I see it, is in my work." There is an honesty in choosing English, an honesty in terms of history.

**R.D.:** Have you then never written in Kannada?

Rao: Yes, I have. I have written a novel in Kannada, some twenty-five years ago. But then I translated it into English, and it seemed much better.

R.D.: Has this been published?

Rao: No, not in either language.

R.D.: Why do you think the novel improved in translation?

Rao: In English, it seems as if one can do what one wants with the language. There are fewer rules, it's a newer language, and therefore has more freedom for invention. I lived in France for a long time and know French almost as well as I do English, but this freedom is not available in French at all. French is so strict a language that there is hardly any freedom there.

R.D.: So you have not written anything in French?

Rao: Only a few essays.

R.D.: But *Comrade Kirillov* was published first in French, was it not? Was any of it written in French?

Rao: No, it was translated from the English. But I wrote the novel in France.

R.D.: Did you have anything to do with the translation?

Rao: No, the translator is a close friend of mine, but I didn't help him. In any case, I didn't have to, as it was so good.

R.D.: One of the reasons I ask is that there has been a good deal of question about the status of translations by the author lately. For instance, Czeslaw Milosz, whom we just mentioned, Isaac Singer, Vladimir Nabokov, and others have translated or cotranslated their own work into English. Do those translations then belong in English literature?

Rao: I don't think that works very well. A certain authenticity is lost in the translation process.

R.D.: Yet you were just saying that you translated a novel from Kannada yourself.

Rao: Yes, but it belonged to English, not to Kannada. It wasn't something I had taken to a finished state in one language, then re-created it in the other. In each language, there are some things it is easier to say. I want to write my last novel in Kannada, as there are certain shades and delicacies of expression there that aren't available in English.

F.J.: But you've said before that when one dies, one prays in one's own language and that you would pray in Sanskrit, not in Kannada.

Rao: Seventy percent of the important words in Kannada are Sanskrit.

When Gandhiji said "Ram Ram" when dying, it was Sanskrit, not Gujarati.

**F.J.:** You have talked and written before about how we all know reality through a language. What about all the different languages in India? Does this mean there isn't a common Indian consciousness?

**Rao:** There are very small differences in India. All Indian languages are born of Sanskrit except perhaps Tamil, which is 30 percent Sanskrit. I think all those who speak Indo-European languages think alike; Indians are closer to the Europeans in thinking than they are to the Chinese.

**F.J.:** Did language patterns condition the way you write?

**Rao:** Some things can be said more easily in one language than another; some things can be said more easily in Kannada, especially the silences.

**F.J.:** Is this more important in oral versus written cultures? There is a lot of discussion now about "the oral tradition," which of course you draw on in *Kanthapura*. Do you think that "orality" is the same everywhere?

**Rao:** Oral traditions are similar because they are concerned with love and death. Here again we are talking too much about internationalism and interculture.

**F.J.:** The tradition of the oral tale itself has changed as a result of culture-contact.

**Rao:** *Kanthapura* is doing that.

**F.J.:** In Africa, people gather in the same manner but tell oral tales in English, for instance, or read from contemporary works.

**Rao:** Those who can read *Kanthapura* can do that. But there are enough wonderful stories in India. Why should they tell the story of *Kanthapura*?

**R.D.:** Would it be easy to write in Kannada here in Austin, in Texas?

**Rao:** No, I find that I must be hearing the language, hearing the language on the streets, to write in it. When I go to France, it takes me a day or two to adjust or switch to French. And the same is true when I return to India.

**R.D.:** Here, in tracing the various languages you know and could have written in, we're moving into an area of particular interest to me. I'm fascinated by multilingualism. One of the questions I'm seeking to answer is why so many of the good writers in English seem to come from the margins of the English-speaking community and in many cases have English as a second or a third language.

**Rao:** Why do you think that is so?

**R.D.**: I wanted to ask you that.

**Rao**: No, I'd like to know your answer first.

**R.D.**: I know of two ways of tackling the problem. One would say that after modernism, British and American—particularly American—writers have been so caught up in formal experiments that they have forgotten they have anything to say. Forms are all that count in their work. In contrast, Third World writers—for a variety of reasons—have a great deal to say.

The second explanation is that having English as a second language, or as one among several languages, is somehow an advantage because it makes the writer the master of the language, not its slave. We usually feel that to learn a language well enough to write in to, one must learn it from childhood and speak it as a mother tongue. But in this century at least, the good writers seem to come to English from the outside, and that seeming disadvantage is really an enabling force.

Do you think that coming to English as a second language has helped your work?

**Rao**: I don't think I agree with either explanation. The important thing is not what language one writes in, for language is really an accidental thing. What matters is the authenticity of experience, and this can generally be achieved in any language.

**F.J.**: It's interesting to hear the word authentic linked to a defense of writing in any language, because usually in non-Western literature, it is used by those insisting that one should return to writing in one's mother tongue. Ngũgĩ in Kenya, Parthasarathy in India, Mazisi Kunene in South Africa have all argued that authenticity requires writing in one's mother tongue.

**Rao**: For me, this has not been true. They are however right in that one must stay in touch with one's language.

**R.D.**: Both the African writers would push it much further than that. They feel now that African literature in English is simply a mistake, that the minute one begins to write in English, the language imposes its forms on you, and that what emerges in English can only be colonialist in expression.

**Rao**: I can't speak for the Africans.

**F.J.**: I'm sure they would extend this to the Indian situation as well.

**Rao**: But we are here after Joyce, and Joyce was very daring, very creative. Now we must all be very daring, and do what we want with the language we use. After all, T. S. Eliot and Yeats did not write like Wordsworth or Tennyson.

**R.D.**: But can't that in turn become a new trap, the trap of being experimental at all costs?

**Rao**: Yes, but again authenticity is everything here.

**R.D.**: But it sounds as if you would agree with the suggestion that having English as a second language is an advantage and this is why the good writers in English are increasingly not English and American.

**Rao**: My answer would be this. England and America are industrialized societies and therefore have a very superficial culture, what do they call it, a "horizontal" culture. They have lost touch with themselves, that is with a deeper, spiritual dimension. It is only out of this deeper experience that great literature arises.

But some great writers from the West still have this dimension. Dylan Thomas had a deep spiritual sense; Gerard Manley Hopkins, of course. Eliot's religious search accounts for much of the depth of his work, and one could say the same for Yeats, with his unusual spiritual seeking. I am not speaking here of organized religion but a search for the transcendental. D. H. Lawrence has this, even though he subscribed to no very orthodox religion.

**R.D.**: And he got out of England.

**Rao**: Yes, which was very important for the spiritual aspect of his work. It is hard to be truly spiritual in a country like England today. Except Kathleene Raine, who writes authentic poetry in England today?

**R.D.**: Is that why Lawrence felt he had to get out of England?

**Rao**: I think in his case it was mostly the class system. In England, he was never allowed to forget that he was a miner's son. So he married, I think, this aristocratic German woman as a way out of that situation. That got him out of England, out of the industrialized world. France is a less industrialized world than England, or at least it industrialized later, which is why there has been more good French writing than in English—Levi-Strauss, Foucault, for example. But there doesn't seem to be much there now.

**R.D.**: Is that why Beckett went from writing in English to writing in French?

**Rao**: No, I think it was because he was so close to Joyce. He could get away from Joyce by writing in French. He is a special case. But it always helps to be able to hear the language you write in. For example, when Rilke lived in Paris, he wrote in French.

**R.D.:** When Joyce lived in Paris, he wrote *Finnegans Wake*.

**Rao:** And that's in another language entirely. Isn't it so? I didn't know Joyce well, but I knew lots of people who did. Joyce wanted to be a musician. That is his struggle for honesty—the music in his work. Honesty is the equation between experience and expression.

**R.D.:** What is the future of English in India? Are Indians likely to go on writing in English as well as in Indian languages?

**Rao:** It is important to recognize that Indians are good at writing in other languages. Indians wrote in Persian, you know, for hundreds and hundreds of years.

**R.D.:** Yes, but now they have stopped.

**Rao:** I am not very much interested in this question of how long we will write in English or in any other language. How long does anything continue when judged by a long perspective on civilization? We are here, and later someone else will take our places. I can't worry about whether Indians will use English or not in the future.

**R.D.:** But at the present do you think English is losing ground in India?

**Rao:** Not at all. The English we use in India today is a much better English than it was some forty to fifty years ago. Then it was just Victorian English. When the British left in 1947, 1 percent of the population could speak English; now it is 3 percent. Most of the English I read in magazines in India today is very much better indeed. Some of it is worse, of course, as the standards of education have fallen. But English in India is so much more interesting and much freer than it used to be.

**R.D.:** And Indian writing in English, the creative work?

**Rao:** I don't read very much contemporary literature, from India or from anywhere else. Most literature today is pure form without contexture. That is why I am not very interested in contemporary literature.

**F.J.:** Can there be such pure form?

**Rao:** There cannot be. If I had to describe a stone which I see there, the texture of the stone and my poetry has to be the same. The experiencing of an object has to have the texture of your concern. A man who has both texture and form today is Wilson Harris, but a good deal of modern literature is simply journalism. I always prefer to read the classics.

F.J.: How do we define the classics?

Rao: Whatever talks of realities, not supposed realities, interests me. I read the classics because of their concerns with fundamentals. The classics are concerned only with fundamentals; otherwise, they wouldn't endure. I would much rather read a great spiritual writer like Dostoevsky or Valery than what is written today. Why read a superficial novel when I could read the *Mahabharata* or Shankaracharya?

R.D.: In Sanskrit.

Rao: Sanskrit on one side and English on the other. That way when I am tired of the Sanskrit, I go to the English, and vice-versa. There is so much more to the *Mahabharata* than to what is written today.

F.J.: Do you think the *Mahabharata* could speak to an American freshman with immediacy?

Rao: If he is sincere. I saw Peter Brook's play, *Mahabharata*, in Austin. It is contemporary. This is true of the Western classics as well as the Indian ones. All classics are contemporary.

F.J. Could you name the key classics for you?

Rao: The *Odyssey*, *Tristan und Isolde*, *Genji* in Japan, Chinese classical poetry, and of course the Indian literature of all ages. The revival of old Greek myths, in the contemporary literature of France, is very important. The classics are always contemporary because they speak of our essential relation to love, life and death.

F.J.: Is the cultural context important here?

Rao: There is no cultural context to love, life and death—Hamlet is universal. Orpheus, Oedipus—these are the fundamental myths of man.

R.D.: What of the writers of your generation in India? You are from the same area in India as Narayan; do you know him?

Rao: I see him whenever I am in Mysore, and we are very good friends. But our works are very different. He writes of the social world; I do not. I am only interested in the Vedantist search for Truth, in metaphysics.

R.D.: But some critics have seen Narayan's work as metaphysical as well.

Rao: Metaphysical? I don't see how. There is a complex sense of social irony in his work, but I don't see any metaphysics.

R.D. And Mulk Raj Anand?

Rao: I know Anand very well also; I knew him from London. He is like

Narayan: he is interested in the social world. He is interested in changing the social world. I am not.

**R.D.**: So we could make a distinction between you and G. V. Desani on one side as writers interested in the Indian spiritual tradition, and Narayan and Anand on the other.

**Rao**: Yes, but there is a distinction between Desani and me. I know him well too, of course, as I brought him to Texas [where both writers taught philosophy and where both still live at least part of the year]. He was born in Kenya, I was told. So he was born outside the tradition, whereas I was born inside it and have largely stayed inside it.

**R.D.**: But there is an irony here: the more philosophical of the Indian writers, you and Desani, both went outside India to live whereas Anand and Narayan have stayed inside India.

**Rao**: Anand was in England for many years also. But that is irrelevant, a matter of chance. I could just have easily been in India all my life. I happen to be in America because I was invited here, but it doesn't matter to me whether I am in America or in Alaska. But it does matter to me if I am in India. At the depth of India, not according to the geography of India.

**F.J.**: You have said, "My India I carry with me." Would you say that you are in India now?

**Rao**: I am always in India.

**R.D.**: How old were you when you went to France to go to university?

**Rao**: Nineteen.

**R.D.**: At that point, was going overseas still a big thing, involving going over the black waters, losing your Brahminhood, and all that?

**Rao**: Yes, at least for the older people.

**R.D.**: Did they oppose your going?

**Rao**: Of course! But then I was continuing our Vedantic tradition, even in France. Tradition is not static; it is an absorption of deep human experiences into a contemporary social context.

**R.D.**: So after a break, they came to accept your going?

**Rao**: No, there was no break. And this is the difference between Desani and me.

**R.D.**: Have you seen Desani at all lately?

**Rao**: No. You know, I think, he is a Buddhist monk? He lives in great solitude.

**R.D.:** Where was he when you brought him to Texas?

**Rao:** In India, in meditation.

**R.D.:** What of the contemporary Indian poets?

**Rao:** I don't know very much of their work. The best Indian poet I know is Parthasarathy. He is capable of some tremendous work; I just hope he does it, with all of the other things he is doing.

**R.D.:** What of A. K. Ramanujan?

**Rao:** He is a very fine translator, very fine indeed! I only disagree with his choice of Western forms to translate the texts into.

**R.D.:** And his own poetry?

**Rao:** I haven't read his work in Kannada. His poetry in English is like his translations, too caught up in Western forms, too Westernized.

**F.J.:** Is that always a problem, in your judgment, to attempt a mixture of Western and Indian forms? Is there a place for multicultural authors such as Zulfikar Ghose, Rushdie, and other such authors? Can they ever be the classics?

**Rao:** Honesty can always create a classic. A gifted man could create a classic by being honest to himself.

**F.J.:** What about those authors—such as V. S. Naipaul—who are struggling to express the many things they are?

**Rao:** Naipaul knows where he belongs, but he is struggling not to belong to where he belongs.

**F.J.:** Is he attempting to deny himself?

**Rao:** He is trying to fight against who he is.

**F.J.:** Why would he do that?

**Rao:** The Parsis tried to imitate the British, and Naipaul hasn't gotten out of that. He is a British subject and will always remain so unless he discovers who he is.

**F.J.:** Writers like Naipaul and Ghose—how are they to manifest themselves?

**Rao:** The Self has no nationality; they are to find their self-nakedness. Naipaul is a very fine man but is afraid to see himself in real context, just as many Jews in the diaspora do. Some writer friends of mine declare that they are French, etc., but essentially they are Jews. I don't know if you know Freud and his *Psychopathology of Everyday Life*. It has great truths in it. *The Psychology of Early Life* gives depth. Without Freud, there would be no

Joyce, also no Proust. A Jew remains a Jew after 4000 years of persecution. There is a great esoteric meaning in this. In my new novel, *The Chessmaster and His Moves*, I try to give pictures of Jews who went to the gas chambers and of one who escaped this destiny.

**R.D.:** The Jewish people and culture seem important to you. Did you know Jews in India?

**Rao:** No, just a few. I know the Jewish poet Nissim Ezekiel.

**R.D.:** What do you think of his work?

**Rao:** It is very clever, very clever. But again it is too Westernized for me and not very profound.

**F.J.:** If you were laying out a formulation for Indian writers, to avoid the superficiality you're describing, what would that be?

**Rao:** To be honest.

**F.J.:** About what?

**Rao:** Yourself.

**F.J.:** The way you stand historically?

**Rao:** No, in yourself. In *The Serpent and the Rope*, I talk of history. But history is only politics deeply assimilated. I am concerned with man and his sufferings.

**F.J.:** Are life, love, and death all suffering?

**Rao:** Suffering, and escape from suffering and happiness. Love is happiness too. I am interested in fundamental questions. The fundamental questions are, "Who am I?" and "What am I about?" in terms of life and death and immortality. In French, l'amour et le mort.

**F.J.:** Why is love essential?

**Rao:** When you love, you become deeply yourself. All objects are known only inside yourself. Even the one you love. Love is a way of knowing yourself. Loving is pure self-realization.

**F.J.:** And how is that important to living?

**Rao:** Being oneself is truly living. Gandhiji said, "If I don't live the truth, I am and will never be free." And being free is the essence of expressing oneself and Being. This is Moksha—Dharma and Moksha—that is what I am interested in. Dharma is the honesty of oneself with oneself.

**F.J.:** Where does one find the words to describe that?

**Rao:** Honesty creates the word. But what you don't say in life is as important as what you say. The full stop is silence. Hiatus in poetry is silence. The universe is vibrant silence.

**F.J.:** In India, when people are sometimes sitting together, they are silent.

**Rao:** I was married in France, and when I brought my first wife to India, she was very shocked at the silence. When we went into the houses of friends, they just sat and said nothing. In India, behind the chatter, there is silence.

**R.D.:** Yet sound—or at least voice—is also important in your work. Much of *Kanthapura* reads as if it were translated from Kannada; the syntactic patterns are those of Kannada, though the work is in English. Was any of it translated from Kannada?

**Rao:** A very small part was written in Kannada, but most of it was written in English.

**R.D.:** Did you sound out those sentences in English, the ones that have Kannada syntax in them?

**Rao:** Only in the sense that one can hear the language in one's head as one writes. But sound is very important to me; in my new book, I have many meaningless words that are just sounds, invented as part of a Jewish liturgy.

**R.D.:** So Judaism is important in the new book?

**Rao:** Yes. The book was first called *The Brahmin and the Rabbi*. I hope the new book ties everything together, the Kannada that was so important in *Kanthapura*, the Sanskrit of *The Serpent and the Rope*, the French tradition. In *The Brahmin and the Rabbi*, I become universal.

**F.J.:** What do you see as the differences between *Kanthapura* and *The Serpent and the Rope*? What accounts for those differences?

**Rao:** They differ the more I become authentic, that is in the expression of my growing authenticity. The levels of thinking changes, matures, also. There are about two levels to *Kanthapura* and about eight to *Serpent*. No one has yet written of the eight levels. It is also politically liberal. But these subtleties escape people. Most writers and readers today do not have the patience for depth. The writers today explain rather than state.

**F.J.:** But what about the accessibility of literature to the common reader?

**Rao:** I'm not in the least interested in that. The people who wrote the Vedas didn't say, "Would the common man understand?" Everyone doesn't understand Shakespeare, but that doesn't mean he was not great. Greatness is that which helps you to be yourself, whosoever you may be, from your depth, not from your egocentric self. Depth is what permits you to go back to real honesty. Real honesty is pure experience. And pure experience is forever ontological.

# Anita Desai

Indian writing in English seemed for a long time to have been the product of a particular moment and a particular generation, the generation of writers born in the first decade of the century who began to write in the 1930s, that of Raja Rao, R. K. Narayan, Mulk Raj Anand, and G. V. Desani. This generation of writers has indeed cast a long shadow, producing important work not just in the 1930s and 1940s but up until the present. The seeming failure of younger writers to emerge out from under their shadows fit in with a growing perception that English had lost ground in India after Indian independence in 1947 with the rise of Hindi and the regional Indian languages. Even though the writers such as Rao and Anand had been critical of British rule, of the Raj, it seemed as if Indian writing in English was going to be limited to those writers who grew to maturity under the Raj.

That might have been the perception up until 1960 or even 1970, but no one would argue that now. English plays as important a role in Indian cultural, political and economic life now as it ever did. In a country with fifteen official languages and over five hundred different spoken languages and dialects, link languages are essential. Hindi, the only indigenous language that more than 10 percent of the population speaks, is still strongly resisted in non-Hindi speaking parts of the country. Because of this and because of the advantages of English for international communications, there has evolved what is called the three-language formula, whereby Indians are taught the language of their region, the national language Hindi and English as well. For people with a different mother tongue from the language spoken in the region, these three languages can easily increase to four or five. Anita Desai perfectly exemplifies this situation: with a Bengali father and a German mother, she grew up in Urdu- and Hindi-speaking Delhi, where she has lived most of her life and still lives. She speaks all four languages, Bengali, German, Urdu and Hindi, but she writes in English.

Moreover, just as English retains its important official role, it retains its role in Indian literature, and Indian writing in English is as exciting and vigorous today as ever. Anita Desai is one of the crucial figures here, as her probing psychological novels beginning with *Cry, the Peacock* (1963) quickly established her as the first major novelist in English to emerge in India after independence. Though she was born in 1935 and has now published ten books, she is still sometimes thought of as a relatively young writer, since she is nearly thirty years younger than the generation of Rao and Narayan. But her breakthrough as a novelist representative of contemporary India was followed by the emergence of other talented novelists in the 1970s and 1980s, most prominently Salman Rushdie but also others such as Nayantara Sahgal, Amitav Ghosh, Shashi Tharoor and others. A fair number of the good contemporary Indian novelists and poets are women, and Desai is also a crucial pioneer in the exploration of feminist concerns in Indian literature.

Ironically, it was not until the late 1980s, with the publication of *Baumgartner's Bombay*, that she became well known in the United States. This coincided with her coming part of each year to live in America, as she has taught one semester a year for the past several years at Mount Holyoke College in Massachusetts. However, despite this residence in America and her having a German mother, Desai does not consider herself part of the Indian diaspora or anything other than an Indian writer. In this respect, the contrast is quite strong, not just with Rushdie and other Asian writers resident in Britain such as Farrukh Dhondy, but also with her exact contemporary Zulfikar Ghose. It is her concern for Indianness and for an Indian identity that connects her in at least this respect with older Indian writers such as Raja Rao.

**Feroza Jussawalla:** *In Custody* is a novel about a fictional Urdu poet being interviewed by a scholar/critic. Does *In Custody* convey some of your own reluctance to be interviewed?

**Anita Desai:** To say that I don't like to be interviewed is beside the point. I don't like dealing with technical things like tape recorders and even telephones for that matter. It's also that I think a writer writes and isn't necessarily gifted with speech and isn't very good very often at explaining the work.

**F.J.:** So you would prefer not to try to talk about your work as it progresses? Is that right?

**Desai:** I suppose most artists have a certain superstitious fear of this kind of interference. It's such a very private, almost secret, connection one has with the subconscious that one has to be careful about any interference. One's always living in fear of it being broken into.

**F.J.:** How do you mean broken into?

**Desai:** For instance, I don't read any critical theory. I shock all the academics I meet by telling them this, because for them it is "the" thing in literature now. They're shocked to hear that it isn't so for me at all. I have a superstition about reading analyses of my work. I think my work comes from such a different source; critical theorists operate in a completely different area. I feel we clash and collide rather than coincide most of the time, though there are a few happy exceptions.

F.J.: Tell me about the superstition. You're superstitious that it will break into your work.

Desai: Yes. I think when one is writing a book one is living in a very, very intensely private world which nobody shares with you. Nobody can share it with you. Theorists would like to seize upon it and analyze it and tell you what the sources are, and you know that they are not so at all. They are bringing to bear a whole load of their own scholarship whereas your work doesn't depend on scholarship.

F.J.: If your work doesn't depend on scholarship, does it come from the heart, from the analysis of people?

Desai: It doesn't come from analysis at all; that is something you avoid. It comes from instinct and impulse.

F.J.: Instinct and impulse about understanding people, or —

Desai: It's not always understanding. Sometimes simply trying to understand, hoping for that moment of revelation, but often it's simply a search or a quest with no goal in view.

F.J.: So with a character like Deven in *In Custody*, who wants to take charge of the great poet Nur's life and even begins at one point to boast that he's going to do the biography and the analysis, is he the one who puts the artist "in custody"? Is that the metaphor of the title?

Desai: There's an ambiguity in the title, as there is in the word; it has more than one meaning. Deven feels himself the custodian of Nur's art and then discovers at the end that he is in Nur's custody. Nur is the custodian and has complete power over his life.

F.J.: And demands that he come through and do certain things for him.
Desai: Yes.

F.J.: It strikes me almost as though *In Custody* picks up where *Clear Light of Day* ended. As Mulk says in *Clear Light of Day*, the artist lives for his art. *Clear Light of Day* ends with "in your world I am subjected and constrained" which would be the critical world, the taking apart of the artist world—"but over my world you have dominion"—and that's where *In Custody* picks up, that switching of one having custody and dominion over the art and the artist. So there are connections where the one book picks up from where the other ends?

**Desai:** In fact, *In Custody* comes not so much out of *Clear Light of Day* but out of a story in *Games at Twilight*. I wrote a story called "The Accompanist" which is about a man who accompanies on the tampura, the great soloist, the great sitar player, the ustad. I wrote about him because I was always fascinated by the figure of the accompanist on the concert stage. I thought what kind of person could this be who's obviously an accomplished musician himself, but is content to play in the background, only to accompany the great singer? How can it be that he never blossoms into a soloist himself, but always remains in the background? Which made me think a lot about the relationship of the guru and chela, the guru and shishya. So I wrote a short story about this relationship, but it continued to tease my mind. I kept thinking I hadn't fully developed it, there was still so much I wanted to say about it, so I wrote a whole novel on the same subject.

**F.J.:** As someone from Hyderabad, I'm quite interested in the great love you manifest for Urdu poetry and literature. Where does that come from?

**Desai:** I grew up in Delhi. Islamic languages and literature are very much a part of Delhi life, and one cannot live in Delhi without being aware of it. It may be a thing of the past and Delhi is a city of ruins, but it's still being kept alive by the Urdu language. Even though historically, the Islamic part of India has moved to Pakistan and long after its people—the people who speak it—have dwindled and even vanished, that language has remained and people still compose in it, write poetry in it. That's what fascinates me, that there is this trait running through the centuries and which language keeps alive. I really don't know very much about Urdu literature. I understand the language, but I don't read or write it. My knowledge of it is very limited, but I think of it as the repository for a certain period of Indian history and a certain culture.

**F.J.:** A sense of loss comes through in *Clear Light of Day* where Raja, the character from the Hindu family who is infatuated with the daughter of the Muslim neighbors, is trying to protect these neighbors, Hyder Hussein Sahib's family, during the religious riots at the time of independence. His loss is not just a personal loss but the loss of all the culture and literature that these people stand for. Do you sense that loss personally?

**Desai:** Certainly it was an enormous change and an enormous loss in old Delhi when suddenly all of one's Muslim neighbors vanished. They fled over the border and were lost to us, because many of them we never saw again. The school I went to had been made up of 50 percent Muslim girls and perhaps 50 percent Hindu girls, and suddenly every Muslim girl in school had left. It seemed to me completely unnatural and an abnormality that there should be a society so divided.

**F.J.:** It's been said that In Custody is your most political novel, because you're talking about the tradition of Urdu and how it's being killed by Hindi. In the fictional college where Deven teaches, the Hindi department comes along and the Urdu department is killed. Would you agree with that? Is there a political thread in In Custody?

**Desai:** When I wrote In Custody, the situation between Hindus and Muslims was much more subdued than it is now. It was something in the air, but not as overt as it is now. Think of what is happening in India at the moment. I'm thinking of the riots over the building of the temple where the Mosque built by Babar stands, which has set off riots and killings all over the country, which shows what a precarious position Muslims have in India. It disturbs me immensely to think that it's a country with a monolithic religion, a monolithic society. It's no longer the composite society I knew.

**F.J.:** There is the sense, isn't there, that the Muslims are beginning to lose their place, that India's not multicultural anymore.

**Desai:** Yes.

**F.J.:** In Village by the Sea and in various other places also, your work reveals a very strong sense of India having deteriorated. I'm thinking of course of the poverty and the conditions under which Hari lives in Bombay. Is it just that India has become very difficult to live in?

**Desai:** That is my sense of it certainly. It seems to me a place of increasing violence and of tremendous change. The change is coming about with a great deal of pain, it seems to me. It's an economic revolution, of course, more than a political one at the moment. My sense of it is a place where life has become extremely precarious and extremely difficult to endure. I'm aware that there's a new book out by Naipaul in which he says the opposite. He's far more optimistic and cheerful than I am.

**F.J.**: Does this anti-Muslim feeling, this intolerance, we have been discussing trickle down to other minority groups also? Both in *Baumgartner* and in *Fire on the Mountain*, you show the intolerence towards the Anglo-Indians or the Christians.

**Desai**: It's always been at heart a very intolerant society. It's tolerant only as long as the majority has its way. Yes, I've been aware consciously or unconsciously of this intolerance and hypocrisy for a very long time, and it's only just surfaced and taken on this very violent form in recent years.

**F.J.**: Is that the reason you have a character like Deven who says "Look, I understand Hindi, I am a Hindi teacher, but I love the Urdu literature and I love the people"? He manifests the underlying love that Indian people have (or ought to have) for each other, would you say?

**Desai**: No, I wasn't writing in such general terms. He was a very specific individual to me, an individual who lives the life of a perfect worm really and is despised and crushed. What I wanted to bring out was that he had a heroic side to him. He did show a certain heroism, partly in his insistence of being loyal to the Urdu language no matter where his life led him and then being loyal to Nur in spite of all Nur subjects him to.

**F.J.**: That's what I've sensed in your work most of all, because even though I think *In Custody* and *Clear Light of Day* are probably your two most political novels, they're also novels about characters who are quirks. Bim, the older sister who lives alone and who's quite quixotic in *Clear Light of Day*, is someone who wants to pursue her own individualism and Deven I suppose pursues his own individualism. Would you say then that it's the individual angst and the individual alienation from society that comes through in both of the novels?

**Desai**: If they are simply representatives, they would be like cardboard creatures, they would be posters rather than paintings. They would simply stand for a certain society or a certain moment in history, which of course they don't. One goes about creating characters very differently. They tend to be an amalgamation of different ideas and responses of your own.

**F.J.**: In what way would you say that Bim is an amalgamation of responses of your own?

**Desai**: Well, that's a fairly autobiographical novel in that I took up the old Delhi I grew up in and the neighborhood I knew, although I didn't really write about my family and my sisters and brother. She has elements of people I knew certainly. In that sense, she's a very personal creation. Once you've written a book and it's published and it's in the hands of readers, it becomes their property. Readers take it over and read things into her and—

F.J.: You're in custody again—

Desai: Yes, she becomes for them something she was never for me. It's inevitable. I cease to own the book.

F.J.: Would you say that she's feminist in any way? Is she bringing out any of the feminist qualities in you? Or do you even think of yourself as a feminist?

Desai: I don't label my characters at all. I never do. I'm always astonished when they are returned to me with these labels pinned on them. (Laughter) I have to take a look and see, "does that really fit?" That is what I mean by saying a writer doesn't go about writing a book through analysis or any kind of rational thought really. I think that can follow the writing of it, but it doesn't precede it. It hardly exists when you are writing it.

F.J.: If Bim is like some of the people who were close to you as you were growing up, would you put yourself maybe in the younger married sister Tara's shoes, the kind of cosmopolitan person who goes in and out of Bim's life, bringing the children with her?

Desai: I wrote that book long before I left India or became at all a cosmopolitan person. Perhaps it was prophetic in that way, but it never entered my head at that time that I would live abroad. The book was built on the idea of what a family shares no matter how divided they may become later in life and how separate their paths may be. They have something in common which they don't with anybody else. And in that sense one remains closer to one's family than anyone else no matter what the divisions are.

F.J.: So that even if brother and sister or sister and sister had then fought over the house or the business or whatever they—

Desai: Yes, they still share that childhood, which no one else can share with them. They have memories in common no one else knows about, and memories are a terribly important thing to a writer.

F.J.: Is that why the memories as they come out in *Clear Light of Day* form the narrative technique of the novel?

Desai: Well, I'll tell you what the purpose of that book was. I wanted to write about the family certainly, but not as an ordinary narrative, beginning at the beginning and ending at the ending. I wanted to try and write the book starting at the end, and then tunneling my way backwards. So I thought of starting with people fairly old and then going further back into their adulthood, then returning to their youth, to their childhood. In fact, my intention was to go still further back into the ancestry which had made them. And the image I had in my mind was a tunnel. I felt I was burrowing. I was first digging a little hole in the ground and then burrowing deeper and deeper. And I wanted to arrive at the source, at the ancestry. But as it happened, the book took a different form. When I had gone as far back as their infancy the book just ground to a halt; it lost its momentum. It told me that this was done, that I couldn't carry it further. But I still have a sense of disappointment about that book, because the intention had been different.

F.J.: In the sense that it doesn't get beyond Tara exploring her relationship with her mother or her father or her aunt Miramasi?

Desai: In that sense, it remained conventional. I had wanted to take it even further back. But by then it had achieved a certain form and I couldn't do anything with it.

F.J.: What do you mean by take it further back?

Desai: I meant to go into their parents' lives and show how—

F.J.: How it came to be that the mother was diabetic and the father kept giving her injections.

Desai: Not only that. I wanted to explain how they all came to be what they were, such individuals in their own right.

F.J.: *In Custody* also seems to be a stylistic experiment, at least in the sense that, for the first time I think, you have a male point of view. Was that difficult to do, putting yourself in a man's perspective and then telling the story from that perspective?

Desai: It was a very deliberate act. That was not anything unconscious. By the time I wrote *Clear Light of Day*, I began to feel I had gone over the same ground so many times, and I myself began to feel how restricted it was, how confined it was. I felt as though I were a woman living in this enclosed garden with these high walls and never writing about the world beyond it. And it struck me that the only way I could step out into the world and write about wider concerns and experiences was by assuming a male persona, becoming a male character, because whereas men in India go out to work and lead the life that working men lead, very few women do.

Women are still chiefly confined to family and domesticity. It was the only way I could write about that larger experience, so I very deliberately took on the male character as the central person, the narrator in the book. Once I talked myself into doing it, it wasn't difficult at all. In fact, in the first draft I wrote of that novel I didn't have any female characters at all because I thought, male society is like that in India. Women are simply creatures in the background who provide food and comforts of various kinds but don't impinge on their lives, don't influence their lives in any way. I wrote the first draft in that way, and then I decided that this is unnatural, that the women have to enter even if only as mothers and wives, but they must have some presence in the book. So I allowed them to step in, and I thought of them as being marginal characters. Then it quite shocked me how very shrill and how demanding these women were. I didn't like them at all. I was very worried because I thought, why have I created such awful women? Then I thought, well, this is how the women would be if they were always being repressed, always being shut out, locked away. This is exactly what they would do—they would scream and throw tantrums and be extremely unpleasant.

F.J.: You just gave me a clue to something that I've been wondering about. *Voices in the City* for me is your most powerful novel. And the most interesting thing to see in *Voices in the City* is how the women don't support Monisha, the new daughter-in-law who comes into the family. Monisha's suicide, or her traditional bride-burning, however you look at it, comes out of—to fit in with what you just said—being repressed by those women—mothers-in-law and sisters-in-law—who are themselves repressed. Is it because these women are so repressed that they repress other women?

Desai: I think this is something you have to face about Indian society. Women are as responsible as men are for all those old orthodoxies and traditions having been kept alive through the generations.

F.J.: For tyrannizing other women.

Desai: I'm not sure if it's always an impulse to tyrannize, or whether it's simply fear of wrecking the traditions that they've lived by for so long, or finding something comforting and supporting in those orthodoxies. It's what they've lived by for so long that they've come to believe in them, and really it's very hard to persuade them that they could live differently, that there is much more to them than what men have ever allowed them.

**F.J.:** But for Monisha, or for the people who are around her, there's no comfort really in those traditions such as that of the arranged marriage and the inability to get away from it.

**Desai:** No.

**F.J.:** They just prey on each other.

**Desai:** Because everyone believes in this tradition of marriage being complete and irrevocable, and no one helps out at that situation.

**F.J.:** Amla, Monisha's more liberated sister, wants to help out, but when she goes to talk to Monisha the mother-in-law insists on being present, and so Amla doesn't make any effort to get beyond her own interests, such as cartoons and painting her toenails, to connect with Monisha, who is feeling quite lost and alone, even more so after visiting with this "liberated" sister.

**Desai:** You know, the feminist movement in India is very new. It didn't even exist at the time I wrote that book. It does now. A younger generation of readers in India tends to be rather impatient of my books and to think of them as books about completely helpless women, hopeless women. They find it somewhat unreal that the women don't fight back, but they don't seem to realize how very new this movement is.

**F.J.:** I see their point in that most of your books are about women who are helpless, suffering from their own angst as it were, unable to break out of it. In *Fire on the Mountain*, the older woman Nanda living by herself on top of the mountain is killed in a fire. It's been argued that Nanda has committed suicide. I see it more though as her little granddaughter, who's really a pyromaniac, is playing with the matches, and just sets the house on fire to see the fire on the mountain, to see the blaze. In a way, she liberates Nanda.

**Desai:** I never meant the book to end in suicide or even death. I'm perfectly ambivalent about the ending myself. *(Laughter)* I have no idea what happens to Nanda Kaul.

**F.J.:** If she's saved or if someone comes along—

**Desai:** I don't visualize her end. It's over for me with that fire. The fire is a real fire, but it's also a symbolic fire of course. It's the little girl who's grown more and more impatient through the summer with Nanda Kaul's fantasies and fabrications. She senses that they are all lies and illusions, where she herself is only interested in the truth of things—stones, pinecones, solid objects—and finally she sets fire to that whole illusory world, from the ashes of which some kind of truth should show through.

F.J.: Would you also see her then as being the liberating generation for the older generation of women?

Desai: I don't like to generalize about my characters; for me, they're individuals, and an individual acts out of her own impulses.

F.J.: She's a beautifully created individual, because she's almost cat-like, almost like a tiger on the mountain, more than a fire—

Desai: I meant her to be like an animal really, without any received notions because all the notions she has seen existing in the adult world are horrible ones for her. They are all so awful that she rejects them. She lives without any ideas and notions, she lives very, very close to the actual physicality of the world, because it's the only thing that means anything to her.

F.J.: Is that in some way similar to what you're seeing in the younger generation of women in India, as you were just saying, the younger generation being impatient with your generation or with the women who let themselves be locked up in high gardens?

Desai: Well, now that you say so, yes, I should think that matches certainly what is happening in India. But again, I have to remind you that I wrote this book much in advance of the feminist movement. This generation didn't really exist at that time. It would have been just an individual act. It was certainly not a part of a movement. It was not influenced by ideas that were in the air at that time.

F.J.: Yet on the other hand, I've heard people say, "well, women in India have always been liberated for a long time." We had, say, Queen Razia or the Rani of Jhansi who led the 1857 mutiny against the British or of course, the classic example, Indira Gandhi. How do the two come together?

Desai: I think it's ridiculous to think that they are representative of Indian women. They were outstanding or exceptional women, and any society has exceptions. Societies aren't herds of sheep. But I think such women came to be because of the extreme suppression of women in general. I think if you study someone like Indira Gandhi, she was very much created by all the suppression she had to suffer, or her mother had to suffer, in a traditional Kashmiri Brahmin household. I see them as going together, one setting off the other. Whereas most of the Indian female society lives according to the rules, lives in a very conservative, conventional fashion, there always have to be some individuals who take revenge for it.

F.J.: Can you elaborate on the idea of Indira Gandhi being made by the repression?

Desai: I think she must have suffered from all the sacrifices that were asked of her as a child in a very political family where she herself was not as important as the political ideals pursued by the males in the family, and I think she saw her mother suffer a great deal. So that when power was finally put in her hand and it came to her by reasons of heredity and family, she used it the way she did—whether she knew it or not—I'm sure, out of an impulse of vengeance also. I see this very much present in most Indian women. The powerful ones are so powerful they seem to make up in a way for all those who have no power.

F.J.: But the vengeance is not on behalf of women, but against women almost.

Desai: Yes, it is personal. That is why I don't think of people as able to act as representatives. It's their personal impulses that lead them to act the way they do, although they might like to explain and justify those impulses.

F.J.: How does it feel that you've been writing for well over twenty, twenty-five years, and now you've finally been picked up in the West with *Baumgartner's Bombay*. Would you say that or would you say you've always had Western readers?

Desai: Actually, that's a very American perception. (*Laughter*) The first novel I wrote I just sent to England because there was no publisher in India who would be interested in fiction by a Indian writer. They were all reprinting things from abroad. I think my books have been known in England ever since I wrote *Fire on the Mountain*. My earlier books certainly didn't get much interest in India or in England or anywhere, but *Fire on the Mountain* won a literary prize, and it's the first book I published with Heinemann's. Ever since then, I think every book of mine has received a great deal of notice in England. Not as much in America. That's because America hasn't the same interest in India as England has, and the reason that *Baumgartner* has had any success over here is not because of its Indian material but because of its Jewish material. It's aroused a great deal of curiosity and interest amongst Jewish readers. It won a Jewish prize in fact, the Hadassah prize, and people are interested in the element of the war, the Nazis and then the Holocaust. India is really superfluous as far as American readers are concerned.

F.J.: I sense a little bit of criticism in your voice, that the readers are not really interested in India, but interested in the person caught in India who might be of European background.

Desai: That's definitely the reaction here in America. I don't think for Americans India has ever figured very largely in their imagination, except for a very limited area which is South Asian studies in a few of the universities. Apart from that there is no interest whatsoever in Indian writing. England's always had a great fascination with India because of the empire and that isn't over. Because that goes generations back, there is very much more inclination to read about and much more knowledge of India than there is in America. And they've had their own English writers for whom the source has been India, people like Forster and Paul Scott. On the whole, they're able to read Indian writers with far greater ease, without the sense of foreignness that American readers bring to this book. American readers would always prefer to read books from their own part of the world.

F.J.: So does this foreignness distance or attract the readers?

Desai: Over here it distances. In America, it definitely distances the reader.

F.J.: Because they're not able to get into the world of someone like Monisha who is so oppressed and has a traditional arranged marriage.

Desai: That's right. I think there's a lot of incomprehension really, and the reason that *Baumgartner* is readable to them is because the key to the work is a European key, a Western key.

F.J.: Yet it strikes me that your work has always been in part in a European key. I'm astonished at the wide range of literary allusions to Western literature that you make. In all your books you refer to poets from Burns to Eliot. You've spoken about your resistance to analysis of your own works, but all your work seems to draw on literature as well as life.

Desai: Literature's certainly one of the richest sources I know of, but my response to it is a private response. It isn't based on analysis.

F.J.: Like the character in *Clear Light of Day* who loves the poetry and wants to recite, Bim's brother, Raja.

Desai: Yes. It's more a coming together of moods or minds. It's a sense of closeness with certain poets and writers.

**F.J.:** And there are certain poets you turn to over and over again.

**Desai:** Yes.

**F.J.:** Who are they for you?

**Desai:** Different ones at different times. I think each writer to be absolutely honest ought to at one time write a book about all the writers and all the work that's influenced him, because every writer is influenced by all other work. I could write an autobiography based on the reading I've done. When I was a very little girl, the only books I had were my parents' books on their bookshelves. I remember being swept off my feet by the Bronte sisters and living in the imagination in their world on the moors which was on the surface so empty and sparse of life yet so rich imaginatively. Of course I moved on from there and in my student days read a lot of D. H. Lawrence and Virginia Woolf and James Joyce.

But I think the first discovery I made for myself which I didn't necessarily share with my family or my friends, but came upon myself, was Russian literature. I've always felt very much enthralled to writers like Dostoevsky, especially, and Chekhov. In later years, modern Russian poets like Pasternak and Mandelstam and Akhmatova have meant a great deal to me, poetry more than prose. There was a time in my life when I was enormously influenced by Camus. *The Outsider* influenced a great deal of my early writing. Some of it was posturing, of course. I read a lot of Proust and Rilke. At a certain stage I was reading a lot of Chinese and Japanese poetry and the Japanese novelist Kawabata, and trying to achieve the same effects as they did through a minimal use of imagery and metaphor. Really, it depends at what stage one's own writing is. Now that I am in America, I'm trying to grapple with the American material. I find it useful to read all the American classics all over again and to read American literature quite differently from *Huckleberry Finn* through *Lolita* and onwards.

**F.J.:** You put Nabokov in the category of American literature?

**Desai:** Of necessity, yes. I have a feeling probably he himself saw himself as an American writer. After all, he deliberately began to write in English — abandoned Russian and wrote in English. I think his richest novels are the very earliest ones, which he wrote in Russian. But I reread *Lolita* recently, and it seemed to me a masterpiece, and it's an American masterpiece.

**F.J.:** How were you shaped by European literary influences growing up in India?

**Desai:** I grew up in old Delhi and when I was a small child it was still a capital of the British empire. It was a curious world. It seemed very, very orderly, and yet it was made up of all these different fragments. There was the British element, there was the Islamic element in Delhi, and there was the ordinary basic and enduring Indian element—the Hindu element I suppose—although I don't like to call it that. And the world was made up out of these different fragments, but brought together in a very orderly manner. And for me, the world took on a completely different shape in August 1947, when the British left, and at the same time, the Muslim population of Delhi left, and it became the modern city of Delhi, what it is now. And although I was a child when this happened, I still don't feel entirely at home with it. I think I am very much a product of what it had been in the 1930s when I was born, and the 1940s when I was going to school. I went to the nearest school, the neighborhood school, which happened to be a mission school, and it's there I was taught English, and I think I instantly fell in love with English literature. It was a lifelong obsession of mine. I think it's what you read that most influences what you write. Of course, my material was Indian, and I had to bend it and adapt it somehow to the English language. The reason I'm so fascinated by the English language is that it's really possible to do this with English; it is so flexible, it is so elastic. It does stretch, it does adapt, and it does take on all those Indian concepts and traditions and ways. In those years, it was very much the tradition for Indians who went to mission schools to grow up reading more English literature than they did the literature of their own country. And I have to admit that as for older Indian literature, I've only taken an interest in it and read it very recently. For instance, Tagore didn't mean very much to me until I was asked to write an introduction to a new edition of his novel *The Home and the World*, which made me go back and read Tagore and read his biographies and become aware of this amazing Tolstoyan personality. Of course, I read the work of my contemporaries. I was interested in what else was being written in India.

**F.J.:** Who were the contemporaries you read and how did they influence you? This is part of a larger question, I suppose, how do you connect with the field of Indian literature in English? How does a woman like you become a writer in India?

**Desai:** When I was a young woman writing in India, writing was a completely private and almost, I should say, a secret occupation. No one thought of me as a writer, and I barely thought of myself as a writer. It was simply something I went away and did in secret. I had no sense of community with other writers, possibly it's got something to do with writing in English. There were so few of us writing in English, and we were so scattered. There was Narayan living in the south and Raja Rao living abroad. There was no sense of community. I shared nothing with them, hardly ever met them. Although I read their work it didn't influence me because it seemed to me each of us was experimenting along completely different lines. We were all handling the English language differently, we were all handling very different material. We had nothing in common. So I lived as a writer in complete isolation.

F.J.: So you really didn't have any role model?

Desai: I was following my own direction, my own bent, which the others of my generation were also doing. We were all very isolated from each other. But I think things have changed tremendously in the last decade, in the last ten years. There's suddenly been a whole new crop of Indian writers, far more confident—confident about handling English, far more sure of themselves as writers, actually being able to earn a living as writers, which was all unheard of when I was starting off.

When Salman Rushdie published *Midnight's Children*, it seemed to set tongues free in India in an odd way. Suddenly, younger writers realized that they didn't need to write correct and perfect English in the English tradition, but they could use Indian English and use it for any purpose whatsoever—for writing comic books, satiric books, or even for writing serious books.

F.J.: Even though G. V. Desani's *All about H. Hatterr* had come before.

Desai: Yes, somehow that never had any influence upon Indian writers at all. It just remained a flash in the pan.

F.J.: It's funny to think about Rushdie as having influence, because one thinks of him as at the tail end of the youngest of the Indian writers.

Desai: Oh, no, there are still younger ones, there's a whole crop of younger ones like Amitav Ghosh and Vikram Seth and Allan Seelye. They've all written I'm sure, whether they acknowledge it or not, under the influence of Rushdie, particularly *Midnight's Children*.

F.J.: Narayan gets very angry if you say he's the Jane Austen of India.

Would you get very angry if someone said you were the Virginia Woolf of India and you "mothered" the psychological novel in India?

**Desai:** No, I would be denying something which is fairly obvious. One is the influence of Virginia Woolf upon my own work, and the other is that there weren't very many women writers in India at that time writing psychological novels.

**F.J.:** There seems an obvious difference between you and Narayan, Rao, and the writers of that earlier generation, which is what I would call your multicultural background. You put yourself squarely in that tradition when you refer to Nabokov. Do you see yourself as part of that cross-cultural drift of intellectuals moving around the world and learning different languages by circumstance? In your situation, you learned different languages even before you were moving around the world. Your father was German and your mother was Indian, right?

**Desai:** No, it's the other way around. My father was Indian, my mother German.

**F.J.:** Did you grow up speaking any German?

**Desai:** It was my first language. It was the language my parents spoke to each other, so as children it's what we spoke at home. We spoke Hindi to friends and neighbors because we were living in Delhi. I only learned English when I went to school.

**F.J.:** Your father was in the great tradition of Bengalis educated in a European language.

**Desai:** Yes. He went to Germany as a student, came back with my mother and speaking the German language, and certainly that's a reason why my home had a larger European element than other homes in our neighborhood. For instance, we listened to Western music and we had Western literature on our bookshelves. But it was never emphasized that this was foreign and Western. It was very much a part of my home. I took it completely for granted and never noticed that other homes did not share this with me.

**F.J.:** Did it in any way make you different from the other children in your school or the other people who were growing up around you?

**Desai:** Not really, no. I don't think so.

**F.J.:** Because the educated elite in India were all intellectual and Westernized to some extent?

**Desai:** Well, there are several reasons. One is that apart from the fact that we did have a lot of Western music and literature and spoke a foreign language in my home, at the same time it was a very, very Indian home. We lived just as our Indian neighbors lived. It's true that the friends we had were at the same level of education as my parents. They also moved in a circle where there were other European women, other foreigners who had lived for a long time in India as my mother had, so my life was always made up of Western and Indian elements.

F.J.: How did you end up creating a work like *Baumgartner*? You must have known someone like Baumgartner from the German diaspora community from your family.

Desai: No, no, I didn't. It comes together out of so many different things and from so many different directions. For years, I wanted to write a book about the German part of my background and to put to use the German language which was a part of my childhood. I had no idea how to do it. I didn't want to write a biographical book about my mother, so I had no idea how to go about it. It seems such eccentric material when you consider the Indian background. Of course, my mother was not the only German I knew in India. She had this large circle of friends, German friends, who had also been washed up in India for one reason or another. They were extremely colorful and eccentric people. I always wondered what made them so eccentric, if it was India or if they had been eccentric even in Europe. Certainly they had led the strangest lives and had strange histories. But I couldn't write about them, they were too personal, they were too close to me—they were the aunties and uncles of my childhood. Then, when I was an adult in Bombay I used to see this old man shuffling around and feeding cats in the streets the way I've described. I didn't know him personally, but a friend of mine did know him and once told me that he was not nearly as poor as he looked; he was actually quite rich and owned a race horse. It stuck in my mind as a curious piece of information. This man died a natural death and he had no family in Bombay so this friend of mine had to go and clear up his effects. He brought me a packet of letters in German and asked me to look through them and let him know if they were of any importance, if they should be preserved or what should be done. So I looked at them, and they were just little notes, affectionate little notes, with no information at all, simply how are you—and I'm well—don't worry kind of letters. So, I gave them back and said no, they're not important at all. I began to read quite a lot of Holocaust literature a little later, and one of the things I learned was that in the early years of the concentration camps the inmates were allowed to write letters, and those letters were always stamped with the number they had in the camp. I remembered that these letters had all been stamped with the same number, and I only realized then that they had come from a concentration camp. Because there was no information about them—the man was dead, I couldn't question him—I began to think a great deal about it and felt the need to supply them with a history, so I invented a history for this figure whom I had seen but not known. In doing that I was able to use all my mother's memories of prewar Germany which had been told me as a child. It used to be our bedtime story—she would talk about prewar Germany. So I was able to put that into the book and use the German language again, which gave me a wonderful feeling of liberating a part of my mind, of my self, which I'd had to keep silenced for all of those years.

F.J.: Was your mother Jewish?

Desai: No, she wasn't. She had left Germany in the late 20s, before the horror of Nazism.

F.J.: Was the character you had known Jewish?

Desai: He was an Austrian Jew. What I had a lot of trouble about in that book was trying to find material about the internment camps in India. There was no material at all.

F.J.: Were there internment camps in India?

Desai: Oh yes, there were. And I had known Germans who had spent the war years in those internment camps. You see, it was the British Empire at that time, so the British rounded up everyone with a German passport and put them into internment camps. Later on Jewish societies came to their aid and helped the Jews to get out of them. But the British simply thought of them as Germans and therefore enemy aliens. But there's no written documents of that period at all. So I read a lot about the detention camps in England and in Canada in order to give me a sense of what these camps were like. Also my mother had known people who were in these internment camps, and they had talked to us about it. So I knew something about them. But after I had written that chapter I was able to send it to a few people who did know these detention camps. One of them is a Jewish professor in Israel who had actually been in such a camp.

F.J.: And what did they tell you about those internment camps in India? Were they mistreated?

Desai: They were not mistreated, no. They were by no means concentration camps, they were simply detention camps. But it was boring for one thing. It was so many years taken out of their lives, and the other thing was if there was any mistreatment, it was from the other Germans in the camp.

F.J.: The ironic thing in *Baumgartner* is that—though there are the kids in the street who make fun of him and throw stones at him and so on — you have him killed off by a German hippie traveling through. Why is that?

Desai: It's something which worried me extremely. Although I knew he would die in the end, I had no idea who was going to kill him, and right through the book I was playing with two alternative endings. The other person who could have killed him was that beggar who lives in the street in front of his house, in whose eyes Baumgartner is wealthy. He could easily have robbed him and killed him. I had, in fact, written two alternative endings for that book. One was his murder by this beggar, but that dissatisfied me because that was simply random violence, it was the kind of murder which does take place in big cities. It had no real meaning and Baumgartner was left incomplete or unfulfilled in a certain sense, because all through he has a sense of having escaped death in Germany. His mother was killed but he escaped. The reason for his sadness through the book is this death that he escaped so that it pursues him and stalks him right through the book. I had to have it catch up with him in the end, and it seemed right and justified in the Greek sense if that death would be death by a Nazi, by a German. That gave me a certain satisfaction, that he had met the kind of death which fate had devised for him anyway. He had fooled fate for awhile and escaped for awhile, but in the end it got him.

F.J.: I didn't pick up on the aspect of that German hippie traveling through India with his dirty feet, etc. being a Nazi. I thought of him just as a representative of the Germans.

Desai: He is simply a German. He probably doesn't think of himself as a Nazi, he's too young to have been a Nazi.

F.J.: As you say at some point in the book, he has no memories.

Desai: No. His mind is quite destroyed by drugs anyway, he's only after drugs. But in some sense one shares one's nation's history. The Germans now, even the younger generation, are aware that they haven't escaped the consequences. They haven't managed to sever themselves completely, but they are still burdened with guilt. Partly this is what others do to them. They would love to escape from that guilt, but no one allows them to, and this young man shares that sense of complicity.

F.J.: How does his killing Baumgartner fulfill him then? Baumgartner had to be killed by someone who was German?

Desai: Yes.

F.J.: So it fulfills Baumgartner or fulfills his past—

Desai: He's at last met the death that he should have met earlier and didn't. He is that way because he bears guilt from having avoided the death his mother had.

F.J.: I see—I see it now.

Desai: And I know that the Jews who did escape from the concentration camps or who survived them have never been able to get rid of the sense of guilt for the death of all those who didn't survive. They all suffered for years from feeling that they should have died instead of or along with the others.

F.J.: One of the themes in your work is clearly the character from a marginal community. What Baumgartner experiences is the same kind of intolerance towards minorities and other communities that you said is developing in India.

Desai: I think every writer does tend to use a handful of characters and a handful of themes over and over again. In a way, it is one's obsessions that one walks over and over, and rarely feels one is finished with the subject. There's always something left over from the last book which you reuse because you feel you haven't really developed it fully, that's there's still something left unsaid, and so you write the next book.

F.J.: Do you see your work then as moving towards a more international dimension? Is *Baumgartner* representative of your work moving into being about people who are made up by these many cross-cultural trends?

Desai: Yes, I do.

F.J.: Why would you say that?

Desai: It's coincided with my own leaving India for large portions of the year and living much more abroad now. In a way, that intervenes with my Indian life. It's like a screen that has come between me and India. I can't simply ignore this experience abroad—it's too overwhelming, it demands to be dealt with, somehow grappled with.

**F.J.:** What was the first time in your life that you left India? How old were you?

**Desai:** Oh, I didn't leave India until I was an adult and then only on short visits. It's only when I started publishing my books in England that I started visiting England regularly, but always for very short visits. Yet I had no sense of being a writer or belonging to a community of writers until I went to England, which was the first time people looked upon me as a writer.

**F.J.:** When was that?

**Desai:** I think I went there first when *Fire On the Mountain*—no actually I'd gone earlier when *Voices in the City* was published in 1965, and then I went regularly whenever my books appeared. I was received there as a writer. I gradually, in England, built up a sense of myself as a writer, which I hadn't had in India. The first time I spent any length of time away was the year I spent in Cambridge as a fellow at the University. I wrote *Baumgartner* there.

**F.J.:** And then when you went back to India, you saw India with different eyes?

**Desai:** After I spent my year in Cambridge, I then came to America and started teaching here and now I go back to India every year—

**F.J.:** Is this your home then?

**Desai:** No, it isn't my home. In fact, from this year onward I've cut down my time abroad. Instead of teaching full time I'm going to be only teaching a semester a year, which cuts down from a year to simply four months—in order to spend more time in India.

**F.J.:** Because your material continues to be in India?

**Desai:** Yes, for that reason and for personal reasons. Of course, a part of my life is still in India, a part of my family is there.

**F.J.:** Looking at India from having been in England must have been very different from looking at India from having been in America, because England still has a large Indian community.

**Desai:** England's much more in touch with the outside world. Perhaps it's something to do with the past, the empire and so on. But when I'm in England, I feel very closely in touch with India there. When I come to America I feel very far removed from it all—very, very distant. I don't enjoy that feeling of distance.

**F.J.:** Could you say why?

**Desai:** I feel extremely isolated, I feel removed to a society with which I have no natural link whatsoever.

**F.J.:** Why would you say that is? How would you explore that sense of aloneness or difference?

**Desai:** Well, it's something I'm trying to explore in another book which I am writing, but which is not about Indians in America at all. It's about the sense of isolation an individual has within a society. But I've begun to wonder how writers like Nabokov and Derek Walcott and Joseph Brodsky have been able to take on a whole new continent and make it their own. I'm finding it very, very difficult to do that.

# Zulfikar Ghose

This interview took place at Zulfikar Ghose's home in Austin, Texas. Ghose lives in the beginnings of the Hill Country, just west of Austin, in a verdant landscape that seems more than miles away from the urban bustle of Austin and the University of Texas campus. We talked for a couple of hours in the late afternoon and early evening, sitting outside, first with a pot of tea and then with a bottle of wine. Listening to the tape afterwards, one can hear birds, insects, and an occasional airplane flying overhead, creating a suitably pastoral yet modern backdrop to the conversation.

The real beginning of Zulfikar Ghose's literary career was perhaps the inclusion of three of his poems in a special number of the *Times Literary Supplement* in 1962. Before 1962, Ghose had published perhaps a dozen or two poems in various journals and a regular column on cricket written as a sports journalist for *The Observer*. In the three decades since this landmark issue of *TLS* noting "Commonwealth literature," Ghose has ranked with and outranked several of the best English language writers in England and America. In the 1960s, he was an important figure in the literary life of London, working with the experimental writer B. S. Johnson on a collection of short stories, *Statement against Corpses* (1964), publishing several volumes of poetry and an autobiography, *Confessions of a Native-Alien* (1965), and beginning his career as a novelist with two novels set on the Indian Subcontinent, *The Contradictions* (1966) and *The Murder of Aziz Khan* (1967). Since his move in 1969 to the United States, Ghose has increasingly devoted himself to full-length works of fiction, with only an occasional poem, short story or essay interrupting the flow of highly original, unusual and fascinating novels. For this remarkable output consisting of a major trilogy, *The Incredible Brazilian*, and seven other novels, Ghose has received little critical attention. Yet his work is known on three continents and has been translated into Norwegian, Dutch, German, Italian, and French.

A writer who has been read widely may not have been studied widely. One reason for this may be that Ghose is a figure who evades most of our accepted ways of talking about and grouping contemporary literature. Though he was born in 1935 in what is now Pakistan (but was then British India) and brought up in Bombay, his work has steadily moved away from typical concerns and themes of contemporary South Asian writing in English or of Commonwealth writing in general. Educated in England at Keele University and for the last twenty years living in Austin and teaching at the

University of Texas, Ghose has nevertheless displayed little or no interest in the dilemmas of immigration and transplantation that have so occupied other South Asian writers who have moved to Britain and the United States. Most of his recent fiction is set in South America, but his use of that locale is sufficiently his own to distinguish himself from the South American writers of the present generation. What separates Ghose most sharply from most of the other writers of the British Commonwealth is his responsiveness to experimental modes of fiction; but his work with its broad range of cultural references and strong narrative interest is not really typical of modern experimental or "metafictional" writing either. Ghose's work is *sui generis*, in short, and he is a unique figure in contemporary literature.

**Reed Dasenbrock:** In your *Hamlet, Prufrock and Language*, you have written that the ultimate business of literature is to test relationships between language and reality. But when we were talking last week, you said that everything in your work is purely imagination with no relationship to reality. I'm wondering then how this testing takes place?

**Zulfikar Ghose:** Without wanting to evoke an image of literature as some sort of diagnostic machine which tests reality and examines its broken parts, what I can say is that there is no reality without a perception to conceive it, that literature is one mode of perception—together with other modes, such as painting or theoretical physics—and that the best literature has a revelatory quality about it, creating the impression, briefly and sometimes only as a passing illumination, that we have experienced something true. Each mode of perception is a language with its signs and symbols and built-in idiosyncrasies. Incidentally, these have evolved to such a complex degree that there are obscure languages within each language, so that the most crucial areas of knowledge must remain inaccessible to people who are not themselves devoted practitioners. However, this is another matter. The statement you quote from my *Hamlet, Prufrock and Language* was made in the context of my theory about *Hamlet*, that from the very first scene where the word "speak" is uttered frequently to Hamlet's last word, "silence," the central idea of the play concerns language and reality. I draw comparisons with the work of some modern writers, like Beckett, to show that Hamlet's compulsion is the compulsion of literature—the driving urge to speak, that is to discover a language that always seems to promise a relief from the anguish of not knowing and the writer's failure to arrive at that language: one ends always with the overwhelming despair of *silence*. I do not know a single writer, I mean among the great ones, who has not lamented his failure to create a work of real worth. Chekhov and Conrad, for example, berate themselves in their letters for not having done justice to their minds, and this after they've produced their masterpieces! What this suggests to me is that a writer has an expectation that a language will come to him of such unutterable perfection that the magical combination of the words will contain wisdom, beauty and truth. But it never does. Beckett realized this early, creating his *Texts for Nothing* where language becomes *stultior stultissimo*. What I said about my own work the other day, that everything in it is purely the work of the imagination without a relationship to reality, that is not, or cannot be, literally true, of course. One inevitably draws upon experience, including perhaps most importantly for a writer the experience of literature, one creates a world of real matter. It's just this: I'm more interested in creating a language that appeals to me than in depicting a particular reality.

The great writers have always been the creators of language. When we think of Shakespeare or Pope or Dickens or Joyce, we think of their language. In each case, we hear a particular voice.

R.D.: So a great writer creates a new language which is a new way of seeing in the way that a scientist or a discoverer does.

Ghose: Yes. It's a form of perception. The subject matter of literature is very limited. It's birth, copulation and death, as Eliot wrote. Add to that a few incidental details—a bit of violence here and a bit of sex there. It is only the capacity of the mind to create a language which has its own interest, which releases thought in excess of the reality referred to, that gives a work its quality. The subject matter of a Shakespeare is the same as the subject matter of any popular writer. The language of one makes him lastingly interesting, the language of the other makes him trivial and ephemeral. We are always looking at language.

Feroza Jussawalla: What then becomes of the relationship between language and reality?

Ghose: I do not think we could have any reality without a language, surely. And I think also that language is prior to thought and that language is sometimes prior to perception—as linguists have shown, sometimes we do not see the things for which we do not have the words. The quality of a perception, therefore, depends very largely on the quality of the language if that is indeed the envisioning medium. This is why I maintain that the struggle of a writer is not with the subject matter—with finding something to talk about—it is always with the creation of a style, the working out of those sentences which have a peculiar ring and shape to them where the thought, as Flaubert would ideally have it, cannot be separated from the style. It is given to very few writers to arrive at a distinctive style—partly because most of them are too eager for success, they're interested, as Flannery O'Connor said, in seeing their name in print and not in art, and what's more, they have the presumption that they have something important to say that will significantly change the world. This is nothing but vanity, of course, the proportion of which increases the less a person has read. However, I didn't mean to embark on a tirade against popular writers—for all I know, it might well be envy on my part! I was talking about a distinctive style. Ponge has a fine image for it when, writing on Braque, he says that "the world has begun to enter his furrow." *Furrow.* That's good. In the same essay, Ponge also says that an artist is someone "who in *no way* explains the world," that a painting "does not *represent* anything." And so one scratches away at the words, hoping that the faint outline of the furrow will one day emerge. Language and reality appear in my mind as two figures in a courtly dance, reaching towards each other, coming into a momentary formal contact, then inevitably parting and receding from each other until the music gradually fades into silence.

**R.D.:** So your quest for a language is really a quest for an individual style whereas many, perhaps more content-oriented writers are trying to be more of a voice of a community. And you would very strongly separate yourself from that.

**Ghose:** Yes, I would agree with that—though I must add that I have no separatist program, it is simply that I find uninteresting to do what content-oriented writers do. Also, I would find it pretentious if I myself said that I was on a quest for an individual style; it sounds too grand, and I'd find the necessary armor too uncomfortable. I read, and then I write: that is all. Some disposition in my mind, or some quirk perhaps, prefers Henry James to Thomas Hardy, James Joyce to E. M. Forster, Faulkner to Hemingway,

Thomas Berger to Saul Bellow . . . . Perhaps it's the same disposition that makes me prefer mangoes to pears.

**F.J.:** I think this is probably what distinguishes your work from other world literature written in English because you have attempted very consciously to transcend those very roots that tie some writers down.

**Ghose:** I think the writers you have in mind are the chroniclers of their time and place. To them, their subject matter is of paramount importance.

**F.J.:** And attempting to convey that subject matter through the language of the recognizable world.

**Ghose:** New versions of the nineteenth-century novel, yes. They are so concerned with recreating the sociological and political content of their world that they pay no attention to style, to the extent even of having grammatical errors, to say nothing of a language defiled by clichés. I could show you such errors and reams of such pollution among some highly acclaimed novels that have been the recipients of a Pulitzer or a Booker. I could even show you some stylistic horrors in Forster and Hemingway. But this is a large, passionate subject, and I'd better control myself! You said that I write about another culture, meaning, I take it, not about the one in which I was born. The fact is that, apart from my second novel, *The Murder of Aziz Khan* (which was deliberately written to prove that I could do it, too, and therefore need not do it again), and my earlier poems that had as their subject my original attachment to India, I do not write about a particular culture at all. I cannot say what I do write *about*, if anything. All I do is to record some images that present themselves and then attempt to discover the imagery that must follow to complete a formal structure that is pleasing to my imagination. From my childhood, I've been forced into exile, a condition become so permanent that I can never have a homecoming; I've no nationalistic attachments to any country, and indeed have very little to do with the world at all. One of my favorite images in literary biography is of Raymond Roussel arriving at some exotic port like Hong Kong during a voyage around the world in an ocean liner, taking one look from the porthole of his stateroom and returning to his desk, quite content that he had seen all there was to see of the mysterious east. What a wonderful madman he was! An ideal writer, really, one who created an extraordinary language exclusively out of his imagination. The majority of my waking hours are spent reading and writing. It's the best way I know to amuse myself. This house is some distance from the city and as you can see the garden we're sitting in is sur-rounded by a forest. Sometimes it's hard to imagine that sitting at my desk and glancing out the window at a forest I'm really in Texas. It could be a view from the porthole of a stateroom. And so I follow the images that get written, finding some distraction in the creation of sentences. Gradually, the accumulating sentences reveal the secret obsession emerging from the imagination, the larger meaning taking shape that I recognize as belonging to myself, my inner world, though the story that might have begun to estab-lish itself might be about some eccentric Brazilian of the eighteenth century.

F.J.: How do you want the reader to get at these larger meanings?

Ghose: I have no interest in the reader. I never think of the reader. I don't know who the reader is. In one's earlier work there might be some images or expressions put there to please or make an impression on a particular writer friend, but in one's later work the impulse comes from within the art where one writes in the company of the dead writers who become one's most intimate associates. Sometimes I receive a letter from a reader who has liked a book; that is always gratifying, of course, but not as gratifying as the reflection that a sentence I have written would have pleased Flaubert or Proust. It will perhaps be meaningless to most people to say that without the company of the dead writers a living writer can have no life at all. My most constant companions in recent years have been Tolstoy, Balzac, Dick-ens, Chekhov, Flaubert and Proust. Sometimes during a pause in the writ-ing I'll have a quiet little chat with one of them. Proust has perhaps been the most dominant figure ever since I first began to read him—I think it was when I was beginning to write A Different World, the third volume of the Brazilian trilogy. If you look closely at my sentences—even in Hamlet, Prufrock and Language, where there is a long sentence on the opening page about a dessert—you'll find in them a sensuous quality that is essentially Proustian. And some recent poems, like "A Dragonfly in the Sun," are one long Proustian sentence. Proust can be dangerously seductive, of course, and so I have the good doctor Chekhov in constant attendance and hearing him laugh when a sentence gets too complicated, cut it down to prevent him from leaving in disgust.

R.D.: So your ideal reader suffering from an ideal insomnia, to use Joyce's phrase, is more the great writers of the past.

Ghose: Yes, the great writers without whom one's mind, one's very perception of the world, would be very different. Incidentally, our perception of reality is very much conditioned by what we know of art and literature; we are all like Swann who found Odette beautiful only after he recognized in her a face in a painting by Botticelli. As for the present, there are many very fine writers in the world but—

**R.D.:** But you don't write to them.

**Ghose:** I cannot say that because I do not know what might not be going on in my unconscious mind. Of course, one likes to think one has acquired a degree of control, but no one can be certain that his exercise of that control is not being undermined by some subversive preoccupation of the unconscious, or by some contradictory hidden impulse which might be the vital factor shaping one's style.

**F.J.:** What's very interesting to me is to hear you name off the writers who have been interesting to you, even, could we say, influences?

**Ghose:** Yes, I would not deny that.

**F.J.:** The element of influence is all Western, from the large tradition of your Western education.

**Ghose:** If you include the South Americans as Western as well, yes.

**F.J.:** Yes. OK. What do you see as the place of someone like yourself, a multicultural writer?

**Ghose:** I'm not multicultural, I'm British. I'm really more Anglo-Saxon than the Anglo-Saxons. I cannot speak my native Punjabi or Urdu or Hindustani because I have been uprooted from India for three-quarters of my life now.

**F.J.:** So English is the language that you are comfortable in?

**Ghose:** English is the only language that I have.

**R.D.:** Yes, but if contemporary content-oriented American writing is insular, contemporary English writing seems far more insular. Do you really place yourself in the world of contemporary British or English writers?

**Ghose:** It's not for me to place myself anywhere, really. When I say I'm British, I don't mean to align myself with Kingsley Amis or Philip Larkin— no more than, were I to say I'm American, would I align myself with Updike or Mailer. All I mean is that my education has been British and that it was such a powerful conditioning force that I cannot see myself apart from it. In spite of this Britishness, of having been shaped by minds such as John Stuart Mill's, of course one cannot escape one's background and therefore I cannot deny that the culture behind me is multifaceted. I might have forgotten the Indian languages but certain elements of those languages must be there within me.

F.J.: And the images of your childhood must pervade.

Ghose: Yes, they are there. And in fact I'm writing a novel right now in which I intend to go back to those images. You know, as you yourselves know better than I do, some of the best new writing in English has come from the Commonwealth. Much of it goes unread in America and Britain. And much of European and South American literature goes unread, too. The odd writer, like Naipaul or Calvino or Márquez, gets taken up and read widely, but who reads Wilson Harris or Juan Goytisolo or Maria Luisa Bombal? Well, I do read some of them, and I suppose they must do something to the way in which my words get put together.

R.D.: It strikes me that almost everyone you mention there is from the nineteenth or early twentieth century, but one of the ways in which your work really delights me is that it brings back what—this is probably a stupid pigeonhole—I would call more of an eighteenth-century or perhaps picaresque love of just pure plot or pure narrative that is conspicuously missing in much contemporary writing.

Ghose: To tell you the truth, I keep myself so sublimely ignorant that I wrote *The Incredible Brazilian* without knowing what *picaresque* meant—I had to look it up when all the reviews of that novel so described it. Later, when I looked up Claudio Guillen's description of the picaresque form, I was astonished that my novel had included in its structure each of the elements described by Guillen. I suppose my mind had simply acquired a knowledge of the form while reading early novels—though at that time I had not yet read *Don Quixote*.

F.J.: For instance, again getting back to *The Incredible Brazilian*, you could transpose that whole thing to a large Hyderabadi or a large Bombay family with pretty much the same change of names because you know Gregorio's father's bride is coming in the same kind of procession as might be in a Muslim bridal procession.

Ghose: That is true and what you've hit upon there is what somebody else has suggested, which is that Brazil in my novels is simply a substitute for India. There might be something in that perception, but I don't really know. I have not consciously said to myself, "I'm not going to write about India but if I have a desire to do so I'll disguise it as Brazil."

**F.J.:** Would your schooling in a school like Don Bosco [in Bombay] have influenced some of your thinking, in terms of Portugal and Brazil?

**Ghose:** I don't really know. It was an Italian-run school; it wasn't Portuguese. The priests were Italians, though some of them were Indian Christians and so they would have been of Portuguese descent. And also half the students were Christians, Christian boarders, with Portuguese names. So maybe there was something in the atmosphere there that breathed of Portugal at several removes that I picked up. I don't know.

**R.D.:** There's been some talk of calling Commonwealth literature the literature of the British Empire, and it strikes me that one might connect Bombay with Brazil and call your work to a certain extent literature of the Portuguese Empire, much more than of the British, in the sense that there is that connection between Bombay and Brazil.

**Ghose:** I always feel very much at home in Latin America, especially in Brazil. There are certain streets in Rio with shops and restaurants which appear almost identical to what used to be in Bombay in the 1940s. And the way in which people gesture when they talk. And something in the Portuguese language. The rhythms are very close to what I used to hear as a child in Bombay. So maybe something of that comes across. Or perhaps I'm imbued with a natural sympathy for that particular world. But, again, we're sitting here rationalizing. I don't really know.

**F.J.:** We've been talking about Latin America and its influence on your work. Do you see yourself as a magical realist writer? Has García Márquez been a major influence on your work?

**Ghose:** Magical realism is a label that's got adopted, that's all, and like all labels it conveys only a very partial truth. Everybody's great example of magical realistic fiction has to be *One Hundred Years of Solitude*. But if you look at it closely, you'll find that all that Márquez does is to have something extraordinary happen from time to time. In the opening chapter, there is the man who brings magnets with him, goes rushing down the street with his magnets, and the pots and the pans come rushing out of the houses. Some pages later there is the episode of the butterflies. And some pages later still, another "magical" episode. It's all very delightful and carries you across the rather wide gulfs of straightforward narrative without your noticing how ordinary that narrative is, until you read the book a second time when you realize it's really a very boring book. I must add that I'm talking of the book in English translation. The bulk of its narrative contains some very dull writing. It's redeemed only by the magical episodes. I think the Márquez of *Chronicle of a Death Foretold* and of some of the short stories is a glorious writer; but *One Hundred Years* is overrated and a lesser known novel of his, *In Evil Hour*, is downright bad. But he caught our imagination with *One Hundred Years*, he changed us with it, and though we now see its limitations it remains an important book in that it gave us a new direction. Actually, the best examples of magical realism are in Shakespeare, in the plays grouped as The Romances. Last year I was invited to contribute a piece to a special number of *Latin American Literary Review* on Márquez, and I wrote a story called "Lila of the Butterflies and her Chronicler," a magical realistic pastiche. I end that story with a quotation from *The Winter's Tale*, a little hint that magical realism was there long before Márquez.

F.J.: What would you say are such images in your work?

Ghose: If there are any, they aren't a matter of conscious influence. When I wrote *The Incredible Brazilian*, I had not read Márquez or indeed any other Latin American novelist.

R.D.: Had you been to Brazil?

Ghose: I'd been to Brazil on a visit of three months. The imagery of *The Incredible Brazilian* came not because I'd been to Brazil but because, on returning to England, I happened quite by accident to discover a book about Brazil. It was *Masters and Slaves* by Gilberto Freyre, the distinguished Brazilian anthropologist—though I didn't know who he was when I picked up his book. It simply looked like an interesting book. It's a wonderful book, and if you read it you'll see the sources of my plantation imagery. *The Incredible Brazilian* was suggested primarily by Freyre's book and also by a desire to amuse my friend Thomas Berger who had recently published *Little Big Man*, the structure of which very largely influenced my novel. I was miles away from magical realism. And even in my recent novels—*A New History of Torments*, *Don Bueno*, and *Figures of Enchantment*—all written after reading Márquez and all set in Latin America, what might be taken for magical realism is actually drawn from Shakespeare.

R.D.: So is magical realism another one of those pigeonholes that doesn't really say very much?

**Ghose:** It does not. You know, one can take a label and somehow twist all of literature to fit into it. I should think that if you took a very realistic, naturalistic work like *McTeague* by Frank Norris, you could find magical realistic elements in it.

**R.D.:** I think that's true. I've always been very uncomfortable with the term "magical realism" because it doesn't seem to me to indicate anything very precise. Your saying that you hadn't read García Márquez when you wrote *The Incredible Brazilian* seems to me just right. I would say you'd read a great deal of picaresque narrative more than—

**Ghose:** The only picaresque work I'd really read then was *Little Big Man*. I hadn't read Fielding or Cervantes then.

**R.D.:** So what is it, then, that has transferred or seeped into or been borrowed?

**Ghose:** For myself, I think it's nothing more than simply a desire to write a story which strains the imagination of the reader and to fill it with a kind of matter that is visually exciting, a vivid imagery that captures the living presence of things.

**R.D.:** I guess what I would like to at least ask or suggest, perhaps, is that it may be your subcontinental or South Asian background that enables you to make use of the Latin American material and setting in some ways. If you think of contemporary English or American literature, I think many of those people are reading García Márquez or whoever, but I don't see them really doing anything with that. Whereas you or other multicultural writers, perhaps alone among British writers, if you want to call yourself British, are really making use of that world.

**Ghose:** That sounds perfectly true, though it could be that other British and American writers who have read Márquez are not interested in taking anything from him. But we're uttering a huge generalization here, taking an omniscient stance when the truth is that we simply cannot know all the literature of our own time. Consider, for example, the situation in Britain in this century. After Joyce and Virginia Woolf, fiction of any quality seemed to die out. Such puny men as D. H. Lawrence and E. M. Forster acquired the status of giants. After the Second World War, the scene seemed particularly dead. The worst examples of parochial fiction were held up for the admiration of a credulous public as examples of British literary genius. That, however, was the surface, the public phenomenon as witnessed weekly in the *TLS* and the other papers. But Beckett's first novel had been published in 1938—much of the stock apparently remained in the publisher's warehouse where it went up in flames following an air-raid during the War. The fifties seemed on the surface the worst decade, a time that saw the very worst fiction hugely acclaimed; well, it was in the fifties that Beckett's trilogy was published, one of the masterpieces of our times was brought to life, but very few of us living then in London even heard of it. In that which remains hidden from us is sometimes the catalyst for an important change that takes place in the future. And incidentally, the situation in Britain is much more vivid now, much more lively and exciting. Alasdair Gray's *1982 Janine* has a terrific imagination behind it and Angela Carter's *Nights at the Circus* contains some wonderfully energetic prose. There's a breadth of imaginative range in them that draws upon wide sources, perhaps including Márquez.

**F.J.:** We've been talking about what one might call the trajectory of your work, which is from the South Asia in which you were born to the Latin America of your recent work. Some writers would say that this cannot be done, that you cannot experience a reality except that you experience it out of your own language and that the language you grow up with shapes the reality as you perceive it.

**Ghose:** Is that any different from saying that I am what I am because I am I and I have been influenced by the environment in which I was born? This seems to me a fairly circular, tautological and empty statement.

**R.D.:** Not just that you are you but you also share some of that "you-ness" with the other people coming from the same context.

**Ghose:** Surely the sharing of the "you-ness" is not confined to the people with whom one spoke one's native tongue? If I met my cousins with whom I grew up speaking Punjabi in Sialkot during my first seven years, some Punjabi phrase uttered by one would be bound to evoke an association exclusive to that group; if I met my school friends from Bombay with whom I grew up during the following ten years and shared with them the first broken attempts to speak English, which became the language of our daily intercourse, then surely there would be a similar evocation of exclusive associations; if I met my fellow undergraduates from Keele, if I met the writers who were my companions in London, surely, it is self-evident and not at all remarkable that with each group one has shared a language that has been charged with meanings which possess exclusive subtleties. A line from an

Urdu poem may make me respond in a deeper way because I grew up in an Urdu context, but I would assert that a line from an English poem would affect me as deeply, perhaps much more deeply because with English poetry I also know the intellectual background which I do not with Urdu. Proust is perhaps more to the point when he says, "reality takes shape in the memory alone." And memory is constituted not only of the accumulation of the images of experience but also of the accumulation of nuances, tones and private meanings of words that give one a sense of one's self. One's "you-ness," if you like. What a horrible word, *you-ness*. Reminds me of Eunice Grayson and a Pakistani cricketer named Younis—much more interesting subjects!

R.D.: So out of all that totality of experiences, the early, first ones aren't to be privileged over later experiences, as yours in London which come after the early ones in Sialkot.

Ghose: You're pushing me into a corner where you expect me to enunciate a law applicable to all mankind. I cannot possibly do that. I'm not an intellectual at all. All I do is read a great deal, absorb it, and then try to shape with words the fancy prompted by my mind. It's only in the classroom when I have to teach that I pretend to have clever ideas. Otherwise, I refuse to have ideas. I despise ideas. Ideas have never helped mankind. Only *things* help. Things like penicillin and flushing toilets.

F.J.: Yet let me get back to this question of language. You don't believe, then, as some Commonwealth writers are beginning to voice, most clearly Ngũgĩ, that one has to turn back to one's *own* language, to develop literarily. You don't think that's necessary?

Ghose: I would say that if a way works, a way of writing works for Rao or Achebe or whoever, fine, good luck to him. That may not be my way. I can only do it in the way I know how. But I would not go on to formulate a generalization based upon one way or the other since neither can be exclusive.

R.D.: One of the laws that I think perhaps a writer like you has suffered from is the law that everything should fit in a nice, neat national category. I don't think you personally have suffered from it but perhaps the degree of awareness of your work has suffered from it. To find your books in a library, for example, one has to look in three or four different places. Some of your books are found in British Literature, others in American and still others in

South Asian Literature. Do you think there's a way around that kind of pigeonholing?

**Ghose**: You're quite right in saying that I suffer from such pigeonholing. And yes, I suffer *personally*: my books don't sell, and I receive very little serious critical attention. It is very rare for a reviewer to remark upon the quality of my prose or to reveal a comprehension of the imaginative structure of my work.

**R.D.**: Most of the best writers in the world seem to me to be in your situation. One thinks of a Beckett who doesn't fit or a Nabokov who doesn't fit. The list could go on and on. We all would have different names here.

**Ghose**: Yes, Nabokov and Conrad would be my great companions in this. I aspire to their position in the world of letters where you are accepted for what you have done and not because you have conformed and put yourself into a pigeonhole.

**R.D.**: I'm wondering if there's a way we can reconceive of writers in order to avoid this kind of negative pigeonholing.

**Ghose**: You cannot because any such "reconceiving" would have to begin with the teachers and professors of literature and the majority of them will not even know what we're talking about. They have no conception of the art of fiction since their focus is primarily on the subject matter. They spend their time on such irrelevancies as studying the sources of an author's material—as if, for example, one's appreciation of *Lord Jim* is going to be profoundly enhanced by knowing that a pilgrim ship sank in the Arabian Sea in 1880 involving unprofessional conduct from its British captain. And you might have noticed that the academic fool who does this kind of "research" is invariably more honored than the poor author ever was. Another teacher will take the biographical approach; another the sociological; another the Marxist or the Structuralist. I see graduate students every week in the building where I work. They look like a haunted lot with Bercovitch and Culler and Derrida and Fish buzzing about their tormented brains. Is there anyone left who loves literature more than some imbecile theory that can be woven around it? Hasn't anyone noticed that just about *all* the critical theorizing of the past has proved to be worthless? All the teachers and professors of literature ever do is to pass the time with talk of varying degrees of apparent sophistication, but talk that to a succeeding generation is quite empty. I'm reminded of something Conrad said in a letter. Let me go find it. Here it is:

"The question of *art* is so endless, so involved and so obscure that one is tempted to turn one's face resolutely away from it." He, of course, did not turn his face away from it; the artist's obligation to his imagination won't let him turn his face away; but your professors begin with their faces turned away—and when you wrench at their jaws and twist their necks so that they can be forced to look at the question of art, all they do is to stare dumbly. There won't ever be a "reconceiving," I fear, because there never was any "conceiving" in the first place. The situation gets worse because the numbers increase. Each year thousands more of "trained" teachers and new PhD's are on the march, armed with the latest *-ism*, setting out to create a new pigeonhole, their own little exclusive area on which to build their ephemeral reputation.

F.J.: This is getting back to what's refreshing about your work for me, which is, again, that you're the embodiment of what's getting to be an increasingly multicultural world. What would you say the role of the writer is in this situation, where we are products of culture contact, language contact?

Ghose: I don't know what the role of the writer is except to sit down and write. I'm made very uncomfortable by *talk*. But let me simply say that in spite of appearances, ours is not a new or a unique situation. I've had no more culture contact, as you call it, or language contact than did Chaucer who travelled to Europe and took back Italian forms and created a new English poetry. Shakespeare, Dryden, Byron, Browning—who is there of any significance who did not raid other cultures to enrich his own, who did not take what knowledge that was currently available from wherever he could find it and add it as one more facet to the millions that already constituted his imagination? Tolstoy, sitting in his estate in Yasnaya Polyana, read magazines and books from other European countries. Graciliano Ramos, stuck in the barren northeastern region of Brazil, scanned the newspaper ads from Rio and discovering a bookshop that did mail-orders was able, in the remote and inhospitable and at that time largely barbaric interior, to discover the works of Dostoevsky for himself. The greatest master of South American fiction, Machado de Assis, who came from a poor and an underprivileged background, discovered Laurence Sterne. And finally, I need say nothing about what shaped T. S. Eliot, what shaped Ezra Pound. Therefore, this talk about the importance of the multicultural background that supposedly makes some Commonwealth writers so remarkable is utterly inconsequential. The only thing of consequence is the quality of the mind of the writer. You can be Robert Bridges, and not the best education of England and not the high esteem of your contemporaries and not the Poet Laureateship is going to make you a good poet; and you can be Pablo Neruda suffering from the lonely exile of a minor diplomatic post in Ceylon and out of the dejection of that vast loneliness create a great poetry. Henry James called this "the very obvious truth" when he said that "the deepest quality of a work of art will always be the quality of the mind of the producer." He also said, "the province of art is all life, all feeling, all observation, all vision." What else can there be to say after that? Only that I need to go and fetch a new bottle of wine. A *very obvious truth*—and written a hundred years ago!

# Bapsi Sidhwa

One of the concepts behind this book is that our habitual division of literature in English according to nationality obscures important differences within the literature of a given nation and obscures important similarities across the panorama of world writing in English. One important factor creating resemblances across national categories is emigration: Buchi Emecheta, of Nigerian origin but long resident in Britain, obviously shares many things including the Igbo language with Chinua Achebe, but her residence in Britain establishes a commonality with other black British writers such as Roy Heath that our categories, African, West Indian and South Asian writers in English, help obscure. But a writer's relation to his or her country of origin can vary greatly as well. Writers from distinct minority communities within a country are likely to have a different relation to it than writers from the majority community or culture, and this is as true of countries like India and Pakistan as it is of the United States and New Zealand.

The Zoroastrian community is a perfect example of this. The Zoroastrians or Parsis are a small community of less than one million comprised of followers of the ancient religion of Iran, Zoroastrianism, most of whom left Iran for South Asia after the Muslim conquest of Iran in the seventh century. Long concentrated in Bombay and other areas on the northwest coast of the Indian Subcontinent, today they are spread all over the world. There are a remarkable number of good Zoroastrian writers, from India, Pakistan, and South Africa, some now resident in Britain, Canada, and the United States as well. They encompass a double migration—they are "diaspora" writers in South Asia and in America.

Bapsi Sidhwa is the best known of these Zoroastrian writers. Born in 1939, Sidhwa is from Pakistan and writes both in the United States and Pakistan. And Sidhwa's insistence on seeing herself as a Pakistani writer, though writing with an awareness of a Western audience, is one sign that our monolithic national categories no longer work. For one's immediate assumption would be that a Pakistani writer would be Muslim, but that would be to ignore her distinctive Pakistani yet Parsi and distinctly individual voice. Feroza Jussawalla was able to interview Bapsi Sidhwa twice, once in Houston when Sidhwa was teaching at the University of Houston and a second time in New York when she was teaching at Columbia. In between the two conversations, her third novel, *Ice-Candy-Man*, was published in Britain, receiving considerable attention. It has just been published by Milkweed Editions in the United States as *Cracking India* to very good reviews in *The New York Times Book Review* and elsewhere.

**Feroza Jussawalla:** I want to start, Bapsi, with your most recent book, *Ice-Candy-Man*, which has been published in the United States as *Cracking India*.

**Bapsi Sidhwa:** *Ice-Candy-Man* is a story about Partition, and I'm writing in the first person, from a child's point of view. This has certain limitations, but, of course, it has a lot of advantages too. Among the limitations was how to place the child in another part of the world. The child is based in Lahore, and because of that, she can only witness what happened in Lahore, which was the looting of the Hindu and Sikh community and the killing largely of the Hindus and Sikhs by the Muslims. Now, to give a fair picture of it, I had to also show the atrocities committed in East Punjab, which is now in India, against the Muslims. The Muslims were peasants there—a majority—and suddenly it was divided and the Sikhs and Hindus drove them out. You don't drive peasants out easily except by being rather brutal, and the aggressors were very brutal in doing that. I wanted to depict this, and I didn't know how to until, very luckily, I met this person in Houston. The long and short of it is that he was wearing a wig because as a child his village had been attacked and he was scalped. He'd been through everything I wanted to describe of what happened to a Muslim village family. I wove his story into *Ice-Candy-Man*, and through him, through his voice, I could present the facts of what happened to the Muslim community, the atrocities against them.

The Hindu-Muslim tension was like the splitting up of a family and of course the tearing apart of one country. The title *Cracking India* comes from a part in the book where I say, "There is much disturbing talk. India is going to be broken. Can one break a country? And what happens if they break it where our house is? Or crack it further up on Warren Road?" And the ayah reinforces this by saying, "They'll have to crack India with a long, long canal."

**F.J.:** Was *Ice-Candy-Man* already in the making when you came up on him and his story?

**Sidhwa:** Yes, it was almost one-quarter through when I came up upon him, but then I embedded him, or rather him as a child, from the very beginning, into the story.

**F.J.**: Did you have a clear idea what you wanted to do in *Ice-Candy-Man* when you started?

**Sidhwa**: I don't have a very clear idea when I start any of my books. But I do seem to know where I'm headed. In the case of *Ice-Candy-Man*, a dramatic incident I witnessed has been incorporated into the story as a climactic scene—the kidnapping of Ayah. When I was a child living in Lahore at the time of Partition, my maiden name was Bhandara, which sounded like a Hindu name. After most of the riots were over, a gang of looters came in carts into our house thinking it's an abandoned house. They were quite shocked to see us and my mother and everybody there. At that time our Muslim cook came out and said, "What do you damn people think you're doing? This is a Parsi household," and they said "we thought it was a Hindu household," and they went away. I decided to write a story about Partition because this scene was vivid in my mind. Another scene that haunted me was one when as a child I was walking with my gardener to my tutor. The gardener just pushed a gunny sack lying on the road and a body spilled out of it. The man was young, good looking, well-built. There was no blood, just a wound as though his waist-line had been trimmed. These scenes and the fires all over Lahore were part of my memory. The fires were like blood coloring the sky. It was a fearful sight. The chanting of slogans was again something very horrific to my child's ears. It was a threatening noise, full of danger to my family and my friends. So these emotions and images were in my mind, and I wanted to write a story of Partition. Nothing has been written on the Partition in English fiction from my part of the world—from Pakistan. Very little actually has been written in English, besides Khushwant Singh's *The Train to Pakistan* and Chaman Nahal's *Azadi*, which was written in English, or perhaps in Punjabi and then translated, I'm not sure.

**F.J.**: Yes, it was written in English.

**Sidhwa**: So there is a lot of room for more writing on the subject. I attempted to write it from a somewhat more dispassionate perspective than that presented by some Indian and some British authors, who naturally conveyed their own bias. So I just waded into writing it, like I do in most of my novels, with a vague sense of direction.

F.J.: Is that why you chose a Parsi narrator, to keep the situation objective, rather than a Hindu or a Muslim narrator?

Sidhwa: Yes, certainly.

F.J.: The Parsis were torn between the Hindus and the Muslims, and in your earlier book, *The Crow Eaters*, you talk at the end about how Faredoon in his dying days says we have to give our loyalty one way or another.

Sidhwa: Well, the Parsis, in a sense, made the best of things. If they were in India, they became patriotic Indians. Those that were left in Pakistan remained there and were loyal Pakistanis. Because of their tiny minority status, Parsis have learnt to adapt to whichever country they belong and to take on the color of the predominant culture.

F.J.: Did you start out maybe writing an autobiography and then turn this into a Partition story, or did you start out with a very definite idea of Partition?

Sidhwa: I started out with a definite idea of Partition. The trouble with the first person child's point of view is that it is very easy to mistake it for autobiography. The child, Lenny, in the book is very distinct from myself. The incidents in her life are often taken from my life, but Lenny is a much more astute child than I was. Even if it's a child's point of view, the narrator's voice is sophisticated, and the reader knows there's an informed adult behind it. The incidents, like the scene where the looters rode into the house, have been totally fictionalized—as in the case of Ayah being kidnapped in that scene. So every incident taken from my life, or perhaps from the lives of people I knew intimately, has been embroidered to create the larger reality of fiction.

F.J.: Is the illness autobiographical?

Sidhwa: Yes, I did have polio as a child. I did not go to school. But the way the book interprets this is quite different from my reaction to it. I didn't even know what it meant not to go to school at that point, and there is just so much fiction in it that I cannot really honestly say that the reaction to all that was mine. It wasn't.

F.J.: It's very interesting in that there are many Bildungsroman written about boys growing up—of course, the one we know very well is *Huck Finn* where he comes to knowledge about himself and his country—and this seems to be the dominant mode for Third World literature. There is Narayan's *Swami and Friends* where Swami comes to an awareness of himself and his family and his culture at the same time as political events, but there certainly aren't as many works where a girl's point of view is established. It is tied in with coming to maturation, with puberty; that sense of the breasts budding at the same time that political knowledge is being gained.

**Sidhwa:** As a novelist I like to link my work to the dramatic situation. The whole subject of the Partition of India and Pakistan is dramatic. At the same time, another very dramatic event is the maturation of a child, and these are intricately linked in the book.

**F.J.:** So the dramatic political events tie in with the dramatic personal events in Lenny's life.

**Sidhwa:** Yes, that is the meat of the story. It comes about automatically because the events are having such an impact on her life and thoughts: they are maturing her, she is losing her innocence and with it comes her sexual awakening. She's learning about good and evil from the adults inhabiting her world, and this forms the intrinsic rhythm of the story. The reader sees through her child's eyes how the turmoil affects the people around her and alters them, and that is what the book is about. I think it is perhaps the first time a girl child's awakening to sensuality is presented so frankly from our part of our world. This sexuality has elements of humor: I think humor is especially important to me. Nothing is that grim.

**F.J.:** Do you see a connection between this sexual portrayal and current feminist theory?

**Sidhwa:** I do hate preaching about feminism although I'm a very ardent feminist and western feminist literature has influenced me greatly. In this case, as in the case of my other books, I have let the events speak for themselves. Whatever happens to the little girl is naturally colored by my sensibility as a woman, and so, in a sense, it presents a feminist sensibility. I hope it does so naturally.

**F.J.:** Would you say that your analysis of Lenny's coming to her maturation is indebted to Freud?

**Sidhwa:** I haven't read Freud. As for sexuality, it is so much a part of growing up. I think if we all look back to our childhood, we don't need Freud to tell us how inextricably sex is wound up with the process of maturation. From childhood, almost, the awareness of the opposite sex was always there without my knowing what it meant. Sex is so wound up with life that you cannot talk of almost any experience without having the shadow of sex on it. But, for example, the cousin character who plays such a big role in the sexual awakening is a totally created fictitious character. I didn't have any male cousins of that age in Lahore, but he was a character the story needed to show the young girl's awakening to her maturation.

F.J.: But the cousin and the brother are both "other" in the sense that they are different, as Lenny is "other" or different for them. And the same kind of parallel seems to go into the religious divisions, in the sense that the Sikhs are also "other" and different and that she's trying to understand them, and the Hindus are also different.

Sidhwa: They start off as a very friendly group, and then they start separating into "others" when the Partition movement gathers steam. Suddenly Lenny realizes the "otherness" growing within them, which gives her an insight into the undercurrent that will tear the country apart. Suddenly, Hindus are being more obviously Hindu, Muslims more obviously Muslims, and they're showing their differences, their prejudices, much more strongly. These normally congenial people are, because of their religious and political differences, turning into something a little monstrous. That is how I gradually lead into the events that will overtake them. Unless I first portrayed them as ordinary people leading normal lives, I don't think the impact would have been the same.

F.J.: I was just struck by the nice way in which the psychology and the political events come together. Just when Lenny becomes aware of her body, she becomes aware of herself, of her gender, as being different from cousin and brother and Hari. At the same time she becomes empowered because she has gained both knowledge of her body as well as knowledge of politics and otherness.

Sidhwa: That's true. Cousin's obvious infatuation empowers her—and these are the little things that do empower women, children even, you know, when they start getting aware that somebody is dependent on their affection or their good behaviour. And there is a parallel perhaps between Lenny's awakening sexuality, and the Ayah and her lover's reaction to each other.

F.J.: In the sense that Ayah becomes aware that her lover—she has been going on with Ice-candy-man for so long—is really just making a tool of her—using her as a prostitute?

Sidhwa: Her lover, Massure, dies, and Ice-candy-man, though he loves her is never loved by her—so, in that sense, he is never her lover.

**F.J.:** There are two other strong women characters, or major women characters; one is, of course, Lenny's mother and the other is Godmother. But they're very different. Lenny's mother is not an empowered woman the way in which Godmother is. Why is that?

**Sidhwa:** Godmother's role in this book is quite different. She has to be empowered in order to save Ayah, in order to support Lenny's isolation. She is again a great learning experience for Lenny, a kind of role model which her mother is not. Her mother is dominated to such an extent by her husband that she is in no position to have much say in Lenny's upbringing. So Godmother is needed as a more powerful figure here. Godmother is based on a character I knew, as Mother is partially based on my real mother.

**F.J.:** Is Godmother more empowered or more powerful or stronger because she's not married?

**Sidhwa:** She is married but she's got a very old husband, who is now retired, so she has become empowered because of this condition. This generally happens to women in our part of the world. They come into their own either when they become widows or when their spouses are not so much in control of things. Often, the husbands are much older and by the time they drift into their dotage, the wives usurp their roles. *(Laughter)*

**F.J.:** What is "Slave Sister" a translation for?

**Sidhwa:** "Slave Sister" illustrates an aspect of power play—how one person can dominate another, and appear to do so with intelligence, benefit, compassion, and humor. That is how Godmother exercises power over others. It brings out her power.

**F.J.:** But the word itself—I was trying to translate slave sister back into Gujarati to know what it was. Is there such a word?

**Sidhwa:** No, this is not a translation from Gujarati. It's a concept in my mind—that this woman is comfortable in her role as—

**F.J.:** A slave sister? She's always doing Godmother's bidding.

**Sidhwa:** She's a servant in a way. She's a person Godmother can dominate and draw her power from. But these are deep ties of affection—she is like a daughter too.

**F.J.:** That's a very typical Parsi setup though. There are two sisters—one is older, one is younger and often unmarried or married to an older husband—and the two are together at all times.

**Sidhwa:** I think it is a Parsi situation, yes.

**F.J.**: Why did you give *Ice-Candy-Man* a happy ending? They find Ayah again and she's liberated from prostitution, and she's set free from this women's camp. Or is it a happy ending?

**Sidhwa**: She's set free, but she's emotionally dead. Her eyes are dead; her reactions are dead; she's no longer able to relate to Lenny with any love. She's become a cold person. She has changed; her experience has changed her. Ice-candy-man too is changed because he has fallen in love with her, and this coldness of hers is making him a more devout adorer, and he's miserable. One doesn't know what happens, after all. Ayah's taken across the border to India; Ice-candy-man follows her there, and we have no way of knowing that he achieves her in marriage. In fact, this is again based on a true story except it was played out by a Sikh man and a kidnapped Muslim woman. This story was reported in our newspapers. After kidnapping her, the Sikh did marry her, but then when the people went around recovering Muslim women from that part of the world, she said she wanted to go to Pakistan. She didn't want to live with her abductor, but he followed her and pitched a tent in front of her house. Her family soon arranged her marriage to somebody else, and the figure I based Ice-candy-man on lay down on train tracks and committed suicide. But I didn't want to bring that into the story; it would change the complexion of the story as I'd woven it.

**F.J.**: If Ice-candy-man is so much in love with Ayah, why was he using her as a prostitute, do you think? Just for the sustenance?

**Sidhwa**: Those were very tumultous times and very cruel times, and I'm showing how man's nature changes into something very bestial when savage things happen. But it wasn't just he who kidnapped Ayah, it was a gang of people. And it was inevitable that they would rape her. That was part of the syndrome of Partition events. Ice-candy-man here played his role as having belonged to Hira Mandi—the area of prostitutes in Lahore. He forced her into prostitution as a lot of kidnapped women were forced into it. From the beginning he had lusted for her, and at this point, affected by the bestiality around him, he took advantage of the situation. He wasn't a very savory character to begin with in any case. But he soon realized he was doing her a great wrong and his conscience acted up because he had genuinely fallen in love with her.

**F.J.**: Does Ayah at all blame Lenny, do you think? This little child has burst out and said, "Yes, Ayah is hiding on the roof," trusting the Ice-candy-man, and the kidnapping takes place as a result of that. Does she blame Lenny?

Sidhwa: I don't think so, because it was normal during the Partition riots for a Hindu woman in Pakistan to be kidnapped just as Muslim women were kidnapped across the border in India. I should think it was one of those things that Ayah and other women knew could happen. Lenny's divulgence of her whereabouts is very crucial in the story, but it is perhaps more crucial in her mind than it needs to be. She blames herself inordinately for it as a child would, but in any case, the rioters were infallible hunters, and they would have found Ayah. That's why they came to the bungalow.

F.J.: Is there in your mind a contrast between the way the Muslims treat women and the way Parsis treat women?

Sidhwa: This is a very complex point. I cannot just generalize about it. We are in such a class-structured society. I don't think Parsi women are all that emancipated in Pakistan or India, and in certain classes of Muslim society in Pakistan, women who are educated do have a greater deal of liberation as well. So, we're talking of class structures here, and it just becomes too elaborate a field to go into very briefly. Parsi women seem to be more overtly liberated. When they come out into the West, I think they become very liberated. But then again, Muslim women coming out West also become very liberated, because they also partake of the atmosphere of the dominant people of the country of their domicile.

F.J.: Yes, you certainly show in *The Crow Eaters* that Parsi women are not quite so liberated because there's the one woman whose marriage is arranged. She doesn't seem to be very much a feminist.

Sidhwa: Do you mean Tanya? In those days, given her circumstances, her background, she couldn't possibly be a feminist. She hadn't heard anybody giving talks on feminism; she hadn't read anything about it, and here I'm drawing a parallel between my awareness about feminism. I wasn't aware of what was happening to women in my part of the world until I read *The Female Eunuch* and books on feminism by Friedan that transformed my personality overnight and brought an awareness of, "my God, what we have suffered as women!" So it wasn't something you just spontaneously erupt into knowing. It's an awareness that dawns through hearing people, reading and through discussing things with other women perhaps.

F.J.: What do you think went into molding your voice as a Parsi?

**Sidhwa:** As a Parsi, as a Pakistani, as a person who was brought up among the Muslims—all these influences molded my voice. It was not just the Parsis. There were only about one hundred and fifty Parsis in Lahore which now has about five million people. And there were only three or four Parsi girls my age. So mainly my friends were of the Muslim and Christian communities. Of course, the strong home influence was the Parsi influence. That was the "motherlode" influence, if you'd call it that, but the other influences were very strong as well. Among contemporary writers, I was influenced by Naipaul, by Raja Rao. I have been influenced by whatever I read. My young age reading has seeped into the fabric, the structure of my sentences, the way of expressing my thoughts, but I have somehow absorbed it and made it very Parsi/Punjabi/Pakistani, very indigenous, and it has come out in my voice, in a distinct voice apart from the voices I read.

**F.J.:** Did you grow up in a typical Parsi joint family where the mother-in-law and the family live together and the grandmother also raises the children, or do you think your pattern was changed a little bit from being Pakistani?

**Sidhwa:** Not from being Pakistani. It was changed from being a Parsi brought up in Lahore. If I were brought up in Karachi which is again very much a part of Pakistan, my experience as a child would have been totally different. I would have been brought up among the Parsis. I was brought up apart from my cousins and other relatives. My family was not a big joint family. My mother had an enormous family, but they were all in Karachi or Bombay. My father's family had also moved out of Lahore, although they belonged to Lahore. In my home, my paternal grandmother was with us for a few years, but there was not much influence of the joint family calibre. I was largely brought up by the servants.

**F.J.:** How did you come to write *The Crow Eaters*? That's your first book, isn't it?

**Sidhwa:** It's the second book I wrote. After *The Bride* I wrote *The Crow Eaters*.

**F.J.:** I had them switched in my mind. Wasn't *The Crow Eaters* published first?

**Sidhwa:** Yes, there were certain political reasons for that. They said that if Parsis get angry, they won't shoot you at least. But I wrote *The Bride* first.

**F.J.:** You said *The Bride* came out of a specific situation that had happened.

**Sidhwa:** It's based on a true story I heard when my husband and I were invited to a camp in the remote regions of the Karakoram Mountains about eighteen years ago. The people there were just locked in by the mountains. They'd seen nothing; they didn't even know what a transistor was, what a truck was. The army was building a road from Pakistan into China which followed the old silk route along the Indus. We stayed at a remote army camp, and the person who'd invited us told us of a young girl brought to the mountain area by an old tribal. The conscripts building the road were fascinated to see a girl from the plains in the wilderness. The tribal said he was taking her across the Indus into the totally unadministered territory to marry her to his nephew. A month after her marriage they heard the girl had run away. This is in the Karakorams, you know, the world's most rugged mountains. No tracks, very little habitation, no vegetation. And the girl had run away in these trackless mountains. She survived for fourteen days. By some instinct, she found her way to the Indus. But her husband was out hunting her; a runaway wife is an intolerable insult to the tribesmen, and these are infallible hunters. The whole clan was hunting her. She came to the rope bridge that would take her across the river to the army camp. But the husband was waiting for her there and he killed her when she was so very close to being helped and rescued. He severed her head and threw her into the Indus River. And his clan were satisfied that he had vindicated their honor.

**F.J.:** But in *The Bride*, she isn't killed, is she?

**Sidhwa:** In *The Bride*, she is not killed. *The Bride* has, as it happened, two endings. I first ended it where there's an illusionary scene, in which she has a nightmare vision of being killed. That's where the book was supposed to end. But by this time, I had a different feeling for the book. I'd inhabited this girl's body and her emotions for so long that I felt it was a shame, considering all she had been put through, that she should be then killed off. One of the privileges of being the author of stories is you can change the ending *(laughter)*, and I did just that. At least in the end she lives—she barely survives, but she lives.

**F.J.:** Yes, so there is some hope.

**Sidhwa:** Yes, she's not dead. She is alive, after all. But when I heard the story and heard about her death, it was something which touched me very deeply. When I came back to Lahore, I felt I had to tell her story. I had not written before. The beauty of the Indus, the very tall peaks, the rarified luminous air had their own almost mystic impact on me, and this brought out a latent creativity. I had a compulsion to write this girl's story and the story of the tribals hidden away in this very beautiful part of the world. I started writing a short story about the girl, and without my really being aware of it, it was developing into a long story. It was an obsession. We had a very busy social life in Lahore. And I would try and take whatever time I could to get off and work on the book: between visits by friends, between bridge games when I was dummy—late at night—

F.J.: It's an interesting situation in which to be writing. *(Laughter)*

Sidhwa: Yes, but I feel that's how it works. When I have too much time, I find I want to enjoy life more than write. But that was a compulsion. And it took about four years to write. So *The Bride* was a difficult book to write.

F.J.: How did you come to write *The Crow Eaters*?

Sidhwa: By the time I'd finished *The Bride*, I had become habituated to writing. It had taken up a vast amount of time in my life, and I'd become, without my knowing it, a writer. And I had this next compulsion: "I want to tell the story of my community. I want to record their charm, their customs, their way of looking at things, their slant on life, their humor, their courage." I knew the subject matter so intimately, I found that *The Crow Eaters* almost wrote itself. I wrote one whole summer, and then I gave it up for a while, and then again I finished it in the spring.

F.J.: How was *The Crow Eaters* received in Pakistan?

Sidhwa: It was received very enthusiastically, but not by the Parsis. *(Laughter)*

F.J.: What do you think the Parsis didn't like?

Sidhwa: The Parsis think I just set out to make fun of them. They were furious! We had a book launching ceremony at the Intercontinental Hotel and the ceremony had to be aborted halfway through because there was a bomb threat.

F.J.: From the Parsi community?

Sidhwa: Yes, from a member of the Parsi community!

F.J.: I wouldn't think that.

Sidhwa: I was surprised myself. It took me some time to accept the extent of their anger. Their reaction was very severe. The irony is that I wrote *The Crow Eaters* with genuine affection for a community that can be termed an endangered species, and I wanted to record something about them. Even here, in America, if somebody says to a Parsi: "Oh, this is Bapsi Sidhwa, you know. She wrote *The Crow Eaters*," they react as if I had written a dirty book. *(Laughter)* Very funny, really. And I've had people say, "Oh, I don't think I'd want to talk to you."

F. J.: Why do you think there was this strong reaction to *The Crow Eaters*?

Sidhwa: I think it was because *The Crow Eaters* is one of the first books which deals with Parsi characters. Parsis are not accustomed to seeing themselves fictionalized. There have been a lot of books about Parsis, by the Parsis, but these tend to be books like all small communities do have, flattering themselves, patting their backs. They aren't accustomed to being portrayed with their vices and their weaknesses also on display. So I think that is partly the reason. Another reason for their reaction perhaps is that the printed word does seem to carry more weight in our part of the world because books are still comparatively rare. They are very seldom discarded. They seem to attain an authority the spoken word does not have, and that is why they seem to mean more to people in our part of the world. It's not like the West, where people have become so inured to the profanity contained in books, that they've forgotten their initial awe of books, the initial awe of the written word, and they've forgotten how strongly they also reacted to them at one stage.

F. J.: I was wondering if there are some themes of alienation, but you say that you wrote it out of fondness for the community, not out of alienation.

Sidhwa: Entirely. This book is not so much a satire, it's just a humorous vehicle for a story I wanted to tell. And the strange thing is that, in Pakistan, it was very well liked by the writing community there and they organized occasions for it. But it probably touches some raw nerve in the Parsis because they have not been written about in this way. They haven't developed that thicker skin to be able to tolerate it because they are, in Pakistan at least, lionized. They are very well respected and they felt, "We don't want to be presented in this fashion." But most of the Pakistanis will tell you, "You know, so-and-so said this about your book and I told them, 'Look, after reading the book, I started to love your community more, even at their worst'."

F.J.: There are also some cross-cultural themes there. There's the one theme of the Parsis going to England and ʼnot being comfortable, which is a very interesting reverse. I think, perhaps, Parsis don't like to face that image of themselves. They have always seen themselves as perhaps more British than the British. Do you think there's that sense?

Sidhwa: That could be, yes. Some of them did give explanations. Now this is only pertinent to Pakistan. And maybe it's pertinent to India. But they feel that it's best for us [Parsis] to keep a low profile there. It's safer politically to keep a low profile. They admit that whatever is in the book is authentic, but I have sort of exposed them. I don't look at it like that at all, but they feel that everything about them has been laid bare. But I think their main objection, this is my final analysis, was that they hated the title *The Crow Eaters*.

F.J.: Why is that? You have the crow-eaters coming again in *Ice-Candy-Man* where they say, "kagra khao," and Lenny says, "Why are we called the crow-eaters?" Which I remember too. I remember being raised with the kids teasing me saying, "kagra khao."

Sidhwa: Well, as far as I knew, the Parsis were called that. To say that you've eaten a crow, in India and Pakistan, is to say that you're talking too much, that you're going on, caw-caw, like a noisy crow nonstop. At one point I realized as a child, when I mixed with Parsis after I moved from Lahore to Karachi for a year, that they do talk a lot and loudly. This is something that strikes one who's slightly removed from the community and suddenly comes upon it. And I thought this was an apt title, but the Parsis, for some reason, didn't connect it to this idiom. They thought it had something to do with the towers of silence and the burial system in which Parsi bodies are left to the elements and exposed to the vultures and the crows, the birds of prey.

F.J.: There's a strong movement now developing in the Third World, in Africa and in India and Pakistan and elsewhere, where people from the Third World are becoming increasingly resistant to any critical portrayals of them, whether it's the Islamic community as with, say, Naipaul's *Among the Believers* or with Rushdie's *Satanic Verses*, where they reacted strongly to it, or whether it's the Parsi community or whether it's West Africans—they are saying, "Why are our own people criticizing us?" For instance, there have been strong reviews of the movie *Salaam Bombay*, where people are saying, "Why are they showing that we Indians are prostitutes and drug dealers?"

**Sidhwa:** There's a distinction to be made between those who have been brought up in the West writing and those who are writing within their countries. Those who are writing from outside their countries do tend to be more critical. It almost appears sometimes that they're pandering to the Western world, reinforcing the stereotypes the Western world would like to see reinforced and perhaps feel they can't do it themselves and would prefer somebody else to do it for them. And here again the question of trust comes up. For one thing, writers who are writing from outside their part of the world are using English as a medium. They are writing in a different language from that of the native person they are talking about, and these people feel that they have to wait and see, "are these people to be trusted because they are writing in a foreign language?" Very often the trust, they find, is misplaced. I do find that each writer has to develop trust within his or her own country individually. I think I have. People in Pakistan trust my writing and accept my criticism.

Then, of course, there's this whole new body of writers who live in England, let's say, or perhaps in France, who write about their countries, be it Africa, be it the Subcontinent, and their way of presenting things, their whole slant on the world and their part of the world, because they're living in a foreign country and they've adopted another country, does change. It somehow alters. There's less compassion. There is less realism, and they start seeing their own backgrounds the way the West has been seeing them. They see them through almost pitiless glasses, not tempered with tolerance and compassion. It's not to say authors who live in their own countries don't criticize, but their criticism appears to be tempered by compassion. They paint the whole image with the faults and the better points, and they bring out a human fabric, the condition of people there in its entirety, rather than just one aspect.

**F.J.:** What is the role of satire in your mind? How do you think satire functions? At what point does satire go over the line of being acceptable?

**Sidhwa:** Well, you know, a writer, especially a satirical writer, is in the business of mocking. But every writer does know, that just as you veer away from the superficial to the perceptive, from the banal to the original, that certain things are acceptable and certain things are taboo. It is a matter of sensitivity and taste. Most often you don't cross that boundary line. If you do cross it in your writing, you very often edit it out. There is no such thing as a totally, totally free world, free press anywhere. You can't have that. There are certain things that are unmentionable. I mean, you can't satirize the Holocaust. You can't satirize a particular race, let's say, nor can you extol child molestation or snuff movies. There are certain things which are taboo, which you can't delve into, and a writer has the sensitivity to know that.

F.J.: Do you see yourself as a satirist or a humorist, and if so, what's the difference?

Sidhwa: Humor is a much wider term. Satire is a part of humor as irony is. Humor, I think, includes buffoonery, caricature, lampooning, satire, irony, sarcasm. In my mind, I feel humor is a gentler way of presenting a situation. It enables you to say things perhaps in a more entertaining manner. Also, things that would be a little harsh or grim if said seriously are somehow relieved of that when they are couched in humor. You can be critical in humor much more easily also by using satire. I don't think I've used irony too often. Buffoonery, yes—burlesque—caricatures to an extent. Buffoonery is where a character himself entertains other people by being a buffoon, by adapting the characteristics of a buffoon, and the Parsis, I think, are born entertainers.

F.J.: In *The Crow Eaters*, would you say there is a bit of buffoonery in Freddy Junglewalla or more so in the mother-in-law who goes to England and goes through all her efforts trying to adapt to England?

Sidhwa: Well, Jerbanoo, the mother-in-law, is an out and out performer. She acts to the gallery; she is a zestful woman, and she gets her way a lot of the times by being a very dramatic buffoon. She has a definite sense of humor in the way she presents her point of view. You know, she doesn't react in a typical mother-in-law elderly woman fashion. Faredoon, yes, at times he acts the buffoon when he's trying to get his way, when he's trying to do what he says—exercise his wiles and get things through ulterior motives. He plays to the gallery to get around people. He acts the buffoon. Most characters do to an extent in this novel.

F.J.: You made in passing a distinction between the writers who live in England and those who have stayed in their own country but write in English. I wonder what your position is on the question that's come up about whether to write in English and not write in English and how to use English.

**Sidhwa:** I'm really fed up of this question. Every conference I've been to, we seem to get drawn into this discussion and half the conference's time goes into debating this point.

I can explain this only in terms of how I see it. My first language of speech is Gujarati, my second is Urdu, my third is English. But as far as writing and reading goes, I can read and write best in English. I'm a tail-end product of the Raj. This is the case with a lot of people in India and Pakistan. They're condemned to write in English, but I don't think this is such a bad thing because English is a rich language. Naturally, it is not my first language; I'm more at ease talking in Gujarati and Urdu. After moving to America, I realized that all my sentences in English were punctuated with Gujarati and Urdu words.

**F.J.:** Do you write that way? Or do you consciously try to keep the languages separate?

**Sidhwa:** Often without knowing, I do translate literally from Gujarati or Urdu into English. Sometimes it works, but sometimes it sounds very stupid.

**F.J.:** Do you lose something there?

**Sidhwa:** No, in fact I gain something there, because I have access to a totally different idiom which gives something fresh to the book or to my writing or whatever. Then again, we have adapted English to suit ourselves. It has become for people like me our own vernacular. I didn't study abroad ever. The little bit of education I had was entirely in Pakistan, but I grew up using English like my own language the way I did Urdu, Gujarati and Punjabi. So I can express myself in English. I think the writer has the right to say, "This is the language of communication, the tool, I choose to use." And I would argue this is the only language I want to use. It suits me. I don't want to go into another language. But knowing other languages gives me an advantage because I have access to two or three cultures and idioms.

**F.J.:** So you can develop a certain objectivity on the one culture and a certain subjectivity onto another.

**Sidhwa:** I am on the borderline of a few cultures and I'm steeped in a few of them. And that, I think, gives me a certain amount of objectivity. There is also, I think, an element of jealousy perhaps, a point of possessiveness that the English or the Western person feels, "Well, why should the browns and blacks write in English? Why are they usurping our language?" And here I think English is no longer the monopoly of the British. It has become a world language, a language of communication not only between different countries, but between different provinces in Pakistan, different provinces in India. As such, it has gone beyond its boundaries and I think writers from our part of the world are twisting it, changing its inner structure to suit their new expressions.

F.J.: What is the activity in English, literary activity in English, in Pakistan now? Is there poetry created in Pakistan in English or is it mostly the tradition of Urdu poetry continuing?

Sidhwa: There are, of course, a lot of Pakistani writers who write Urdu poetry and prose but very little in English.

F.J.: Why do you think that is so?

Sidhwa: There is a very rich tradition to Urdu poetry. The language lends itself so naturally to poetry that if you know Urdu, you just don't want to create poetry in any other language, and this is perhaps why I don't create poetry in English. I'm so enamored of Urdu poetry and the way the Urdu voice, the Urdu idiom, the Urdu words lend themselves to poetry. It touches me very deeply. Being from that part of the world, I like sentiment; I like the emotion contained in Urdu poetry. I'm opposed to what I think is the Western point of view in this respect as poetry goes, but I'm no authority on that.

F.J.: You use a lot of Urdu poetry in *Ice-Candy-Man*. You seem to be very influenced by that tradition. There are Parsi proverbs, Parsi-Gujarati cadences in the sentences, but you are also very influenced by an Urdu literary tradition.

Sidhwa: Yes, my love of Urdu poetry overflows in this book. I've made it part of this book and woven it into the structure because I feel it gives a resonance to the book, a cultural resonance. Something which is very eastern, very Urdu has permeated the book in the form of poetry. As far as the Gujarati idiom goes, the Parsi idiom translates much more naturally in prose.

F.J.: Who were the major Urdu writers that influenced you?

Sidhwa: The poets of course—Ghalib, Alama Iqbal are strong influences. Iqbal is our national poet, and he's a mystic poet. Mystic poets have generally influenced my thinking. They write in Urdu and Persian. I adore Faiz Ahmed Faiz. I knew him personally. We have some marvellous contemporary poets. Women in particular speak to me—Zehra Nigar, Kishwar Naheed.

F.J.: But what of prose fiction published in Pakistan?

Sidhwa: Again, there is a lot written in Urdu, but not that much in English. We don't have a strong publishing industry in Pakistan, and it's almost non-existent where English fiction is concerned, so there's just no outlet for it. There may be hundreds of scripts being written for all I know which are not published, so we don't know what is being done.

F.J.: Zulfikar Ghose is the other Pakistani writer in English who comes to mind. Do you know his work?

Sidhwa: I reviewed one of his books for the *Houston Chronicle*. And I read a very old book of his, *The Murder of Aziz Khan*, his only novel set in the Subcontinent. It was marvellous. That's all I've read of him. In Pakistan, there has been almost nobody published abroad where English fiction goes, you know. The only writers I was able to dig up were Ahmed Ali and Zulfikar Ghose besides myself—just us. And now Ghose writes about South America.

F.J.: The interesting thing about Pakistani writers is that there, other than Salman Rushdie, there hasn't been—

Sidhwa: Rushdie is not a Pakistani writer. He's an Indian writer, he's a Cambridge man, I don't know. *(Laughter)*

F.J.: He's hard to classify.

Sidhwa: Yes.

F.J.: What do you think of Rushdie's novel about Pakistan, *Shame*?

Sidhwa: I reviewed it for *Harpers & Queen* in England. It confused me so much that I wondered if I should review it at all. I know Salman and I was also published by Jonathan Cape [his former English publisher]. I adored *Midnight's Children* but I found *Shame* much too diffuse and disjointed. It appeared to be a rather hasty work. He was writing about Bhutto's assassination, and this was something we all felt very strongly about. My family and I were aching to run out in the streets and to riot and protest the hanging, but General Zia's regime had all the pro-Bhutto leaders in jail. It affected us as if a loved relative had died; I grieved for a year. I felt that these events were too fresh for Salman to present in a correct perspective. Besides, he was not part of that world, and he has his own Britishized angles, biases, whatever. I think that he doesn't really understand Pakistan; that's why he sticks with the fairy-tale and magical realism gambit. But I think I may be too close to the issue to see his point of view as dispassionately as I should. We were all so much in favor of Bhutto then—he gave the poor people, the minorities, the women some self-respect, a voice. He did a lot to break the strong feudal Sardar system.

F.J.: What about the great playboy image of Bhutto that Rushdie creates?

Sidhwa: Bhutto was a colorful character. The playboy image is based on fact. But this was part of a larger argument. It was really the rich, vested interest which was anti-Bhutto. They just brought him down eventually. At that time, the argument was: "Oh, do you really think he is for the poor people? Look at the way he squanders money—he gets his handkerchiefs from Savile Row and his suits from Harrods." And they would talk like this to the poor voters, asking, "Why are you all for him?" And the poor people, they had the Punjabi way of expressing things, they would say, "But he's a *dhullah*, a bridegroom. He's our country's bridegroom. Let him wear good clothes, let him do this." They idolized him. When he was hanged, many of them fantasized that he was alive, that he'd run away to India and would come back riding a white horse.

F.J.: What made up your reading as a child?

Sidhwa: From the age of about eleven to eighteen, I read nonstop because I did not go to school. I had nothing else to do, no other form of entertainment to fill my life with, and a big slack was taken up by reading. This did turn me, I now realize, into a writer. I must have read *The Pickwick Papers* at least four times during that period. I would laugh out loud. I recently reread *The Crow Eaters* and reread *The Pickwick Papers* and realized there were so many parallels. I subconsciously absorbed a lot of that book and years after, when I wrote the *The Crow Eaters*, it influenced that book without my being aware of it. I think all that I read then was an influence—a lot of Tolstoy has influenced my work, many British writers. And Naipaul was very good to begin with, though I don't care as much for his more recent writing.

F.J.: Why is that?

Sidhwa: Well, he seems to have drifted into some sort of stylistic journalese. I just adored *A House for Mr. Biswas*. There was a creative energy there;

you could see it—he is a writer, a storyteller. I was writing *The Crow Eaters* when I came across it. And I felt that it was just the right thing for me to read when I was writing it. But that seems to be lost.

F.J.: What about other South Asian writers in English? What do you think of R. K. Narayan?

Sidhwa: I've not read too much of him. In Pakistan, one is still removed from a lot of what's being printed elsewhere, especially in India. What really got me interested in him was his criticism of Naipaul's *An Area of Darkness*. And I thought it was a very valid criticism. I can imagine the Indians fuming at that book, because you know Naipaul visited India without knowing anything and delivered these opinionated little vignettes where every Indian woman is cow-eyed and ugly and horrible, but some little American beatnik is the most charming goddess going. As an Indian it hurt him [Narayan] and I felt his criticism of that was very valid. But Naipaul's writing in the book was excellent—as it is in *India: A Wounded Civilization*. You forgive him his opinions.

F.J.: Did you read the section of *Among the Believers* set in Pakistan?

Sidhwa: Yes, I read that and that really disappointed me. I felt that was such a superficial little book.

F.J.: In its treatment of the Muslims?

Sidhwa: Not in its treatment of the Muslims. I have no particular sympathy with any one community, you know. But what does that book amount to, written in any language? It could be condensed into a feature article on a tour into Pakistan, Iran, etc., etc. There's nothing creative in it.

But it may be only in the West that these writers are considered so important. I don't know if you've read Faiz Ahmed Faiz. He's a Lenin prize winner and one of the best contemporary Urdu poets. He died in 1983 or 84. He considered them good writers but not great writers. In fact, he placed me in the same slot as them and that, as far as I'm concerned, tumbled them in my regard! *(Laughter)*

F.J.: What do you think would be his standards for a great writer?

Sidhwa: He would be among the great in our part of the world.

F.J.: No, I mean, if Narayan and Naipaul are merely good writers, who are the great ones?

Sidhwa: After what he said, I didn't even come down to asking him that.

*(Laughter)* He probably would go to the level of Shakespeare or Goethe or Proust or something like that.

F.J.: You're living in America now. How do you see yourself changing as a writer as a result?

Sidhwa: You know, it's strange, but I don't see myself changing so much as a writer. Of course, whatever I experience now does change what I can say. I'm writing a collection of short stories now set in America, but here again, I don't know the Americans well enough to write of purely American characters. I will use people from my part of the world in America—the expatriate, the immigrant experience if you like, how they interact here with the Americans. To that extent it's changed.

The other day I started a story. I was just watching TV, and there was this silly little ad about hemorrhoids. And so seriously done. I thought it would be marvelous if a Jerbanoo or a person like her could be brought here. And the way she could take off on America would be fabulous. I could place a book in America, but I'd have to write of people I know very well, somebody from the Subcontinent. I wouldn't be able to portray the Americans so well. The Americans are much more adept at doing it; why should I do it?

F.J.: How long have you been in the States continuously, or have you been in the States continuously at all?

Sidhwa: I've been here for about five years, but each year, I have spent at least three months in Pakistan. The first two or three years, I used to spend a longer time in Pakistan. I've not been here continuously even for a year. Each year I've gone back.

F.J.: Was 1982–83 the first time you came to the States?

Sidhwa: I visited the States for the first time in 1971 during the India-Pakistan war. I was stuck in England. I'd gone there for some treatment, then the war broke out and I wasn't able to go back to Pakistan. I had some friends in America and instead I came here, and I lived generally with a Parsi family here. My impressions of that visit were totally different from my impressions when I moved here. I enjoyed the experience of moving here and suddenly starting a life here much more than just visiting it.

F.J.: And you did that in—

Sidhwa: This was in 1983 I believe.

F.J.: And you moved to Houston, and you taught—

Sidhwa: No, I first moved to Charleston, from Charleston to Atlanta, from

Atlanta to Houston, from there to Cambridge, Massachusetts, and from there now I am in New York, so I've progressed from South to North. *(Laughter)*

F.J.: But you had actually written *The Bride* and *The Crow Eaters* before you came to the States.

Sidhwa: Entirely. They were published in the States before I moved here. This was in itself a miracle; to live and write in Pakistan and to be published in America is quite unique.

F.J.: Is it easier for an unknown quantity to break through the writing world in America?

Sidhwa: Good God no! It's the very opposite. That's why I say it's a miracle. It's almost impossible for an unknown "foreign" quantity to break into America. It's just that I was published in Britain first, and I was buttressed with very, very favorable and very, very strong reviews. And that is why after two years, they were able to place my books here. It wasn't easy, but the editor at St. Martin's published it. It was a very brave step on his part, because generally American publishers are the most timid in the world. They know their public. America is so vast, the public is generally interested in reading only about America and Americans.

F.J.: How do you see the role of Third World literature today since it seems to be a growing field? We see increasingly writers like yourself or Anita Desai being reviewed and getting a prominent place. What do you think is the role of Third World writers in contemporary literature?

Sidhwa: I think they have a very vital role to play because they express their communities, their countries, in human understandable forms. By the act of writing and telling stories about people in their part of the world, they are turning faceless people and stereotypes into individuals with faces. It's very easy for the West to stereotype people as "the Africans," "the Asians," "the Chinese," "the Arabs." These people become faceless. They become blobs of humanity. They are not individuals, but writers turn them into human beings, and once you turn somebody into a human being, it becomes more difficult to kill that person, more difficult to exploit that person too ruthlessly. The Western world does develop a conscience reading books about the Third World by Third World writers. It is very important to emphasize this. The Western world too often jumps in and defines other cultures for the West, but the Third World voice itself does most for that part of the world, because it is much more genuine, authentic, and it seeps into the subconscious of the reader depending upon the skill of the writer.

F.J.: But of course you don't see yourself as a spokesperson for a community.

Sidhwa: No, I don't. I would see myself as a person who wants to present Pakistan, because I do feel that Pakistan has had its share of being kicked around.

F.J.: Well, Bapsi, just to round it off, how would you like to be known as a writer? How would you hope your literary career and your reputation would be known?

Sidhwa: I would certainly like to be known as a Pakistani writer, and I would hope when anybody wants to know about the Parsis they'd say, "Oh read the book, *The Crow Eaters*, it's entertaining and also tells you a lot about the community." If somebody wants to know about Pakistan, I hope *The Bride* would be pointed out as a novel that displays its culture. Again, *Ice-Candy-Man* is a story of India and Pakistan, and it deals exhaustively with the Partition, and I would like to be known by these books. Then again, I guess there's no end to a writer's ambition. I would also like to be known as somebody who is writing of their experience as an immigrant in America and observations of the American culture.

F.J.: Do you see yourself as a woman writer, a writer writing for women, a particular women's voice?

Sidhwa: No, not at all. In fact, at one point, people didn't know what my gender was by my name, and when they were reviewing *The Crow Eaters* in Britain, they very often called me "he." The reviewers thought I was a man writing, and I think this was one of the most wonderful compliments I could receive—that my gender is buried. My first priority is that of the story-teller. Of course, being a woman, I see things filtered through my woman's sensibility and I have enough, as all writers have, of the man's sensibility in me to create male characters too. It's not as though women writers and men writers are committed to their own genders. Tolstoy portrayed women so beautifully and all great writers have, and I think gender doesn't come into it in a very big way.

# Witi Ihimaera

One of the terms proposed for the literatures in English from around the world is the "new literatures in English." This seems a remarkably inappropriate term for many "new literatures": Indian literature, for instance, is a spectacularly old literature and even Indian writing in English dates back almost one hundred seventy-five years. But there are some situations, however, where the term new literatures seems more appropriate. New Zealand, for instance, had not even been settled (or invaded) by the English by the time Indians had begun writing in English, and literary writing in English by the indigenous Maori population in New Zealand began only in our lifetimes. Born in 1944, Witi Ihimaera is undeniably the dean of Maori writers, the first Maori to write a novel and the first to receive any international acclaim, even though—as the following conversation reveals—such acclaim still puzzles him. Though by now other Maori writers have emerged, Ihimaera's oeuvre remains the most substantial and impressive.

Between 1972 and 1977 Witi Ihimaera burst on the New Zealand literary scene with four books in those few years, two collections of short stories, *Pounamu, Pounamu* (1972) and *The New Net Goes Fishing* (1977), and two novels, *Tangi* (1973) and *Whanau* (1977). His work instantly attracted a good deal of attention, but this early burst of work was followed by a long silence, and it must have seemed to many as if Ihimaera had suffered the fate of many Western writers accorded immediate recognition: that the promise of his early work was not going to be sustained. Ihimaera, in the conversation that follows, gives a rather different explanation of his silence, that he was waiting for other Maori voices to be raised. In keeping with this, his major publication in the intervening years was the anthology of Maori writing, *Into the World of Light* (1982). With the emergence of a number of other writers, most notably Patricia Grace and Keri Hulme, winner of the 1985 Booker Prize for *The Bone People*, Ihimaera ended his self-imposed silence with *The Matriarch* (1986), a massive, ambitious and challenging novel, which has been subsequently followed by another book of short stories, *Dear Miss Mansfield* (1989).

We interviewed Witi Ihimaera in New York, where he was the New Zealand Consul; he was subsequently the Attache for Cultural Affairs in the New Zealand Embassy in Washington. Currently, he is posted back in New Zealand. One of the questions we brought to our conversation with him was if his art had changed as his perspective had become more international. In an important sense, it hasn't; he remains the committed Maori writer he began as. If anything, his work has become more Maori in the sense that he is now consciously trying to carry across certain aspects of Maori art into his writing in English. For, of course, Maori writing is only a "new literature" in a highly qualified sense. There is a rich and old oral tradition in Maori culture; all that is new here is the attempt to carry some of that tradition over into English.

**Reed Dasenbrock**: Most contemporary writers that I know and that I know of teach in universities. But here we are talking to you in the New Zealand Consulate in Rockefeller Center in New York. You are the only writer I can think of who is a consul and works as a diplomat. I wonder how that affects your writing; is that a good combination?

**Witi Ihimaera**: Well, there are in fact a number of writers who do belong to the diplomatic service. I always think the diplomatic service is just like any other job, it takes away one's time between nine and five. So it doesn't really matter that it's diplomacy or if you're a post office worker or whatever you do, it's simply a job that pays the rent. And that is what it is for me. Most writers, especially indigenous writers, if they don't get into a university, tend to work and write only part-time. In my own country, Patricia Grace, for instance, works as a teacher. Most New Zealand writers, because our economy cannot support writing as a professional, full-time activity, are writers who write during the weekends or during the evenings. Keri Hulme, because of her success, has now managed to maintain a fairly good living. But it's only a *fairly* good living. It's not a living that she considers a good one, but still it is now something that sustains her writing full time. The only other writer in the Pacific that I know of in the diplomatic service is Vincent Eri. Vincent Eri wrote a book called *The Crocodile*, the very first major novel from the South Pacific. And the last I knew, he was Deputy High Commissioner for Papua New Guinea in Australia.

**Feroza Jussawalla**: I wonder if there isn't a closer connection than that. Just a few minutes ago, we were sitting in the room for visitors in the consulate surrounded by books about New Zealand, informing readers about the country and the people. Do you see yourself consciously contributing to the knowledge about your area?

**Ihimaera**: Yes, I do. But I must admit that it always puzzles me that in

America people say, "Oh, we must read your work, we must read your books," and I say, "Well, why?" because to me it is not important for the work to be assimilated here. It is more important for it to be known in the place where it originated—where it will most have its effect—and that is in New Zealand itself. One good thing about coming from a tribal background, as I do, is that I really do believe writers in our area are not competitive. We are all cooperative in our activity, and I do not know of one Maori writer who is selfish enough to believe that he or she is better than the others. We all have this great sense of purpose, and I'm not meaning that in any romantic sense at all. We all want to contribute to a better understanding within our region of the Maori people. Most of our work has been directed to the Maori people. But we are beginning now to turn on that and beginning now to direct our work to the Pakeha who is the majority in power. Because if we cannot interpret our needs to the Pakeha in power then we will never, ever, advance the causes of the Pacific.

F.J.: That's very interesting to me because one of the things that strikes me about your first novel, *Tangi*, is that it's not self-conscious at all about depicting the culture. I can think of several other "Commonwealth writers" who are either very precious in their style and in their attempt to depict their culture or are self-consciously working too hard. With *Tangi*, I don't get that sense, even though there are words I don't understand and you're going back and forth between English and Maori. So do you see your audience as the Maori people who would switch back and forth between English and Maori?

Ihimaera: Well, I mentioned that we have begun to turn a little bit. I must give you a copy of *Into the World of Light*, the anthology of Maori writing I've edited. In the beginning, what we had in New Zealand was what I call the pastoral tradition of Maori literature. I don't think we were too dissimilar from the Caribbean tradition, where people generally wrote very small stories about folk incidents. As long as your stories were stylistically excellent and as long as they were without too much rhetoric, then they were acceptable. My first works, which were all published between 1972 and 1974, like *Tangi*, were right in the middle of that pastoral tradition. That is, they were for Maori people, trying to interpret their lives within rural settlements in New Zealand for them, and the race relations component in those stories was not very high. Now, ten years, fifteen years later, most of the work that is coming out of New Zealand is more about the relationship between Maori and Pakeha. We have now, I think, interpreted sufficiently ourselves to ourselves, and it is now time for us to interpret ourselves to the Pakeha.

F.J.: How do you see your style or the content changing for this newer audience you want to reach, the Pakeha?

Ihimaera: I have just launched a book, which has taken me three years to write, called *The Matriarch*. It is an odyssey, an exploration of a Maori family over five generations. Of course, when you begin this exploration into the dynamics of what has occurred in a Maori family, then by implication you are also exploring what has been happening in the dynamics between Maori and Pakeha. The book is about a way of life that was completely whole and completely sustainable until the Pakeha came to New Zealand. Ever since then, the New Zealand Maori and the Pakeha have been at war. That basically is the theme of the book.

F.J.: I remember one time in *Tangi* you said you walked out of a history class, I say you, but the narrator walks out of the history class because of the interpretation of the Maori wars.

Ihimaera: Yes, I was much too young then to argue with the lecturer, so I walked out of the class, which is a passive act, really. But I think age gives you a sense of being able to do anything, so I don't walk out any more. I have begun to be uncompromising in my approach to history, particularly to Maori history.

R.D.: So your earlier work was more about Maori life today. Now you are going back into the past, but you're also saying that's more addressed to a Pakeha audience. I wonder how those two fit together?

Ihimaera: For most writers there is a time lag between the experience they write about and the time the book actually comes out. So, although I was writing in the 1970s as a grown man of twenty-eight to thirty, most of my stories and most of the earlier novels were about childhood experiences which, therefore, put them into the 1950s. Fifteen years later I've learnt enough to widen my range and to explore the dynamics behind my childhood. The work that is coming now is an attempt to try to fit that particular childhood experience into a wider historical, social, and tribal context. That's where the difference is.

**R.D.**: You began with your own experience, and now you are attempting to explain what led to or created that experience?

**Ihimaera**: That's right. What exactly was it that made the world as I knew it between 1950 and 1970 the way that it was? It's been a very exciting assignment, but it's also been a little bit unfair because I've always felt that indigenous writers have to be so expert so quickly. We have to be good writers from the very beginning of our careers, we have to be right on the ball stylistically, technically, whatever else, because our work suffers such tremendous exposure. If you are the first Caribbean writer or the first black African writer from Zimbabwe, people tend to put your work under a microscope. I believe European writers who have written a first book don't get that sort of exposure.

**R.D.**: But that sounds good as well as bad. Most writers would love to have exposure quickly, wouldn't they?

**Ihimaera**: Yes, but it means that we have to aim for excellence from the very beginning. We do not go through a kind of apprenticeship period. The other aspect to that is that we are also seen to be very representative of our cultures. That's another good thing that can also be a bad thing. In my case, when I first started writing, I considered it to be bad because New Zealand has only a population of three million. People in New Zealand were reading my book and saying, "Oh this is what Maori life is really like." But I knew it wasn't. I was writing simply about the experiences of a small family group within a wider tribal framework. So I gave up writing in 1974, and I only began to write again ten years later, in 1984. The reason was that I felt that one person could not possibly have everything to say about one's culture. It was time just to sit back and wait until there was sufficient growth in Maori literature before I could make a reentry.

**R.D.**: So that you wouldn't be taken as the only voice?

**Ihimaera**: There is also another matter, and that is when other people start to come along it becomes more difficult for them, because in many ways what you have done is create a stereotype or create a way of writing or a way of approaching the subject which then becomes the norm. And New Zealand publishing is mainly ruled by Pakeha publishers who have Pakeha preconceptions about what Maori writing is. So, if you do not want those preconceptions to be maintained, then you obviously have to absent yourself from that dilemma.

**R.D.**: Were you writing in those years and not publishing, or doing neither?

**Ihimaera**: I actually wrote an opera. I got to a stage where I was feeling that maybe opera was a good way of showing my own people that a mix of drama, music and literature would not be dissimilar from life on the marae or in the village. The opera, when it was put on in New Zealand, was regarded as being just a slice of life as you would experience it on a Maori marae.

**R.D.**: You thought opera would work better to represent that than a novel?

**Ihimaera**: There are no Maori opera composers in New Zealand. So I thought, "Oh, well. That's not being competitive, let's do something different." Although I took music as a student, I had no composing skills left. A friend of mine, Ross Harris, said he would do the composing for it. It's an ensemble opera. Maori people are not really individual performers. Everybody is important in this particular opera, there are no major roles in it. It's like Mozart, I suppose, like *Così Fan Tutte*. You have a range of people all expressing in their own way what life is like for them in the village. The opera is called *Waituhi, The Life of the Village*. It had a great success.

**F.J.**: Tell me a little about the Pakeha publishers and their preconceptions. Are there preconceptions about language and about style? About how you should write and whether you can use Maori words to a certain extent?

**Ihimaera**: When I first started I went to three publishers who turned my work down because I was quite adamant that the audience for the work was Maori. The second publisher said, "You know Maori people don't read books." So, that was one assumption that was made. At that time, in New Zealand, in 1970, the idea of someone who wanted to present his work simply to a Maori audience, and then use Maori words without a glossary, was rather difficult for publishers to comprehend. Also, I don't think my short stories were really short stories. They were slices of life, I suppose, which didn't really conform to the expectations of literature in New Zealand. And again, that was something that had to be worked through. We have a history, in New Zealand, of turning down books. Keri Hulme's *The Bone People* was turned down by five or six different publishers before a woman's collective actually took it up. Since then it's gone from one strength to the next. But I don't think that's a preconception that is held just in New Zealand. I sometimes fear very much about my own publisher's African Writers Series because, in many ways, publishers also have the power to divert one's work from a major audience and categorize it as being for a specialist audience. I've often thought that the African Writers Series, while it was a good avenue at the time, in that it established a particular look and a particular feel and people understood what they were getting, also limited the work in some ways.

R.D.: In what way? By putting it into a box, this is African?

Ihimaera: Yes, this is black African; therefore, don't touch it, if you're not interested in it; or it's for serious study perhaps. At least in New Zealand, what happens is that we have a small enough population that it is able to absorb our literature now—that is, Maori literature—without any real necessity for it to be in any way indicated as being special.

R.D.: Then things have changed from ten years ago when you felt you were type-cast as being *the* Maori.

Ihimaera: Yes, I think things have changed because New Zealand itself has begun to come to grips with its bicultural heritage. Maori people are not an invisible minority any longer; you see us on the street every day. Nor are we the sort of people who are prepared to be pigeonholed and kept in one particular conceptual framework.

F.J.: So you would rather not be seen as part of the stream of Commonwealth Literature or New Literatures in English?

Ihimaera: It wasn't always the case. I think that as our literature has developed, and as it has become acknowledged as being good in our country, we have started breathing a bit deeper and gaining more and more confidence in ourselves. That doesn't mean to say we think our literature is any better than any other world literature, but it is just as good. I think that we all need to get to the stage where we feel that we are contributing to a world literature.

R.D.: If you see yourself as part of world literature, then what audience do you have in mind? If you write, for example, with a lot of Maori words, then do you feel that by that you are excluding a non-Maori audience?

Ihimaera: I can't speak for others but in my case what I know is that I am tremendously proud of the Maori people. In New Zealand I have yet to hear Pakeha people say that what they are doing is for the Pakeha people of New Zealand. But you talk to most Maori people and they say, "What I am doing is on behalf of my people or on behalf of the people." I guess with that pride also goes a sense of arrogance. It is the arrogance which states "I am not going to make any concessions to anybody." For me, therefore, my culture is as important as Greek culture is to Greeks or Italian culture is to Italians. And nobody ever made it any easier for me when I was reading a book by an Italian and there were Italian words scattered through it. One got the sense of the emotions and the intellectual and spiritual elements behind the work. So why should I in my work not include words from a minority that people hardly even know? And why should I provide a glossary? This is why I don't tailor my work for an international or any audience. But what I do now is write for an audience without any tags on them.

F.J.: How about the decision between writing in Maori versus writing in English? Is that a difficult decision?

Ihimaera: In New Zealand the Maori language has only just begun to be taught. So, all modern Maori writers, without exception, began by writing in English. I mentioned before that New Zealand is going through a period in which it is coming to grips with its bicultural roots. Part of that is now a resuscitation of Maori as a language. *Pounamu, Pounamu*, for instance, is now being published in Maori.

R.D.: Did you translate it, or did someone else do the translation?

Ihimaera: No, someone else did the translation. It is now the first book that has been published in the Maori language.

R.D.: Could you see yourself writing in Maori?

Ihimaera: Yes, I can. But if I did, it would be for a specific educative purpose rather than for a literary purpose.

R.D.: So that people would have texts in the Maori language to read?

Ihimaera: Yes.

R.D.: Why not for a literary purpose?

Ihimaera: Well, not a European literary purpose anyway. When you write in English, because there are narrative forms to consider, you tend then to have a beginning, a middle, and an end. But in Maori, most of our work has to do with different literary forms, with genealogy. The Maori language is always full of genealogical references and references to what we call whakapapa or historical connections. Because of that, the work will obviously be in a different tradition. I can't think of any parallels, but I would imagine that it would be difficult for a black African writer to write chants and maintain a primarily European literary focus for them.

R.D.: Then the language itself brings with it certain kinds of forms. You can't imagine doing in Maori the kind of literary work you do?

Ihimaera: What I would be doing would be writing within traditional frameworks and—I guess—within traditional inhibitions because Maori people believe that the word is very sacred. Luckily for Maori writers who write in English, the English word is not sacred, it's profane. English is a profane language.

R.D.: You would feel much more constrained by those traditions writing in Maori, whereas writing in English you feel freer.

Ihimaera: Yes. More respectful, really, not constrained. Part of this, from a technical point of view, has to do with the fact that the Maori framework for its literature, apart from being heavily allusive in drawing these references from the past as all languages do, also has a very short line. It's a line that in singing isn't very obvious because what you hear is a voice continuing one line after another line. But in English the line is longer and therefore shows a wider range of forms. That's really quite important.

R.D.: Let me just change this question around a little. Some Indian writers and some African writers, I think, if they were sitting in this room, would be very upset by what you just said, so let me speak for them a little bit. They would say that everything you've just said says that to write in English is to a large extent to be caught in English language forms. And I think you've said that and would agree. But they would then go on and say, therefore, if you want to depict maoritanga, or a Maori ethos, you must write in Maori, that to write in English is necessarily to falsify that kind of experience. So, for instance, the Kenyan writer Ngũgĩ has gone back to writing in Gĩkũyũ because he feels that English is a language that you can use only to depict a kind of Anglo-Saxon or Pakeha world view. I wonder what you would say to them? Ngũgĩ could put this argument much better than I could, but—

Ihimaera: I mentioned that word profane before, and I think that's what I really do mean about writing in English. It is profane enough for me to do whatever I want with it. But Maori, you cannot do whatever you want with it. It is a tapu language. It is the language of the people, it is a sacred language. It has spiritual connotations to its usage. In that respect, I agree with what you've just said, what Ngũgĩ would say. I agree that the only way to present an unadulterated view would be to do it in Maori. But I still make the distinction between it being educative or "real" in Maori and being literary, because literature is a falsification of the "real" or an alternative reality to the truth. In my own language, the word can only be the truth; there can be no interpretation. It has to be absolutely factual, and it has to be constrained. If it wasn't constrained and if it didn't fit into the traditional framework, then it would become non-Maori.

F.J.: Can we perhaps exemplify that with the form of *Tangi*? Are there freedoms that come with this profane English language that let you go back and forth in time and in mind and in the actual situation. Is the thought consciousness going back and forth because of the English language or is that a certain kind of Maori form?

Ihimaera: I earlier mentioned about my first books being in a particular pastoral tradition. That was fine as far as they went because they were dealing with Maori life in the way that Maori people would understand. But once I began to use literature in a wider sense, as I have begun now, then I also brought into the experience more developed Maori concepts of time, of narrative, of style. Perhaps that's good in that it ensures that our literature marches with the times. We also have an inbuilt sense, all of us, an inbuilt fear that if we don't continue to reflect what's happening in our society then our work will become dated. It won't have as much importance in New Zealand as it should have. It won't have as much relevance. The relevance of the times means, in my case, writing in English. But the purity of the tradition would mean that I would have to go back to writing in Maori. When that time comes.

R.D.: Your own work in English then exemplifies the kind of biculturalism that you think New Zealand is moving towards. In other words, it's caught up in certain kinds of Maori traditions but it also reflects Pakeha traditions as well?

Ihimaera: Yes. In that respect I think that our literature is a little different from the literatures of other peoples in the Pacific. The Polynesian community in New Zealand is the minority in my country. In the rest of the Pacific the Polynesian community is the majority. No other island group in the Pacific has more than 30 percent English; in our case it's 90 percent English and 10 percent Maori. So we have always been a minority under stress whose major dilemma has been to continue to interpret our culture to ourselves within that 10 percent framework. We have done that in Maori for ourselves but in English for the majority who rules us. So in many ways our direction is perhaps a little bit different from the rest of the Pacific.

**R.D.**: What about the situation of someone like Albert Wendt, then, who now is living in Fiji, right? He writes only in English. Has he ever thought of writing in Samoan?

**Ihimaera**: Albert is now at the University in Auckland. He has a year-long fellowship there.

**R.D.**: The political situation for him may be different, but the language situation is really not, because he has written in English. In fact, you use much more Maori in your work than he uses Samoan in his.

**Ihimaera**: I think that maybe Albert was caught up in the same educative process that I was. He was born and brought up in Samoa, but his education was in New Zealand. So he went through much the same literary, social, and intellectual upbringing as I did.

**F.J.**: What do the majority of Maori children now learn? Do they learn English, do they learn English and Maori? If they're talking in a situation in a novel, should we presume they're talking in English?

**Ihimaera**: We have to get the context right first. Nowhere in the Pacific is the indigenous language the first language. The first language in the Pacific is English. That's the reality of the situation in the Pacific. The second language is the local language. Marjorie Crocombe, from Rarotonga, was very, very upset about four years ago. She told me that for the very first time in history English had become the first language of her islands. She and I went into a virtual tangi for a whole week, just realizing that that was what had happened to all of us in the Pacific. In New Zealand, that has always been the case for Maori children. Only recently, in the last few years, have the Maori people—and they are the ones who really had to do it in the first place—begun to establish what are known as language nests for Maori children. At first they were nests that were exclusively just for Maori children—preschool children—who would be brought by their mothers into a particular group. They would only be spoken to in Maori. Now that kind of framework has extended throughout the country and Pakeha children are now, also, participating in these language nests (which have now had official blessing). The Maori language, hopefully, at the end of this year, will become an official language in New Zealand. If that is the case, then we believe that we can begin to speak Maori wherever, for official purposes, even in the Ministry of Foreign Affairs. Once that happens then I think we will see a restoring of the balance of languages in New Zealand and Maori returned to its rightful place. That will be the time when I will begin to write in Maori.

**F.J.:** You make reference in your books, also, to a pidgin. What sort of pidgin is existent? You have that nice scene where the brother and sister say to the mother and father, "Don't speak in this language. Speak in English," and they say something about pidgin at that point.

**Ihimaera:** Maori, like all minority languages under stress, went through a period when there were a lot of transferrals of different words and different ways of saying things Maori in English. The rhythm remained the same and some of the words remained the same but it sounded like a dialect caught between the two languages. This is the process that occured in the 1950s. Thank goodness it didn't stay for too long, because, although I know that there are some people who defend pidgin now as a language in its own right in the Solomon Islands and Vanuatu and in Melanesia generally, my whole attitude has been that I dislike pidgin intensely.

**R.D.:** Pidgin in this context is Maori that's taken on a lot of English coloration?

**Ihimaera:** Yes. The interesting thing about it is that it has evolved in urban areas as a kind of street language. In New Zealand we have seen, in the last ten years, anyway, the rise of street gangs. And they have adopted Maori phrases as a kind of slang and turned it into a street lingo which has its own sort of "hip" and its own sort of "hype."

**R.D.:** These are Pakeha gangs?

**Ihimaera:** No, these are Maori kids. I guess, for them, it's their way of reinforcing an identity which is not traditionally Maori, i.e., not traditional pastoral Maori, and neither is it contemporary Pakeha English. They fit in a very, very strange inbetween world.

**F.J.:** So when some of your characters are speaking standard English we should presume them speaking standard English, not speaking Maori or being translated by the author?

**Ihimaera:** Yes.

F.J.: And that when you go into the Maori then they are actually speaking in Maori.

Ihimaera: Yes. But in the books which you refer to, which are earlier works, I purposefully held back on the Maori. In my new novel, *The Matriarch*, there are whole chunks of Maori without explanation.

F.J.: How important do you consider knowledge of the context for understanding or interpreting your work? Would the best critics of your writing be those people who know the context, who are New Zealanders, or would they again be like your international audience?

Ihimaera: There are a range of people in New Zealand that all Maori people have to answer to. There's a range of opinion about how fast or how slow our development should be. We have a wonderful radical feminist movement in New Zealand, which is, in fact, forcing the pace in Maori terms in New Zealand. We also have a number of extremely politicized people, for whom literature and the literature of all Maori writers is of no use whatsoever. It is not specific enough. It doesn't deal with specific political goals. The context in that respect is, therefore, an attempt just to show where New Zealand Maori writers are coming from. We are not trying to establish ourselves as being the primary political movement in New Zealand, although we now regard ourselves as being a political movement, nor are we saying that we are a part of a mainstream. Although we are a part of that mainstream, we also believe we are directing the mainstream. It's a way of saying, "these are our credentials, and you need to understand where we are coming from."

F.J.: Then it's important that the critic and the audience understand where you're coming from to put your writing in some kind of framework.

Ihimaera: Right. So that then they can relate it, whether they like it or not, to their own directions.

R.D.: What then about the Pakeha reader? Or, let's say, an American? What do you expect that reader to do with the Maori?

Ihimaera: I've never really thought of an American audience. It just always surprises me, when I get letters like yours, to come to grips with the fact of any interest other than Maori or Pakeha in my work. I am well aware that using Maori could cause a problem for an international audience, but that doesn't change anything because of the tremendous pride that I do feel in the Maori language. It's also that I always feel surprised by any interest overseas in my work. I've never really thought of it as being important overseas.

R.D.: How I would respond to that is that what you have been describing in terms of Maori culture is remarkably akin to other situations around the world. What you are describing in terms of the Maori culture is remarkably similar to Native American and Chicano culture in this country. Everything you've said, I think, would be of great interest to people facing similar situations in this country as well as for African writers and Indian writers. What you are talking about is something a lot of people are trying to find their way through.

Ihimaera: Maybe the way in which I feel stems from the fact that I hate making parallels between Maori literature and Caribbean literature (or whatever) because people always tend then to make comparisons which show one culture as being either less than another or less valid than another. In Maori terms, when I first started to write, people used to say to me either, "Your literature isn't really like Papua New Guinea writing," or "It should be more like Papua New Guinean writing." Or "It should be more like Caribbean writing" or "It should be more like black African writing." I think that we were the last of the minority black peoples to enter into the world of English literature. I think that Indians here, Inuit people in Canada, black African writers were all here before us. So a whole range of assumptions was brought to bear on us.

R.D.: The comparisons have been prescriptive, someone has been trying to give orders.

Ihimaera: Yes. I used to say to some Maori writers, "You know, if you're going to start writing, don't read anything. If you read anything, then you will borrow phrases. What you will borrow from is an internationalism which seems to be pervading all of world literature. Don't read James Baldwin. Because if you read James Baldwin then you will get a particular mindset about black American literature that you might then want to transfer into the New Zealand experience. You have to concentrate just on your own life and interpret it the best way you can without any antecedents other than your own tradition."

F.J.: But what about the reader as opposed to the writer? Do you feel that your work must be interpreted only by those people who know your contextual situation or do you think it should be accessible across the board?

**R.D.**: Or to put it another way, if we would come along and make descriptive—not prescriptive—comparisons, would you then say we were giving you a hard time?

**Ihimaera**: I can't stop anybody from doing this.

**R.D.**: I know you can't stop it, but what would you say about it?

**Ihimaera**: Most of the work that I've seen on *Tangi*, for instance, always compares it with a black African writer.

**R.D.**: Achebe?

**Ihimaera**: You know to this day I have avoided reading Achebe? *(Laughter)*

**R.D.**: Because of the comparisons?

**Ihimaera**: Yes.

**F.J.**: Actually, it's funny because *Tangi* is very different from Achebe.

**R.D.**: I've read at least one of the articles making that comparison. I don't think it's a very good comparison.

**Ihimaera**: I haven't answered your question. I would find it interesting because if I am to reach a new audience, then obviously I need to find out how that audience is reacting. And what we have been talking about in the last hour has been a movement, a personal movement by myself, from an attitude where I was only writing for Maori people to an attitude where I am now beginning to feel competent and confident enough to write for a wide audience. But that audience will have to accept that my writing hasn't changed. In other words, what I have now come to is an understanding that "Maori literature is wonderful, but I shouldn't just concentrate on a Maori audience." As a culture it has as much beauty and as much relevance to provide for everybody. As any other literature it should stand very proudly in the sun. That's where I am at the moment.

**R.D.**: Everything you've been describing works for me in a slightly different way. That is to say, one of the experiences I get reading *Tangi* is that I get a very strong sense of all the things we've been saying about how in New Zealand, at least at that time, certainly Pakeha ways were taken as the norm, Maori ways taken as a fairly marginal sort of thing. In other words, primarily when Tama goes to work, he's on Pakeha ground. He has to behave in Pakeha ways.

**Ihimaera**: Yes.

**R.D.**: So one of the things your work would do to an average New Zealand

Pakeha reader is make him experience some of what Tama would experience every day. Which is to say, for that reader, encountering a lot of Maori that he may or may not understand would be meaningful, educative for him. Because if he thinks about it, he's going to say, "well, wait a minute, I do similar kinds of things to these people every day." So it strikes me that the Maori may be difficult for a non-Maori reader to understand, but that's also significant in the sense that he, then, if reflecting upon it, will realize the kind of experience a Maori person has in that Pakeha culture. Does that make sense?

Ihimaera: Yes. As I mentioned before, I never have glossaries, and the reason is that the work has always basically been for a New Zealand audience. What I am saying is if you do not know these words then you are maintaining a monocultural bias in your lives. I could make it easier for you by translating these words and making the sense more accessible. But if you really do want to become bicultural, then you have to begin to do some research of your own and find out these things for yourself. The will to do that is really a personal choice. I know some people even with a minimal amount of Maori who have thrown the books out the window.

R.D.: Then the reader who rejects it is in a sense being located by your work, located as refusing biculturality. Whereas the reader who does accept it will probably not understand everything but in that process will learn a great deal about the Maori experience as well.

Ihimaera: And I also have to acknowledge, and I have acknowledged this in the last work that was published, The Matriarch, that the people who most matter to me are Maori, and for many of them their knowledge of English is not good. So the Maori that is in the work, as small as it is, is going to be the text that they will appreciate, not the English. Another reason for not translating the Maori into English is that sometimes it just looks awful and sounds awful. The correlation is with Italian. If you've ever been to see La Traviata in English, and heard an English translation of it, it's just terrible. It loses all of its emotional context. In Italian, they sing "O Dio," and when it's rendered "Oh God" it has a totally different sound and has a different aura to it. This is why I like to keep the Maori language tapu or sacred. If you use the Maori language, then it should not be, to my mind, translated. It should be just as it is.

R.D.: A few months ago, in El Paso, we went to see a Chicano writer give a reading. At one point, he interrupted what he was reading and said "this would sound so much better in Spanish," and Feroza asked him later, "Well, why don't you put it in Spanish?" and that seemed to baffle him. He'd never thought of that before. He was telling a certain kind of anecdote that was full of proverbs, and he was right. It did sound silly in English.

Ihimaera: A similar instance is a word that we use, aroha or "love." If you translate that into English, then people will say it is love. But then that locks it into kinds of assumptions about sexual love, or celibate love, or family love in a European sense. In the Maori sense, aroha means love, sympathy, tears, sorrow, laughing. There's a range of connotations and not one single meaning.

R.D.: The semantic field is so different that you keep it in Maori because the English semantic field would be the wrong one.

Ihimaera: Yes, it puts it in another direction.

R.D.: The word tangi is a perfect example of that as well. I suppose an English translation of that would be funeral or funeral rites.

F.J.: Yes, but that wouldn't give it the same sense of tearful mourning; the long period of—

Ihimaera: Yes, that's right.

R.D.: If you had called *Tangi* "Funeral," that would have seemed grotesque and totally inappropriate to the book.

Ihimaera: When you use the word tangi at home, it encompasses not just a word or a feeling but a whole tradition and ritual. That is what most Maori language is about. It's about ritual. Perhaps I should have said that earlier. There is a ritualized sense of use of the language. That is why it is, again, sacred.

R.D.: So writing in English you have the freedom to do what you like but then at those moments where you want the Maori values to come across, then you can rely upon Maori phrases, words, even dialogue to establish that dimension. Whereas to stay in one language or to stay in the other would deprive you of that freedom.

Ihimaera: Yes. Neither would it be an accurate reflection of New Zealand, where now Maori and English are quite frequently used in the same circumstance.

F.J.: May I ask how autobiographical your work is? Are you the boy who didn't go back to take care of the family? *(Laughter)*

Ihimaera: I'm not sure myself how autobiographical my work is. Indeed, I've often asked myself two questions. The first is, "Is my life conforming to the dictates of fiction?" The second is, "Or am I purposely writing a pre-scription for myself, which I am now trying to fulfill?" I still haven't resolved the question. One of the reasons why I did stop writing after *The New Net Goes Fishing* was because I didn't know where my life was going. *Tangi*, for instance, ends with the boy at the railway station. In 1972 I knew where I was going so I could have, at that stage, completed the sequel to *Tangi* which would have seen the boy's return to the village. But because fiction has a habit of reflecting the writer's reality, all of a sudden, in 1972, I was asked to join the foreign ministry. When that happened, I could then no longer complete the sequel until I had discovered just what was going to happen to "the boy." I still have two books to complete the whole cycle after *The New Net Goes Fishing*.

R.D.: You've begun them?

Ihimaera: Yes. I began the sequel to *Tangi* which was called *Maui/Mauri/Maori*. It was a play on three words that we have. Maui was the God who discovered New Zealand. For me, he's always the symbol of self-exploration, of discovery. Mauri is what we call the life giving force which makes us move, which animates us. And Maori, of course, is what we are. And so in the sequel to *Tangi* the boy was coming to grips with himself as a person, realizing that although there was a great big wide world out there, his pri-mary focus should be on his family. And so he was going to return. Well, fourteen years later he is in New York. (*Laughter*)

F.J.: And you can't finish those two books yet, can you?

Ihimaera: No, I can't.

R.D.: What you're describing as a sequel seems already implicit in *Tangi*. It seems quite clear that he's made up his mind to go back and to leave the city. But in *The New Net Goes Fishing*, there's a story where he says that, "my father died and I still haven't gone back." That seemed in a sense to reverse the ending of *Tangi*. Was that consciously a revision of *Tangi*?

Ihimaera: It was written during that time when I was really trying to figure out a direction for myself. In that one, Tama is in a dilemma. That dilemma has yet to be resolved. But I still plan to finish the six books. What do you call it? A sixtology or something. It's going to be an exciting enterprise for me because what I might have to do is to distance myself from the fiction.

**F.J.:** In order to be able to create a fiction that is distant from you.

**Ihimaera:** Yes. Which will round all of that off. It will mean having to go back fourteen years, trying to adopt a style which I have now increasingly left behind, and writing about a "Tama" who isn't like me.

**R.D.:** In other words you think you might finish it with Tama going back even though you didn't go back.

**Ihimaera:** I haven't gone back *yet*. But I'll tell you, all Maori people return.

**F.J.:** How strong is that tension between city and the homeland for the majority of the Maori people?

**Ihimaera:** At one stage we used to believe that the only way in which we could retain our roots was to return to our maraes. And we did that frequently. Now there is this feeling, that instead of returning, the maraes should come to where we are. I'm so pleased that I was able to give you a copy of *Into the World of Light* because the introduction to that will give you an indication of what is happening in New Zealand now. With the change in demographic patterns in New Zealand, where most of our people live in cities and only twenty percent in rural areas, we have had to force our culture to come to us. So we have begun to establish maraes where we are. I think that's been quite a significant development.

**R.D.:** That's close to the movement of your own work also, which began defining a fairly enclosed, rural Maori identity, as you've said, and is now reaching out to broader contexts. What direction do you expect it to take in the future?

**Ihimaera:** *The Matriarch* is part one of a two-part novel. The first part is five hundred pages long and the second part will be five hundred pages long. After I've finished *Tiana*, which is the sequel, then I am going to have to get back to completing the cycle of six books, of which *Pounamu, Pounamu, Whanau, Tangi*, and *The New Net Goes Fishing* are the first four. Once I've done that—

**R.D.:** So that will give you two novels as sequels to *Tangi*.

**Ihimaera:** I've always been fascinated by spinoffs, I suppose. The name of the game today is spinoffs. *The Matriarch* and *Tiana* together are another context for the earlier work because they still deal with Waituhi and with Maori history but over a five-generation span. Because of that they carry with them a lot of historical and social and intellectual material about Maori life. So that's the great, great, great big circle in which the earlier work belongs. And then the two remaining books will be part of the inner circle also.

F.J.: Yes. I see the design, as it were, in my mind. You see two concentric circles. *The Matriarch* and its sequel will be the outside circle and these are the inside circle—

Ihimaera: Perhaps the word spiral is better because the spiral is the major symbol for New Zealand and for Maori people in New Zealand. In New Zealand, in Maori terms, we have what we would call the double spiral which starts off like this and goes in and then comes out. I hope that my work conforms to all of the visual and lyrical elements of the spiral.

R.D.: So they form, in a sense, a kind of double spiral. You are starting from your own experience and then spiraling out to a larger context and then spiraling back in.

Ihimaera: Yes. It's a good image, isn't it? It allows you then to go back into history and then come out again. Back from personal into political and back again. Or in fact from Maori in New York to Maori in Wellington, to speaking Maori in your own community and then coming out to speak English. So it is a good one.

R.D.: Well, we've probably taken much of your morning.

Ihimaera: It's been fun actually. I never did think it would be fun. Most of these things are not fun. *(Laughter)*

F.J.: Is there any kind of final statement you want to make?

Ihimaera: Ah, no!

F.J.: We'll end with the spiral then.

# Rudolfo Anaya

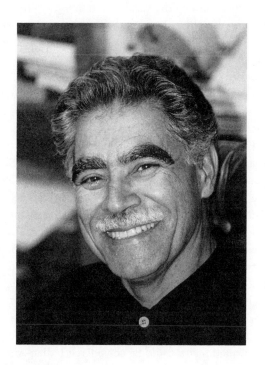

One of the concerns we have brought to the interviews contained in this book is the way the categories with which we divide up literature in English get in the way of a genuine understanding of the richness of contemporary literature in English. "Commonwealth literature" as a term for literature in English other than British and American is—as we have seen—a term generally disliked by the writers themselves. One problem with the term is that it obscures differences among the various "Commonwealth" countries. But if the term "Commonwealth" obscures differences among Commonwealth countries, it also obscures the similarities between much "Commonwealth literature" and American literature, which if not a "Commonwealth literature" by any conceivable stretch of the term, is certainly a "post-colonial" and a "new" literature in precisely the way the other literatures in English around the world are. An indigenous writer such as Witi Ihimaera is, as we have seen, part of a minority under cultural pressure from the majority population of European descent. This makes his situation comparable in interesting ways to that of minority writers in the United States. For the United States, too, has minority and indigenous peoples and languages, and a rich literature is emerging from these minority populations.

This is one crucial reason why we have extended the focus of this book past the easily demarcated non-British literatures of the world to include three representatives of America's fastest-growing minority population, the Chicano writers Rudolfo Anaya and Rolando Hinojosa and the Chicana writer Sandra Cisneros. Such writing is not often put in such a global or comparative perspective, but we believe that such a frame is illuminating, both of the work of these writers and of the other writers in English from around the world. For, indeed, Zulfikar Ghose and Raja Rao as long-term residents of the United States could be considered Indian-American as well as South Asian writers, in just the way as writers of non-British origin such as Buchi Emecheta, Roy Heath and other African, Caribbean and Asian immigrants can be considered black British writers. No neat distinction can be drawn any longer between the inside of English and American literature and the outside of non-Western literature in English.

Rudolfo Anaya is a writer who represents this reversal extremely well. In one perspective, he is the most local of writers, a native New Mexican who has lived in New Mexico all his life and has written extensively about his own Spanish-speaking people. But the Hispanic culture of the Southwest for him is derived overwhelmingly from the pre-Columbian world and from Native American culture. And this is why he sees this local identity in global terms, as part of an emerging New World and non-Western identity that can meet the old European world on equal terms.

Anaya is the Chicano writer who has—with Rolando Hinojosa—created the most substantial oeuvre. Born in 1937, he is the author of three novels, including the best known Chicano novel, *Bless Me, Ultima*, and a book of short stories. But he has also written plays, children's stories, a travel book, *A Chicano in China*, has edited a volume of essays and two collections of stories. He is a true man of letters and has also worked hard to encourage other Chicano and southwestern writers to develop their own voices. The following interview was taped on a visit by Anaya to El Paso (and then followed up on at his home in Albuquerque), where true to this sense of responsibility, Anaya visited with students, taught a class and did a reading of his fiction.

**Feroza Jussawalla:** I've used *A Chicano in China* a lot in my classes because it speaks to my students, here in El Paso, about identity and crossing cultures. In a way you've made identity the central issue in the book. In what ways does China speak to you? There's quite a bit of reference in *A Chicano in China* about the connection between the Chicanos and the Asians. Your grandfather, for example, puts his ear to the ground, and he says that you can hear the Chinese. You have a whole theory about Asian immigration from Asia through the Northwest coast into the Llano area, into New Mexico, establishing a connection between the Chinese people and the Chicano people. I'm interested in this partially because I'm from Asia and I'm living in New Mexico. How did China and Asia become relevant to your personal history?

**Anaya:** I have always been very interested in the migrations of people, especially in the Southwest. This has been a migration path since time immemorial. Basically, the migrations from the Asiatic continent took place from North to South. Those people came across the Bering Strait and then settled all of the Americas and kept going to Tierra Del Fuego. That's a very important migration. If you look at the legends of the Aztecs, they talk of that migration. We came from north of Mexico; we came from Aztlan. That was one of their stopping places in their migration. Then you get the migration of the Español going in the opposite direction, going upstream from Mexico up into Nuevo Mexico. Then finally in the last century you get a new migration of the Anglo-American coming East to West and running into this very important corridor. What happens in these corridors of migration interests me—how people treat them, how they live there, what consciousness and new awarenesses they come to and what kinds of conflict develop when different peoples mix, as we have here in the Southwest. We have the Indio, Español, Mexicano, and finally the Anglo-American. I use the metaphor of being a fish in the stream of migration—which I think blends perfectly into the golden carp and the fish people that I have always used as a theme in my work. So here I was swimming upstream of the original migration, thinking of that part of me that is native American, that is, what I call the New World man, and feeling very much at home because by going to China I had returned to part of my roots, my symbols, and the Sipapu, the homeland. Aztlan might be in China, if you push it back far enough, if you push it back to its original source. I have always traveled and tried to see what I have in common with people, how we all fit into the human salad. It was very natural for me to see myself as a Chicano Chinaman. I became a Chicano Chinaman.

F.J.; Is this a revelation that came to you upon going to China, or had you always thought about this?

Anaya: No, everything evolved naturally. I didn't preplan anything or plot anything. I went with an open mind. The allusions to my grandfather were very important because I've always used a mentor or a guide for my characters in my literature. I felt the need, especially in this trip, to have a mentor, a guide. The place was very foreign, very far away, very strange, and I really knew it only through the stereotypes that we most often have of foreign countries, especially of the East. I alluded to this in the work, to Charlie Chan movies; what else did we know about China? So I was trying to learn the truth about China, not the stereotype, and I felt someone like my grandfather, a wise old person, would be that spiritual guide that I needed, that mentor.

F.J.: Had he any connection with China or Asia?

Anaya: This man lived all his life in a little valley in New Mexico, in the Puerto de Luna valley. He was a farmer, he was born there, he was raised there. The old people didn't know a world beyond that, but they were so intuitively wise enough to know that we are connected to the world out there.

**F.J.:** You've said before that when you're asked about your roots, you look down at your feet, and there your roots are, and that's just New Mexico. So your roots lie in New Mexico rather than tracing any Spanish genealogy? How do you see yourself in that context?

**Anaya:** My roots are in New Mexico because New Mexico is one of the Indo-Hispano cultures of the New World. What I am trying to do in my work and when I talk to people, is—by having them look down at their feet and their roots, at the soil of the New World—to take a meaning and iden-tification from it. We don't have to go to Europe or to Spain to find our roots. We have finally become New World persons. I think if we don't do that, we will never meet our authentic selves. We'll always be rushing to Spain as the mother country. Those connections are important, those roots are there, but we have evolved in the New World.

**F.J.:** Can you give me your definition of the New World man? What does he incorporate?

**Anaya:** The New World man, the New World person, takes his perspective from indigenous history and spiritual thought and mythology and relation-ships. The New World person is a person of synthesis, a person who is able to draw, in our case, on our Spanish roots and our native indigenous roots and become a new person, become that Mestizo with a unique perspective. That's who we are and how we define ourselves.

**F.J.:** That tension is played out very strongly in *Bless Me, Ultima* because you have the Lunas who identify with the Spanish colonizers and who cul-tivated the valley and grew things and made it green, and then you have the Marez, the vaqueros, the people of the Llano. How did you come to working that tension out?

**Anaya:** As I look back in my work, as I said in the essay "The New World Man," which I read at the conference in Barcelona this past summer, it seems to me I have always been in search of this person. I have not been able to feel authentic until I found this person because I was being led to believe I was too many other things by too many foreign, outside influences that didn't even know who I was. So how could they describe me? Looking back at *Bless Me, Ultima*, at least one way to describe Antonio is that Antonio is the beginning of my search for the New World person. He incorporates the Español and the Indio, the old world and the new.

F.J.: I've used chapter six of *Bless Me, Ultima* in my freshman classes a great deal. That's the chapter in which Antonio comes to school for the first time. The teacher looks at him and calls him Tony, and then the students make fun of him when he's eating his lunch of tacos. It's an experience that must speak out to my students because my students respond: "Oh yes, this happened to me, this happened to me," and they respond to it with a genuine gut feeling. Is that a colonization process you're depicting, a new colonization, the way in which someone like Antonio is colonized into becoming an American?

Anaya: Yes, but after all, this area that I speak about and this corridor that I belong to, this Rio Grande spiritual corridor, has always been colonized. There have been successive colonizations, successive migrations. People pass through and make this place their home. When the Anglo-American finally comes here in the mid-nineteenth century, he becomes the most recent colonizer of the indigenous peoples, and so Antonio in that chapter, and I think probably in all of the book, reflects that indigenous person. I think a lot of people have missed this in the book, but my concern is how will Antonio ever find himself, truly see himself?

F.J.: Can you tell me how he will?

Anaya: It's going to be a long process because the reality of the colonization mode or model is to destroy the roots that bind you to the authentic self. Everybody has to search, to continue searching. It happened to my generation, and you're saying your students still reflect on that; so it's still happening. I believe that history and literature and all the arts are important; they feed the person that we really are because they go to our values and our roots.

F.J.: I've talked about *Bless Me, Ultima* with Rolando Hinojosa, and he said that most people consider *Bless Me, Ultima* as a mythical novel, but that it is really a political statement. Do you see a political statement in *Bless Me, Ultima*, and if so what would you say it is?

Anaya: I've just told you that the novel has a structure by which a boy who is very small begins to inquire into who he really is. When you find out who you really are, you become a person of incredible power.

**F.J.:** What I was thinking of was the scene when he finally decides he's not going to become a priest, or does he decide that?

**Anaya:** I would hope that he would be a shaman, but, you know, a shaman is another kind of priest. The point is not so much what he becomes. We can't dictate what people become, but what we can hope to do is to liberate people by having them become their most true selves, their authentic selves, to find their deepest potential. Then you will recognize the models of colonialism that are set over you, and you'll know how to react and how to accomplish your goals in life. So to me the important aspect of *Bless Me, Ultima* is that process of liberation.

**F.J.:** Antonio is essentially shucking off two levels of colonialism—one is the Spanish colonialism that comes through his mother's family, the religious colonialism of the Catholic church, and at the same time the kind of Anglo-American colonialism that's coming to him through the Anglo-American education system.

**Anaya:** I think that's fair to say.

**F.J.:** What about the people of the Golden Carp? Do they ever get set free, or do they just go around in a circle?

**Anaya:** I'm not sure I follow that line of thinking.

**F.J.:** Antonio says at one point that the Golden Carp is never set free from Narciso's mythology. He says it's never set free, it just goes around and around seasonally.

**Anaya:** You must know that in one sense no one is ever set free. This is the nature of our humanity. We struggle to be free, and we struggle depending on the philosophy that we follow, right? If I wish to achieve a total freedom, must I die, or must I turn to the Zen or to Nirvana or to the Buddha or become a priest for the Catholic church? I don't prescribe and tell people what will set them free, but I'm very interested in the process. There is a process by which you can get to know yourself and to be liberated in yourself. That liberation also has a very important component in the community because as you liberate yourself, you liberate others, and you get to know more of your humanity. I am interested in that process; other people will be interested in the political ends of that process.

Culture is something we create. We're creators of culture; we love it, you know. And in many ways, there is as much of a trap there as in anything else. I'm interested not only in the individual, but in the communal group.

I'm also interested in the fact that cultures can be as binding and enslaving as anything else. But they can also provide the context where you explore your relationships with other people, explore the possibility of being that authentic self I talk about. So nothing is good or bad categorically; it's what we make it. I think that we have the possibility of making our culture a vehicle for the exploration of that self, for communal fulfillment. Perhaps I'm being too idealistic, but I really believe that is possible in community because that's all we have. We look around and we only have each other, and how we relate to each other is important.

**F.J.:** So the "Heart of Aztlan" doesn't have any kind of particular specific locus for you. It shifts with communities and people, would you say?

**Anaya:** No, I think it has a definite locus. It is a Barrio which is a definition of community, set in a specific place and a specific time with specific goals.

**F.J.:** I don't mean the novel with that title, *Heart of Aztlan*, as much as metaphorically. Does the culture have a specific locus or can it move to communities and cultures in Northern New Mexico or Southern New Mexico or West Texas?

**Anaya:** Everything we write should be able to move like that. Everything we write should be able to move out into the world and be a reflection of everybody else's community.

**F.J.:** I don't know how you'll receive this question, but is that why you write in English? I'm beginning to get more and more feedback from writers who say, "oh to be authentically Hispanic, we should be writing in Spanish, or to be authentically African, we should be writing in an African language, or to be authentically Indian we have to write in an Indian language." Does your sense that writing should speak to everybody govern your choice of language?

**Anaya:** I didn't have a choice. I was educated in the American school system, and this school system teaches English. So very quickly I moved from my native tongue, which is Spanish, into the English language both spoken and written. So the choice was not there to make. By the time I started writing I was a university student, I'd been fourteen years in the English-speaking world and English-writing world. What choice did I have?

**F.J.:** If you had the choice, would you have chosen Spanish? Or is English part of the New World man's consciousness?

Anaya: No, the New World man's consciousness is language free; he can use any language to express it.

F.J.: So there are really no considerations of audience. It's just that the language that comes naturally to you as you write is English.

Anaya: Yes, by now it comes more naturally of course. I think that in terms of language one does what one can do best with one's resources. I didn't pursue a study of Spanish. The Chicano writers who are part of the Chicano movement generation who took degrees in Spanish-language departments wrote in Spanish. It's easy for those who write in Spanish to use that as a political statement. I try to be more realistic, I deal with reality. I was brought up and educated in this language so I use it, and I didn't think about audience when I started writing in English. It was just that by that time I had been trained and gotten my degree in an English department, so that was natural.

F.J.: One thing that's very natural in your writing style is the way in which you switch back and forth between Spanish and English.

Anaya: I think we're all, in many ways, multilingual people. Most of us Chicanos in the Southwest are surely bilingual. So it comes naturally sometimes to shift back and forth. But it is more important to use the rhythms of Spanish in our work, the rhythms of Spanish in the Southwest, which is a unique blend of Spanish.

F.J.: But then in the *Cuentos* anthology of traditional stories or tales from New Mexico that you've edited you've worked consciously at having one page in Spanish and one page in English.

Anaya: That was an editorial decision. My friend had done the collection in Spanish and he said: "I want to present a book bilingually; will you do the English translation?" and I said yes.

F.J.: Do you think that many Chicano writers feel compelled to succumb to that pressure of having to include Spanish, even though they may have, like you, grown up mastering the English language initially?

Anaya: They might. The only problem with writers who throw in Spanish for effect is that it sticks out like a sore thumb; you see it right away. My advice would be to write with the tools you have, what you can compose in well. The craft of writing anything is difficult enough as it is.

F.J.: Is there a publication problem with using Spanish and English, moving back and forth?

**Anaya:** Absolutely. In this country, you cannot get works written in Spanish published. It's difficult. There are very few publishers who touch manuscripts written in Spanish. Then it would be difficult to market and distribute them.

**F.J.:** One of the things that interests me a great deal in your work is just the way in which you focus on the individual and bring out the individual, and then you bring the mythology in, like you did in the story you read yesterday about the desert and the dust in the mouth. How does all that come together for a writer? How do you mix the mythology with individual characters?

**Anaya:** I have been in training all my life to be this person, to be this writer. I am aware of a goal that I have set in life that I want to accomplish, and I work at it.

**F.J.:** Is it knowledge of myth together with knowledge of human psychology and observation, or is it mostly observation of individuals?

**Anaya:** It's a knowledge, but more than knowledge it's an exploration into what makes us human, the human soul, the human condition, intuition. I don't study mythology. I read myths; I'm interested in mythology, but that's not a real study I have. Myths are personal; they come from your dreams and your subconscious. We all have them, and we all have the ability to know each other, and I'm interested in what drives us. I'm interested in passion and desire and how all these show up in different forms in mythology.

**F.J.:** There's a very close tie-in between landscape and human beings in your work. Does the landscape make people be a certain way?

**Anaya:** Absolutely, yes. If you begin to go back to mythology, one statement, one phrase I have used, and I don't know if I made it up or I read it somewhere, is, "The gods come from the landscape." The gods come from the sea and the trees and the mountains and the caves and the forests, and people responding to those landscapes are responding to those gods. By responding to the gods you're responding to the landscapes. Different landscapes give rise to a different form of gods and demons.

**F.J.:** In your more recent work, you are moving gently off the Llano into the desert. You're not really moving into the Rio Grande Valley, but off into the desert.

**Anaya:** No, I'm moving into the city.

**F.J.:** In your new work? Can you talk about that?

**Anaya:** Well, look around and make a list of every writer in the Southwest. Ninety percent or more of them live in cities, and this has been true since World War II, since the migrations began from the Llano and the desert and the villages and small towns into the cities! So now we have to deal with urban landscapes, or we should be dealing with them. The writers of the Southwest and the West resist dealing with that urban experience, but it is who we are; it is us.

**F.J.:** That's because the landscape has been romanticized in Western and Southwestern literature in a certain kind of way, and that's kind of a colonial factor too. When we talk about Third World literature, we talk about the colonial literature about the area or about the landscape: E. M. Forster about India's landscape versus the Indian writers writing about India. Is it perhaps this romanticizing of the landscape that makes a writer a Southwestern writer?

**Anaya:** I don't know if the landscape and how we use it would be a criteria for definition. I tend to think it is. In reading through anthologies and books of these Southwest writers who live in cities, they constantly place their stories back in the old Rancho, or the little village, or on the highway, or in the cafe in the outskirts of town. It's just something in us to do that. We are part of the myth, and we perpetuate it, you know?

It's good and bad like everything else, right? It can be made to work for you and it can also become a formula that's not very interesting after a while. I've been in the city most of my life, so I can't continue to write *Bless Me, Ultima* of the small town. I am no longer that. I must confront my new landscape which is an urban landscape.

**F.J.:** And in what ways do you confront that?

**Anaya:** By writing about it, by using it as the backdrop, by studying the dynamics of the Southwest city, the new migrations that are coming here, the new models of colonialism. How are the new migrations of the last ten or twenty years into the Sunbelt changing our cultures, our traditional cultures? Who's in charge now? Who's suffering? All of that is taking place in the city.

**F.J.:** Is this a new phase of the diaspora experience in that the Mexican-Americans are becoming part of the larger diaspora, or becoming part of the mainstream? What exactly is it about the urban landscape that engages you?

**Anaya:** The fact that we live in it. Everything about it should engage us. I don't know if dealing with the urban landscape is a return from the diaspora or not. I don't know if the barrio can any more be the focus of our community. The Chicano is entering the mainstream, the middle class. There is no doubt about that. There are people who will argue it, but by and large, that's the drive. And it brings up one more cycle of our history. We are wrapped up as part of the human condition in cycles. The important thing, I think, is to look at this new cycle. What are we like now that we enter the urban landscape, professional jobs, middle-class mainstream? To use your comparison, what will Antonio's role be today? If he had stayed in Ultima's Llano, he would be the new shaman. I think there's a job for him to do in Albuquerque, New Mexico, or in El Paso, where people still need literature to reflect on their condition. That's what literature does.

**F. J.:** What is the job for educators in this new urban landscape when we come across our Hispanic-American students? Is it to bring out their Hispanicity more or to make them mainstreamed? Is it to encourage their use of Spanish versus their use of English, or to get them to use both? Is it to rouse a sense of the colonized individual in them?

**Anaya:** I think our role as educators is to give them a real grounding in what we call the humanities, to help them read the classics and good literature and world literature and the literature of their group—to read the Chicano writers. If we are *not* to become the new colonizers, our role is to set them free. That's always been the role of the teacher. So I don't see that that role has changed; in fact, it's more crucial now than ever because the American popular culture has such a grip on young people. It inculcates them with a world view and a system of values that is so empty and void and has so little meaning that we are poised at a perfect point in history in terms of telling young people look, there is good literature—read it, there is history—read it, reflect on it, find yourselves and go out and do something good for mankind, for people.

**F. J.:** What classics would you have them read?

**Anaya:** World classics from all cultures of the world. If you're talking about Hispanics students now, Chicano students, I would say that would include a lot of the mythology and the classical thought of indigenous, pre-

Hispanic America. Also read the contemporary Chicano writers, but read them always with a sense of fulfilling yourself.

**F.J.:** What tradition do you see yourself writing in, or what tradition would you like to see yourself in? I guess I want to make this a two-part question. What have been the literary influences on you, and what tradition do you see yourself in? Did the influences on you come from American literature, British literature, or indigenous Hispanic literature, or indigenous Native American literature? And should the Chicano writers be seen as part of a stream of American literature?

**Anaya:** I think the influences came from all of those sources, including some of what I call the world classics. I consider myself very much a Chicano writer, but I think eventually we will be one more voice in that make-up of what is the literature of the United States. Eventually, I would like to see that what I have written and what I am writing is a search for a unique person, a person that has not been written about very much in the literature of the United States, and a person that is not known in this country. There is this New World person, essentially he is a mestizo, he is myself and that's what I've been exploring in my writing.

# Rolando Hinojosa

Writers who are bi- or multilingual are necessarily faced with the question of language: In which language do I write? What are the consequences and implications of that choice? These questions that go with the ability to write in more than one language are faced by many writers around the world, as the reflections of Ngũgĩ, Farah, and other writers show. As we have seen, the situation of a Chicano writer, a writer of Mexican descent living in the United States, has some important similarities to that of other writers in English from around the world in terms of this bilingualism and also in terms of biculturalism, the seemingly inevitable tension between Anglo-American and one's own cultural norms. But the choice between languages is somewhat different for a Chicano writer from that faced by other bilingual writers from around the world, because the Chicano writer does not have to choose between a regional or ethnic language and a national language or between a national language and an international language. Spanish is a major international language just as English is, and each has hundreds of millions of speakers and readers in many different countries.

Of all the Chicano writers, Rolando Hinojosa is the one who has best expressed and taken advantage of this situation. Most Chicano writers write in English, though usually with an admixture of Spanish words. Some write in Spanish, and a few write in a mixture of Spanish and English that can be understood only by comparably bilingual readers. Hinojosa began writing in Spanish and was the first Chicano writer to win significant attention in Latin America, winning the prestigious Casa de las Americas Prize in 1976 for his second novel, *Klail City et sus alrededores*. But he has also written several novels in English and is increasingly considered one of the most important Chicano writers in English as well. Most interestingly, he has also translated or re-created, as he likes to say, three of his novels written in Spanish into English. Two of these, *Estampas del valle* and *Klail City et sus alrededores*, were initially translated by someone else and published in this country in facing page bilingual editions; subsequently, Hinojosa re-created them as *The Valley* and *Klail City*. The only thing he has not tried is to re-create some of his English-language works into Spanish.

Born in 1929, Rolando Hinojosa teaches creative writing in the English department at the University of Texas, Austin. And the conversation that follows is a composite of conversations with him in Austin and on a visit to the University of Texas, El Paso. Hinojosa is like Anaya in that he takes his position as a respected senior Chicano writer seriously, so he does a good deal of travelling to other colleges and universities in Texas and across the Southwest and the rest of the country, encouraging younger writers and arguing for the importance of Chicano (and more broadly, Latino) writing and culture. And the sense shared by Hinojosa and Anaya that writers have responsibilities beyond simply writing is one more link between their work and the work of the other writers included in this book. Hinojosa has a sharp sense of the difference between his relation to his culture and that of Anglo writers, and everything he says below on this score would be seconded by Achebe, by Ihimaera, by Ngũgĩ.

**Reed Dasenbrock**: One of the distinguishing features of your work is that you write both in Spanish and in English. As a writer, how do you approach the demands imposed on you by this situation? Do you write in both languages at the same time?

**Rolando Hinojosa**: Well, as you know, the first two novels I wrote were in Spanish, *Estampas del Valle* and *Klail City et sus alrededores*. I wasn't compelled to do one language or the other, but I wanted to write in Spanish and then I found that I had made the right choice because the people I was describing were 95 or 100 percent Spanish-speaking. It felt very natural for me to write *about* them in Spanish and then to have them talk about themselves or their doings in Spanish.

**Feroza Jussawalla**: How did you get to using English in your writing then?

**Hinojosa**: I started to write the third work—*Korean Love Songs* (1979)—in Spanish because I'd done the first two in Spanish. They had been successful and I was going to be talking about the same people. But after I started in Spanish, I wasn't happy with it. Then I realized that I was talking about the Army, which is an all-American institution, which is an all English-speaking institution, and all the orders were given in English, so I said, "My goodness, what am I doing? I'm wasting my time." English was the only language for that situation. Giving an order in Spanish when the order had been originally given in English—well, it didn't function at all.

The fourth work, which was written, completed, but not published, in 1978, carries a Spanish title, *Claros varones de Belken*. I wrote it in Spanish and then I helped the translator translate it into English. And it was right that I write it in Spanish because *Claros varones* has to do with immediately after the Korean War. The present generation has not been born yet, and the generation that I know very well, my generation, we were in our twenties then, so we still had one leg in the Spanish background and an emerging leg into the English background. Because the young Korean War veterans return to the Rio Grande Valley, to their Spanish-speaking milieu, I began it in Spanish. But then when I transfer the novel up to Austin, to the university, English begins to creep in. Then, when they go back home, either on vacation or for the longer vacation in summer, they go back to Spanish.

R.D.: Up to that point then, one could have said that your choice of language was largely determined by the choice of language of your characters?

Hinojosa: And by where they were at the time, and by the different situations. Then with the fifth work, *Mi querido Rafa* (1981; *Dear Rafe* in English), an epistolary work, things begin to get complicated. In it, one of my recurring characters, Jehú Malacara, is working in a bank. When he first writes to his cousin, Rafa (or Rafe), it's in Spanish. Though he wrote his letters in Spanish, because he spent eight hours in the bank where English is spoken at all times, English would very naturally creep in to his letters, as it does. Once you are in the world of business, then English has to muscle in, at all times. And then, as the letters go on, I noticed that English becomes quite natural to him. He maintains the Spanish, but the English is always there. And this is analogous to the whole Texas-Mexican experience: once you leave that Spanish-speaking neighborhood, English is bound to take over.

F.J.: What amazes me about *Dear Rafe* in particular is that the English he writes in those letters is almost the kind of English my students speak, picking up the intonations of Spanish, using colloquialisms, etc.

Hinojosa: Two things are important here. First, he is completely at home in English, so he can use slang or very learned English or foreign languages. But also, the form of the novel is epistolary, and because the person to whom he is writing these letters is his cousin Rafe, with the same age, same background and just as good an education as Jehú has had, he can fool around with the language. Since letters to cousins or friends are not business letters, he goes back and forth in one language or the other. He knows, of course, as bilingual people do when they use bilingual language, that he can be understood.

**F.J.**: Did I miss that then? Is there a lot of code-switching and mixing in *Dear Rafe*? Do they go back and forth?

**Hinojosa**: Not in *Dear Rafe*, the English version, but in the original, *Mi querido Rafa*, there is a lot of English mixed in with the Spanish. He begins with a lot of Spanish, but as the bank job becomes more and more with him, the Spanish begins to be invaded by English. And this is not just because of business. When people at home speak both languages, we tend to code-switch, to mix them. Sometimes we use them for emphasis. Sometimes one word or a set phrase does not come readily in one language but it does come in the other. Knowing that you are going to be understood, you use it. And the other guy is going to respond the same way.

So by the time I wrote *Rites and Witnesses* (1982), Jehú was now more than hip deep into the English-language milieu, so it's completely in English. And the same thing with *Partners in Crime* (1985). Between *Partners in Crime* and *Rites*, I wrote *Dear Rafe*, which was the English version of the *Mi querido Rafa* that started the whole thing.

This is close to a conversation I had with Tomás Rivera years ago. I told him that I had noticed that although he and I spoke Spanish, and we wrote it, and we both had Ph.D.'s in Spanish, because we were both departmental chairmen and later, eventually, deans, and then vice presidents of institutions, that we conducted all of our business in English because that's the way it was. But once we reverted either on a more social basis, drinking beer, eating, or with our families, or going back to the old place, Spanish would return. So, we both agreed that English has made it impossible for Spanish to rear its head again, as it had, in the earlier works.

**R.D.**: If your choice of language is dictated by the language of the community and the evolution of the community over the past thirty or forty years has been largely from Spanish to English, then are you going to go on writing predominantly in English? Or will you continue to write in both languages?

**Hinojosa**: I think that English is an imperative when you have the English language in a majority. But Spanish is going to be the imperative if I decide to go back and tell some more of the prehistory, "pre" meaning prior to, say, the 1930s or 40s. As soon as I go back to the older generation which was absolutely fluent in Spanish, my characters will reveal that. But as I'm coming up more and more to, say, 1972 in *Partners in Crime*, with the changes in the Valley, many of the young Chicanos or Texas-Mexicans are not as fluent in Spanish as I was, or as my generation and the previous generation were. So my novels will always reflect the truth of what is being said, spoken, thought of, in that particular language. I think English will predominate, but Spanish will never completely disappear.

**R.D.**: So there will be Spanish words and phrases, but probably the predominant language will be English?

**Hinojosa**: Yes, I think so.

**F.J.**: Are you speaking here for your own work or for Chicano writers in general? For certainly some Chicano writers feel very strongly that this move from Spanish to English ought to be resisted and is an unfortunate development.

**Hinojosa**: The unfortunate side of it is commercial. If I write in one language or the other, it's usually because of the necessity to present the people the way they are. But this overpublication of English or underpublication of Spanish may be due to the publishers themselves, who are looking for a more marketable product.

But because of the two thousand mile border, Spanish will not disappear. Spanish will not be the overwhelming language of communication of the Chicano or of the Mexican-American. With increased urbanization, English is going to be the language of commerce, and in the city acculturation calls for English. But here it is in the 1980s, and people continue to write in Spanish. It will never be the majority language, not in this country, at least, not in our lifetime. But it won't be disappearing any time soon.

**R.D.**: But someone might—this has often been done in the criticism of African literature—turn around, and then say, to write in a language is to be caught in its values, and therefore you can't transmit the original culture in another language. Translate that into Spanish, they might say—and certainly there have been Chicano activists who said "If you write in English, you cannot transmit those values of Chicano culture." What would you say to that?

**Hinojosa**: Well, the Russians who read Tolstoy were probably not bilingual in French and, as you know, Count Tolstoy wrote many pages in *War and Peace* in French! I think it's a narrow view on the part of some activists, and they don't give the people who read enough credit to think and to make up their minds for themselves. I'm not prescriptive in that regard; I'm not a pharmacist. I still think that people can make up their own minds, and they know exactly how people treat them in one language or the other. I may have thought that twenty years ago, that by using English, I would be playing into somebody else's hands. I wanted to write in Spanish because I thought it was important. I still do. But I also want to write in English because I think that's very important, and I think that people are not going to be easily led or misled one way or the other.

F.J.: This whole discussion of writing in English or Spanish is close to a debate going on in African literature, where the Kenyan writer Ngũgĩ has said that he is going back from English to write in Gĩkũyũ.

Hinojosa: But if he wants to reach people and explain to them about the Gĩkũyũ experience, he needs a common language like English which the majority of Africans can read. He has effectively cut himself off. If Chatto & Windus or Heinemann will publish a Kenyan writing in English, then their distribution and their marketing can reach more effectively more Africans and more of us who are interested in the Third World. He then very effectively cuts me off if he writes about the Gĩkũyũ experience in Gĩkũyũ.

R.D.: So your sense is that we don't need to be quite so worried about the politics of a particular language choice?

Hinojosa: You always have to trust the reader. Five readers are going to read at five different levels. Once you've sold the book and somebody plunks down his or her money, there isn't a thing you can do about it. You have to trust the reader, always. I speak German, but not well, and I read German, but not well, but I've read everything by Heinrich Böll, and I think Leila Vennewitz, the translator, transmits to me exactly what Heinrich Böll wants transmitted. If I were to take the other extremist attitude, then I would never read him or Gunter Grass, or anybody else.

R.D.: Perhaps the question is whether translation is possible or impossible. And you believe it is possible.

Hinojosa: Yes, and that's why I tried it. Writing in Spanish, and then going into English, or writing some in English, as I have.

R.D.: But if you're bilingual and the community you're writing about is bilingual, why not write in both languages at once? It seems to be that someone like Anaya in *Bless Me, Ultima* or Alurista, of course, has enough

Spanish that it's sometimes very difficult for an Anglo reader to understand. They are in effect writing in both languages at once rather than worrying about the choice between them.

Hinojosa: More with Alurista than with Anaya. Anaya is a novelist, so he has to really go 99 percent English, and then throw Spanish words in, say like Hemingway, or anybody else. When you say Alurista, of course, you're thinking of the early Alurista, the Alurista of ten years ago. Alurista narrows down the readership. You have to be absolutely bilingual to read him. I'm not sure whether he cares one way or the other, or cared about it at the time. Now he's moved away from that and on to something else. He's doing all sorts of pyrotechnics with language.

R.D.: Do you think there's a cost to that narrowing of the audience to just a bilingual one? And you don't want to narrow the audience in that way?

Hinojosa: That's something I've thought about, because I know that if I write in Spanish, I'm going to have a good readership in Mexico, in Central and South America, and in Europe more than among Chicano readers in the U. S. If I write solely in English, then the audience in the U. S., Chicano or non-Chicano, will find it more accessible. And if we really want to tell our perspective of our life in the Southwest for the last one hundred and fifty-some-odd years, then we're going to have to have that wider audience.

R.D.: Should the writer try to broaden that audience as opposed to just speaking to his own people?

Hinojosa: Yes, otherwise it's self-defeating. Why should the writer write for himself? It isn't therapy, and you don't want to write for the closet. Writers want to show off. We may not want to show off, but we want to show off what we have, and to tell at least as many sides as we can.

R.D.: What do you feel about the success—artistic success—of those sorts of bilingual or interlingual works?

Hinojosa: I think that the artistic success is always measured by the talent of the person. I enjoyed—and still enjoy—some of Alurista's sixties and mid-seventies material because not only was it interesting—to use that neutral word—linguistically, but it was also pleasing.

R.D.: So you would partially separate the question of success in aesthetic terms from success in terms of communication. The bilingual work can be successful aesthetically, but it just doesn't communicate its meaning to that many people.

**Hinojosa**: Not if the writer wishes to reach a wider audience, and writers write for that particular reason, to prove certain points. But to prove it not to the faithful, because that's old hat, but to prove it to many other people. Feroza reads it, and she's a native of India, and her English allows her then to read it on the same level of comprehension, understanding, and even of pleasure, as someone else five or ten thousand miles away who has a different background even from hers or from mine who wrote the work in the first place.

I am not a romanticist. I know that the kids that I now teach here at the university from the Rio Grande Valley, where I was born in Mercedes, are not as well-versed in Spanish as I am. But if they can still write in English about what's happening to them or what they see and witness, and what lies there before them, then the language will serve as a communicator, but not as a destroyer of the original culture. It's a transmitter, and it's just one of those things. I have no fear whatsoever that English can overtake the culture.

**R.D.** So, what led you to do your own versions of your Spanish works?

**Hinojosa**: People were complaining that the flavor wasn't there in the translation. What they also failed to see was that the translator did the best under the circumstances.

**R.D.**: So you weren't working with the translators at that point?

**Hinojosa**: No. I worked a little with the second one, *Generaciones y Semblanzas*, but none at all with the first.

**R.D.**: So what happens in this re-creation? What's it like? Do you have a sense of a reader when you're doing this? There's been a lot of discussion about who is the right kind of reader of a bilingual text.

**Hinojosa**: For these three re-creations, I was using myself as a reader. Am I happy with what I'm doing? Is this faithful to the original work that I did in Spanish now that I'm doing it in English? I'm completely bilingual in one, and I'm completely bilingual in the other. I can go back and forth, as you know. But, does the writing sound right to me? How truthful am I? How accurate am I? And at the very same time, I obviously want to tell my story. So all of these things come into play. And thus I keep myself in mind. Is this believable? How true is this? Am I getting as close as I can?

**R.D.**: So you hope to create something which will work as well for the Anglo reader as the Spanish will for the Hispanic reader.

Hinojosa: Yes. Whether the Anglo reader has never heard of my work and sees it for the first time, he should accept it as that. And the same goes for the Spanish reader.

R.D.: When you do these re-creations, do you sit there with the original and then translate page by page? Or do you really start fresh?

Hinojosa: I see myself as a re-creator. That's why I think it took me eight or nine years before I sat down to actually do it. When I sat down with the original publication of *Estampas*, I did not look at the English version, I concentrated on the Spanish.

R.D.: But you do go page-by-page from the Spanish to the English? *The Valley*, for example, is so different from *Estampas del Valle* that one might have thought you just started afresh. What is the relationship between the original and the re-creation?

Hinojosa: As I was reading, I said, "You can't say this in English, it doesn't work word by word." I'd use an English idiom. But not only that, I also have to use something else to let the person know that this person is a Texas-Mexican. Once in a while, I will use Spanish words that are universal and therefore need no explanation. But if I think that something needs to be said in Spanish, for whatever reason, I will use it, and then put the English version, or translation, or re-creation, or flavor of it immediately. You'd be surprised! The reader tends to gloss over a lot of things, like "he said."

R.D.: So the reader can gloss over the Spanish that he may not understand in the same way that he can gloss over "he said," "they said."

Hinojosa: And from the context the reader can sometimes understand what the outcome is—negation, acceptance—even if it's entirely in Spanish.

R.D.: But if you leave key words untranslated because they can't really be translated, how does the Anglo reader pick up on the resonances of the word? Here, I'm thinking of a word like *la raza* which you tend for obvious reasons to leave in Spanish. Race doesn't quite work as an English equivalent.

Hinojosa: No, you're right. But one has the phrase "the people" which is different from "people." Or, you use "us" and "us" works well in the created context.

R.D.: So you are freer than a translator of your own work would be, because you're freer to discard what doesn't work in a more literal translation. But you've got at least one eye on a monolingual reader in order to cushion that reader, to give that reader what he needs in order to understand you whereas a translator again would have to stick more to the given terms of the work.

**Hinojosa:** Absolutely. But when I did the re-creation, the responsibility of putting the thing down on paper was as burdensome on me because then I said "Well, wait a minute! I'm responsible for both versions, so I don't want to fool around, and I want to put out what I think."

**R.D.:** You remind me of the story about Borges, that when Norman Thomas di Giovanni was translating his *El Hacedor*, Borges said, "the English title must be *The Maker*." And di Giovanni said, "that's not really a very good translation of *el hacedor*," and Borges said, "No, but I was thinking of the English word 'maker' when I wrote *hacedor*." So there's a similar kind of movement back and forth. Do you see yourself doing the same thing to your English works into Spanish? Could you re-create *Partners in Crime* in Spanish? And I ask this because of all your novels it seems the deepest into an English-speaking milieu, the world of English-speaking banks, the police, etc.

**Hinojosa:** I don't think so.

**R.D.:** Have you ever thought about it?

**Hinojosa:** No, I had not thought of it. I wanted to write it to show the different changes in the Valley in 1972, which is completely different—day and night—from *Estampas del Valle* or *The Valley*. I had never thought of writing it in Spanish. I'm not even sure that I would want to at this stage. Lord knows what I'm going to say ten years from now, because I hear myself saying what I was saying about *Estampas* ten years ago. I said, "No, I'll never translate it!" But no, I don't think that I would like to do *Partners* in Spanish at this time.

**R.D.** I'm thinking here of Vladimir Nabokov, who helped translate his Russian works into English, and then went back late in life and translated *Lolita* into Russian because he said he imagined the problems a translator would have with it and he wanted to forestall that.

**Hinojosa:** He certainly has historical precedent for that. Russian literature in the nineteenth century, when Dostoevsky, Turgenev, Pushkin, Gogol and of course Tolstoy were writing, the French translations of those Russian works were simply abominable. But there must have been something, as poor as the translations were, that let the careful reader and critic say, "This is excellent work! With a good translation this would . . . or this really should be ransomed." And they were, luckily for us. But it doesn't always work out that way.

F.J.: I want to shift a bit here. We've been talking about the issue of language in a fairly technical way. But what about the politics of language? Are the characters in the *Klail City* series a colonized people?

Hinojosa: Yes, they may have a colonized mentality, and it may work in this way. They are so colonized that in the 1980s they are afraid to fight for their own rights because they're afraid that the majority of the population of the United States may look on them unfavorably. The other part of the colonized mentality is that which just embraces a brand new culture foreign to them, without even understanding the new culture and, worse, without even having realized or understood *their* own culture and language. It's those inhibited by this colonial mentality that wish to turn their own back on their own history.

F.J.: Are our Hispanic students aware of this? Do they have this sense of themselves as colonized individuals?

Hinojosa: I don't think they can even think in those terms. They're probably still down to the basics that most of us begin with—food and shelter and clothing. Resentment is there, yes, whether they can articulate the resentment or the reasons for the resentment. But I don't think that they are intellectually sophisticated enough to formulate a philosophy, although they can garner a lot of the culture from their parents and grandparents who can tell them the way things were. The kids can probably say, "Well, it hasn't changed very much for me," while not realizing that they're thinking in English or expressing themselves in English.

F.J.: When I use Anaya's *Bless Me, Ultima*, which I sometimes do in Freshman Composition, they immediately identify with Antonio's name becoming Americanized into Tony and with the scene where his schoolmates laugh at him because he's eating tortillas instead of sandwiches. They immediately identify with this, but they don't see it as a message of decolonization. They miss the politics.

Hinojosa: The statement Rudy Anaya is making there may be too subtle for some readers but it's a strong statement, too. Yesterday, I was in Austin waiting for my plane, and there was a young man and a young woman there. Everyone's waiting for the plane, and she is eating breakfast. What is she eating for breakfast? Flour tortillas with whatever is mixed up in it—just what Tony is being made fun of for eating in *Bless Me, Ultima*. And I thought, "Isn't that nice?" Now that the majority of the population has legitimized eating tacos for breakfast, it's perfectly OK even to eat them in airports.

But the sad part of the scene in *Bless Me, Ultima* is that the kids who are making fun of Tony are also Mexican. They're little city boys from that little town and they're poking fun at this rural Mexican who's eating tacos.

**F.J.**: But they're not all Mexican because he talks about walking into the classroom and seeing a lot of blond heads.

**Hinojosa**: But the kids he eats with, Horse and Bones, are Mexican, and they will discriminate: a city boy versus a country boy. But *Bless Me, Ultima* is a political novel, I have to agree with you. I think it is misread by a lot of people. They like to see the mysticism, but there's really no mysticism. I think Rudy writes in a very straightforward way about what bothers him.

**F.J.**: In your work, you seem less concerned with that theme of city and country than the juxtaposition of the Texas Anglos and the Texas Hispanics. Do you see a difference between the Valley and here in El Paso, in the way in which people mingle?

**Hinojosa**: I don't know the El Paso experience fully, but I can speak of the Valley experience. When I went to school, I didn't have any Hispanic or Mexican teachers in any grade. I graduated from high school in 1946. By now, 90 to 100 percent of all the teachers and administrators are Mexican. That's a vast difference. What I'm capturing in my literature is what was happening then, what is happening now, and juxtaposing those two positions.

What El Paso is doing now, has been doing for the last ten years is what the Valley did twenty-thirty years ago. I turned on the television yesterday to see what was going on locally. I daresay that twenty years ago there wasn't a Spanish-speaking person as a television announcer. But now there are, the staff development people in the schools are Mexican. It's a very subtle thing, but it's in a formative state.

**F.J.**: Yet it's not changing. Last year there was a big fuss because the mayor didn't want Spanish spoken in the City Council.

**Hinojosa**: That's one man. Will this change in El Paso? It has to. Why?

It's in the nature of things to change and if you don't change then El Paso disappears as an important city.

R.D.: There's a related question here to the questions of language and culture, which is the question of audience. Is the communicability of your work connected to that immediate context? Imagine a reader who isn't bilingual, who doesn't know the Valley, doesn't know Chicano culture or the Southwest. What's he going to make of all this?

Hinojosa: I think it communicates beyond the immediate context, because of the theme and the topic one covers. One recognizes justice and injustice, chicanery and abnegation, self-sacrifice and bull-headedness. Those are all universal attributes! *(Laughter)* People are people, and they can see what's there. They recognize the types. They may see it in a different context, because of their own peculiarity or their own political ideology. Whenever I see a review of mine, say of *Dear Rafe* in *The New York Times*, reviewers seem to say, "Oh, well, it's about those people down in Texas." But when they read it, they realize that they're not just those people down in Texas.

R.D.: So it's not just that translation across language is possible but translation across cultures as well?

Hinojosa: Yes. When in Faulkner, Eck or some of those people talk, like the Texan in *Spotted Horses*, it's the native regional speech that Faulkner attributes to them. But what they're doing really binds every culture. When Flannery O'Connor writes about the artificial nigger, you realize that it's not Flannery O'Connor who's against the black in any way, but maybe young Nelson who's uninstructed and *dumb* beyond belief. That goes across any culture. Again, you have to trust the reader.

R.D.: I'm glad you brought up Faulkner because I wanted to bring him up. *(Laughter)*

F.J.: Yes, how did you come to create Klail City, Belken County?

Hinojosa: I thought it was important for me to have my characters living in a place that I knew. So I transformed the Rio Grande Valley into different cities and one big fat county, which is Belken. Even though I don't live there or work there, I needed a place. Once I set the place, I decided I would draw a map to help me. And by drawing a map this gave me a direction as well.

F.J.: This seems to be a trend that has gone through to Third World writers. Narayan created a place, Achebe created a place.

**Hinojosa**: Naipaul created a place.

**F.J.**: Why do you think that's important? Are they just proceeding in a Faulknerian tradition?

**Hinojosa**: Before Faulkner, in the nineteenth century, Balzac created his own Paris. He used Parisian streets and boulevards, but it was the one he had in mind. And right after Balzac, Benito Pérez Galdós wrote about Madrid. In Anthony Powell's *A Dance to the Music of Time*, which begins in 1920 and ends in the 1960s, he creates society in London. So although he's using a real London and Balzac a real Paris and Galdós a real Madrid, they're just as fictional as my Belken or Narayan's Malgudi.

**R.D.**: But I had another connection to Faulkner in mind. It's not just that he set all his books in one place but also that they're interconnected, that characters from one book reappear in the others. One of the experiences I have reading your work is that I keep finding connections between the works. Usually, this is quite satisfying, but sometimes I wonder, "Now, am I going to find out about this in a later work?"

**Hinojosa**: I'm not as psychologically deep as Faulkner is with his characters, but I have more characters because I have another intent than his, which is the way it should be. Sometimes, I don't know where the characters are. I'm not being cute or saying that they control me: no, I control the characters. But sometimes I don't know all their prehistory. First I wrote *Mi querido Rafa*, then I wrote *Rites and Witnesses*, and yet, *Rites and Witnesses* takes place before *Mi querido Rafa*. So in some ways, *Mi querido Rafa* helped me write *Rites and Witnesses*. Then when I wrote *Dear Rafe*, I made some changes to show that Rafe was already a lieutenant of detectives. So by now, I'm already thinking of *Partners in Crime*, don't you see?

**R.D.**: I guess my question would be, is there therefore a "right" order to read your work?

**Hinojosa**: I don't think so. I think they can be read independently. And if you read them linearly, say *Estampas, Klail City, Korean Love Songs, Mi querido Rafa, Rites and Witnesses, Dear Rafe, Partners in Crime*, and then *Klail City* (in English) after *Partners in Crime*, it'll just keep filling more and more. What I really want the reader to do is to know these people well. Many of the people who've read my stuff know the characters so well—as you do—that we talk about them as if we could expect them to be sitting here with us.

**R.D.**: That takes us back to Faulkner. I taught *Absalom, Absalom* last fall, and there is always a big question to face when teaching that novel. It's largely being narrated by Quentin Compson, who commits suicide in *The Sound and the Fury*. So do you let the class know that this narrator commits suicide or not?

**Hinojosa**: Oh, it'd be very hard, wouldn't it?

**R.D.**: My instinct is always to wait and wait and wait, but if you've read *The Sound and the Fury* first, it's a very different book you're reading because you're reading it with the awareness that this narrator commits suicide.

**Hinojosa**: Oh absolutely, yes, yes!

**R.D.**: With your work, as with Faulkner's, comes the question, less whether there's *a* right itinerary, but whether there are better itineraries, or worse itineraries?

**Hinojosa**: I don't think that there would be a better or a worse one. I like to write them independently. And if one is all you ever read, then you'll say, "Well, there it is, whatever this is." But if you read the others, fine. It's not like, say, Anthony Powell's *A Dance to the Music of Time*, which is linear. And when he mentions a minor character, say, in *Books Do Furnish A Room*, well, yes, we met him first in Casanova's Chinese Restaurant. But I wonder how many people really remember unless you write a thesis on it? Well, I didn't write a thesis, but I have that type of memory, and I like to remember, and I enjoy Powell very much, so I know who the minor character is and remember him still.

**R.D.**: But there is one right way through Powell's work, whereas yours is more like Faulkner's where there's this criss-cross?

**Hinojosa**: Yes, and also, as you know, I enjoy having two, three, four, five different narrators. All of a sudden, you discover a new narrator. Then if you know it's Jehú, then you say, "Oh well, I'm back with my old friend." Or if it is Rafe, you say, "Well, I'm back with Rafe," or somebody else. I find that this method gives me a lot of freedom to write.

**F.J.**: But isn't that the world of the oral tradition, in which these stories are passed on? This seems another way your work resembles non-Western writing: Raja Rao has an old woman telling the story in *Kanthapura*.

**Hinojosa**: Yes, the South is very oral. Faulkner does too. And Texas, whether people want to believe it or not, is a very Southern state. J. Frank Dobie made it into a Western state and Hollywood fostered that myth. But

Texas is a southern state: slaveholding, member of the Confederacy, popu-
lated originally by Southerners, a Southern state. Very Southern, very rural,
so with an oral culture.

**F.J.**: But Mexican culture comes in here as well, doesn't it? Your father
was in Mexico during the Mexican Revolution, wasn't he? How does that
form part of your family, your oral history?

**Hinojosa**: My family has lived in the Valley, the Rio Grande Valley, since
1749, so we've been Spanish, then Mexican, then American citizens. But
those categories aren't really exclusive. Because of the proximity of my
home town, Mercedes, we have relatives on both sides of the border. It's a
jurisdictional barrier, not necessarily a cultural barrier. When the Mexican
Revolution started in 1910, my father was twenty-three, I think. And with
the spirit of adventure of young men that age, he leaves home, along with
other men his age, Texas Mexicans from the United States, to fight in the
Revolution. That's bound to affect a whole generation, through stories and
myths and legends. As I'm growing up, these men talked about the Mexican
Revolution night after night after night as if it were still a living, pulsating,
vibrating thing. There are many other Chicano writers who also write about
the Revolution—not to any great length or even intensely but it's usually
mentioned.

**R.D.**: Of course, there's José Antonio Villareal's novel about the Mexican
Revolution, *The Fifth Horseman*.

**F.J.**: Is it as much a part of their lives, though?

**Hinojosa**: I don't know. It was a large part of our lives because my father
was still coming and going back and forth to Mexico. He was still involved
in it in the 1940s. That had become a way of life to him so it was very
important to me too.

But you've been touching on something that's very important—the oral
aspect of this literature. Because of the dual language and because some of
the older folks spoke no English whatsoever, that maintained the oral tradition of passing history on. It's very important to the characters in my
books that they identify by name and place who was married to whom. And
when someone forgets something, the other members of the conversation
chide him and say, "Boy, you losing your head. You can't even recall who
this person is." Then if he makes a mistake again, they correct him and

pretty soon he falls into line and then he knows who he is related to. This is a very important feature of oral literature.

R.D.: But is that being carried on today?

Hinojosa: Yes. What these youngsters, Rafe, Jehú and some of the others, are caught up in is that they are being educated in English and writing in English, but they are very oral, they are not losing their Spanish tradition. Rafe can talk to the old about history, about the Valley. There's a lovely conversation between him and an old, old aunt of his. She says something like, "Do you remember that salt well? It belonged to a family called . . ." and he says, "Oh yes, they lost the land to the Leguizamon family." She reacts and says, "How in the world do you know that?" Well, he has never left the community. He has gone through college, the Army, his professional life, but he is still attuned to the place. Not many youngsters his age would be, but he happens to be.

F.J.: So these themes run through the oral culture, a culture that transmits its history orally.

Hinojosa: Yes, it's a very interesting phenomenon. It's kind of Third World but it's also contemporary, and it's also Western. The commonality of course is that it is a people expressing itself through the written form as well as basing the written form on some form of oral tradition that they inherited.

R.D.: Your work obviously reflects that with its multiple narrators, nearly all of whom seem to be telling their story *to* someone.

Hinojosa: In *Claros varones*, it says on the title page, I'm not sure of the order, but these are the narrators: Rafe tells part, and then Jehú, and then P. Galindo, and then Jehú again, and then Rafe and Echevarria. There are four narrators, and at least three of them speak twice, so this allows me to present something I've always been interested in, which is a multiple perspective. Not only point of view which is what we teach our kids in the classroom, but the same fact seen by three different people.

R.D.: With this "heaping up" of perspectives, is there a sense that you put three or four perspectives together and you can sort out the truth, or is your sense more that, well, you have three or four perspectives, and you have three or four perspectives? *(Laughter)*

Hinojosa: That you have three or four perspectives. It's very difficult to know what the truth is—unless you're dealing with fact. At two-twelve, water boils. That's a fact. It takes longer for that fact to take place in Denver, but it's still a fact. But an opinion can be viewed in many ways. An opinion isn't worth a darn if the guy has no foundation, and it's worth more if he has more foundation. I don't know who is the best evidence, the actual witness, or someone who hears and retains more. I'm always being surprised at meetings that people hear such different things. And I say, "That's completely different from mine, or it coincides." So I said, "But this happens in real life, therefore, it has to happen in the novel."

**F. J.**: You experiment a good deal with form. Do you see yourself working in a kind of European modernist tradition, with the vignettes in your fiction?

**Hinojosa**: I operate that way for different reasons. I wanted to produce not one character in the nineteenth-century novel mode with redemption at the end for the woman or for the man. I wanted to present, say, the whole Texas-Mexican people as the protagonist.

**F. J.**: So it's not a conscious working in a modernist form.

**Hinojosa**: Well, it is a post-modernist form in many ways, too, in that the reader has to collaborate with the writer. It is modernist and it is post-modernist in many ways. But I use form not to do those things, not to show that I can do post-modernist or whatever. I use form as I will use any technique, to help me tell my story the way I think it should be told at that time. When I wrote *Mi querido Rafa* and then when I did the English *Dear Rafe*, I said, "I think that the epistolary would suit me here." But the epistolary is only good for part. You can't have the whole novel written that way. I'll only use it for half the novel because I want to present about twenty other points of view of people. There's a murder in the bar and the man who knifes the other person has his point of view. His brother-in-law, who is a witness, talks third, and in the middle talks the killer's sister who is wife to the witness. She wasn't even there but she has her own point of view. I like point of view because I don't know what the truth really is half the time and it isn't what people tell me it is all the time. Everyone sees things differently.

**R. D.**: Is that why you're interested in the detective story?

**Hinojosa**: Yes, I think so. I also wanted to use a detective story because it's linear. In *Partners in Crime* I decided to write a nineteenth-century novel with a beginning and an end. I just don't like to be restricted in one particular kind of writing. I wanted to show also, and I will continue to show, that the old values, that is those that were entrenched in the mid-eighteenth, held through more or less to the nineteenth, and then up to the twentieth century, are beginning to change. That the old families are beginning to break up. That there's new money, drug money, that presents a very false economy to the Valley. That new money cannot be invested, because it's a false economy. The money is being made in a nefarious way. Therefore, values will also change. The Valley will also change.

**R.D.**: *Partners in Crime* is your only work with an anonymous narrator?

**Hinojosa**: Yes. What I also wanted to do was to make Rafe a narrator. So sometimes, the anonymous narrator in *Partners* steps back, and then Rafe tells that one chapter from his point of view. Or Sam Dorson, his best friend, the other. And I wanted to use that, because I don't think you can get too literary in a detective story. Also I didn't want to say, "Well, it's more than a detective story."

**R.D.**: But it also seems appropriate to the economic changes you're talking about, in the sense that what emerges from the earlier work is a very richly textured oral society. One gets a very strong sense of the form of your novels being representative, not just of an oral culture, but of a small town culture, in the sense that X runs into Y, and they tell a story about Z. The different interviews of, say, P. Galindo in *Dear Rafe* are not that different from what one might experience wandering around that small town, whereas the voice of *Partners in Crime* is more impersonal.

**Hinojosa**: You need that. X stopping Y, as you said, on the street, is a personal thing. You just grab somebody by the arm, and says, "Let me tell you what I just heard."

**R.D.**: But there can't be that "Let me tell you about something" for drug smugglers.

**Hinojosa**: Not in this new society, either, because there you're taught the stories that are told behind closed doors.

**R.D.**: Or never told.

**Hinojosa**: That's better, or never told, yes. Therefore, a policeman, who has more information than anyone else, all he has to do is to look at the public records. Since that's all the policemen do, they usually know what's going on in town. And a banker like Jehú knows more than anyone else eventually because—

**R.D.:** But he isn't going to tell the story in the same on-the-corner way, is he?

**Hinojosa:** No. Even though he's so good and adept at it, now he has other responsibilities, so I have to use the anonymous narrator who takes a cold view of not what's happening to *my* place, but what's happening to *this* place? Look at these people, what's happening to the values? The narrator can't comment on values. He doesn't know what they are.

**R.D.:** It strikes me that the most typical chapter in one sense—though in another, the least typical—is the chapter where you simply list the bullet wounds, the report of the lab man. A chapter of absolute facts or absolute cold reporting.

**Hinojosa:** Yes, on those you can rely because those are observable items, and they are set down exactly. Since you can't really fix facts, I had to put them down that way. But it's also a marked contrast, not only with my previous writing, but also with what's happening in *Partners*. You come to that chapter, and you realize that these used to be human beings at one time, and now they're in bits and pieces. Very cold-bloodedly, no one says this or that, it's just set down.

**R.D.:** And the change from X meeting Y on the street corner to the impersonal narration of *Partners in Crime* is like the transformation from the agricultural economy to these corpses.

**Hinojosa:** That's exactly what I meant. Perfect. Absolutely.

**R.D.:** Going on from there, I just read *The Rolando Hinojosa Reader*, the collection of essays on your work, and I was wondering what you felt about the image of your work that emerges from those essays?

**Hinojosa:** I haven't read them all, I'm afraid. And I'll give you the reason why I haven't read them all. I am afraid of becoming mannered or stylized; where I'll start writing the way they said I write! And I'd rather not do that. I read the interview because I had given the interview, and I wanted to see it. And I have no quarrel with that. The questions were as nice as these here, I mean, where you can really talk. But I don't really wish to read too much of whatever people say about me because I may be inhibited. I don't know, maybe I have some sort of anxiety. But as long as I keep doing what I'm doing, then they're certainly free, of course, to write. That's why I don't write them letters, and say, "Yes, no, or whatever."

**R.D.:** I asked because the picture of your work that emerges from some of the essays—I don't have it here, so I can't refer to specific essays—is a very Marxist sense.

**Hinojosa:** But, then, maybe those critics are too, see?

**R.D.:** That's what I'm wondering.

**Hinojosa:** While I have no quarrel with any school of criticism, they're going to see it from their particular bent and perspective. I imagine that someone from historical criticism would look at it another way, etc.

**R.D.:** There are two parts to that Marxist criticism. First, looking at your work as opposed to many other American writers, one has a very strong sense of your representing a social-historical reality in your work. Certainly economic institutions are a very large part of that, the bank, and the KBC Ranch, and of course, the drug interests, as we have just been saying. But the Marxist line on your work would also say you are representing that in order to offer a critique of that society. And though the first seems right, I wonder about the second part. Is your work a critique of the American economy?

**Hinojosa:** I am interested in the economic thing because of the deprivation of education of many worthy American citizens who didn't receive an education because of racism. I'm sure a lot of it was racism or economic deprivation. I'm also attacking that society. But I'm attacking, not from a Marxist viewpoint that they see, but as a person who's outraged and should be outraged morally as a writer. One who says, "This is wrong, and it shouldn't be done." And I'm going to show how some of these things have deprived these people. But at the very same time, I'm also showing, which is probably going against the Marxist grain, that despite all of that, some of these people succeed, even without joining the other side.

**R.D.:** That's where I think the criticism falls short. It seems to me that one of the reasons why Rafe and Jehú are the central characters that have emerged in *Klail City Death Trip*, at least so far, is that they're the two who can put the two worlds together. This may be too crude a formulation of it, but they can be successfully bilingual, they're not giving up one or the other. They are successfully bicultural, in the sense that they remain deeply Chicano, or Texas-Mexican, or whatever, but they're also successful in that Anglo world. And they're also good.

**Hinojosa:** They're good people, yes.

**R.D.**: It seems to me in Jehú and in Rafe, you're dramatizing the possibility of people who can be a success and still give a damn.

**Hinojosa**: And there are many people like that. As there are many fools such as Ira Escobar, as there are many Polín Tapias, the political hack.

**R.D.**: But that seems to me where the Marxists would either misread you, or disagree with you in the sense that they would have to see a Jehú working in the bank as inevitably a degradation or inevitably a corruption.

**Hinojosa**: And choose not to see him in any other way but in those terms. But the chances are that other critics would see him in another way. That's why I can't afford to get pinned down. Wrong is wrong, and I don't care who does it. And although that sounds simple, it really isn't. Jehú's trying to work himself into retaining what he believes is right, and the only confidant he has who can understand him, in many ways, is his cousin. So he writes him. And Rafe, of course, helps, he counsels him. He says, "Don't forget who you are. Where we're from."

But it's very difficult for me to accept one or the other in criticism, because, to give one example, twenty-five years ago, generational grammar was the thing in linguistics, and it's probably old hat by now. Those people were very convincing to me when I was in Illinois in the early sixties, and now of course, they've been displaced by somebody else. The writer cannot afford to just do this one thing. You have to present everything. Then the critics come, and they do what they wish to do. Another set of criticism, by another school, would probably produce a completely different work.

**R.D.**: So one description of your work would portray the change from the 1920s and 1930s to the 1970s as degradation, as a corrupting, a falling away from an older way of life. Another, focusing more on Jehú and Rafe, could write a very optimistic history, could talk about these characters moving into certain kinds of professions as a triumph over racism. But you would prefer to escape both such descriptions?

**Hinojosa**: Yes, because some people are still being dropped by the wayside, and they don't "make it." But you and I know that Jehú has been many things in his young life. He's in his mid-thirties now. But you and I saw him as a schoolboy, we saw him as an orphan, and we saw him in some very interesting and odd jobs. And there's Rafe, more settled than Jehú. But Rafe has his own devils. His own father was murdered, and though I've never suggested that he became a detective because of that, maybe that's why he did! But we don't know *why* he did. What we do know is, he did not want to practice law. That much we do know. That much, I, as a writer, know.

But they have done all of these things, and yet they've managed to stay out of jail. Remember the Peralta twins in *Dear Rafe*? Same generation as Jehú and Rafe, but limited in their perspective. One of them even chides Jehú to P. Galindo, and he says, "Man, he doesn't even know how to protect his job!" But Jehú, whom they'll never understand, whom Martin San Esteban will never understand, can get up, and walk out of that job, just as he does in *Dear Rafe*! Just walks out of the bank and leaves. Then, of course, everybody starts criticizing Jehú, with or without foundation. But the twins cannot understand when someone who is resilient can do these acts or can take this decison. People say, "My God, he gave up a job at the bank." Or, "My God, that's a very high-paying job, or that's a tremendously responsible job." And then they'll say, "And for a Mexican to have that job, and then for him to walk away!" But Jehú doesn't think about it in those terms. And then three years later, how does he get his job in *Partners in Crime*?

**R.D.**: He just walks in.

**Hinojosa**: He walks into the office, and there's Esther Bewley. Nothing has changed. He has changed. And Noddy says, "What are you doing in my bank?" He swears at him, but in a loving way. No discussion about office or position or anything. The job is his. And people say, "Does that actually happen?" I said, "Yes, it does." All that shows is that some readers are not well versed in life. You can do a lot of things all of a sudden.

**R.D.**: Or, to put it another way, most books have more neatness than life, and you're attempting to escape from that.

**Hinojosa**: Yes, I am. Some things are so simple sometimes that you can just do it. Now it is important that a lot of my readers are in the academy. And admitted or no, like it or no, a lot of our professors, as wise and judicious and certainly bright as they are, are limited in their own life experience. All right, I too am a professor, just as they are, but there are ten years difference between my baccalaureate and my master's, and five years between the master's in 1962 and the Ph.D. in 1969. So, I'm forty years old when I get my Ph.D., so I'm infinitely older than a twenty-seven year old Ph.D., who's brighter and who can really assemble all manner of fact, and has a philosophy and his own critical school. But I wasn't interested in that. So, I know about the Army and I know about business, and all these different things have helped me as a writer. But also, it helped to see people and to see how some things can be quite uncomplicated, once you get into them and realize, "Ah, this wouldn't fool a child!" That's what Jehú says in *Rites and Witnesses* when he memorizes what the lawyer gives him on the transfer of a business transaction.

**R.D.**: But it works!

**Hinojosa**: But it works! I used to hold my chairman in awe, then I became chairman, then I became the dean, then I became a VP for Academic Affairs. I said, "This isn't a joke, but it isn't as tough as many of us think it is."

**R.D.**: I wanted to get to the academic question, and you've brought it up yourself. It seems to me—and this is one of the areas in which I think your work is a wonderful exception—that one of the worst things that has happened to American literature is the academy *(laughter)* in the sense that many writers have gotten university jobs. They end up either writing novels about being a professor or about writing novels and get caught up in a certain kind of formalist gamesmanship. Going back to what you said earlier, they probably take what the critics say about them a little too seriously and get more and more complicated.

**Hinojosa**: Yes! That can happen.

**R.D.**: How do you think you've avoided that? I would say that your work is a conspicuous exception to that.

**Hinojosa**: Well, maybe by just trying to be myself. And by going back in my own mind as to where I came from, and knowing that life is complicated enough without trying to play games internally in a book. I don't like to show off, although I may be showing off by saying I don't like to show off. I like to show off in other ways in the books, to surprise the reader and tell the reader, "You too can see this as well as I can." In short, I try not to obfuscate. Where it almost becomes a game, whose game is it?

**F.J.**: But would you consider your writing purely part of American literature?

**Hinojosa**: It's American literature and it is Chicano literature the way Faulkner's is Southern literature but eventually his is American. It is about people who live and work and die in this country. But at first we had to identify ourselves the way Sidney Lanier identified himself as a Southern poet, as Eudora Welty or Faulkner did. But it's American literature. It's not Mexican, for crying out loud, and it's certainly not Canadian. And it's not even regional because, although most of us came and still come from this area, the Mexican-American, Chicano, Hispanic experience is being felt all over now, in the United States. Kids who never thought of writing in Chicago realize who they are and what they are and begin to write about their experience. It's American; it can't be anything else.

F.J.: But isn't there a considerable debate about whether to call it "Hispanic" literature, "Chicano" literature, "Mexican-American" literature?

Hinojosa: I think the debate is not among the writers. It may be more among the critics. Writers spent enough time writing without worrying about what their work will be called.

F.J.: So you don't have a preference for one term over another?

Hinojosa: No, but I do know that it's American literature after 1846, whether we want to admit it or not. One of the things people were always bothered about was whether "Chicano" literature had been accepted or not. Chicanos were asking this all the time. This is the type of question being asked by colonized mentalities. Writers always spend a lot more time worrying about what they are going to write and where they are going. The assessment is by someone else.

R.D.: But still there is a big difference between the work you do and most contemporary American literature. What most contemporary American literature has focused on are quiet, private lives, psychological dilemmas.

Hinojosa: Yes. Eventually, who cares? On the other spectrum now, we have a lot of writers, as you just said, who are professors, a lot of professors who are writers, or an amalgam, who are writing experimental stuff, but they're not writing it for readers. Maybe for themselves, or their colleagues in other universities, for tenure, or whatever in the world they write it for.

R.D.: Would you link those two things, the kind of privatist, more psychological, often humorless fiction, and formalist gamesplaying? Do you see those as linked?

Hinojosa: Oh, I think that they are linked. I think it's part and parcel of the very same thing. But I don't want any part of it at all.

R.D.: Why has there been this withdrawal from public representation?

Hinojosa: I think it has to with the liquidation of history that we have done in this country of ours. After 1945, "the last war ever to be fought by this country," there was the churning of the product, you know, the market, which is fine. I'm a buyer, like everybody else. And then five years later, our hearts are broken by Korea. And Korea goes from 1950 to 1953, and how many books were written about Korea? You can't name me ten. And I'm not going to embarrass you because you can't even name me five novels that came out of Korea.

**R.D.:** I can name two, and they're both written by Rolando Hinojosa. *(Laughter)*

**Hinojosa:** So, we liquidated 1945 to 1950 because we're churning out housing, and we need new cars, and we need to get the economy going. So from 1950 to 1953 we have Korea, by 1954, we're already in Vietnam with advisors, under Eisenhower, but now we become very rich. So we turn inward, and these novels turn inward. I hope I'm not making too neat a package here.

**R.D.:** So we didn't want to write about these public events because—

**Hinojosa:** We're not well versed in them.

**R.D.:** And they didn't reflect well on us?

**Hinojosa:** And they did not reflect well on us.

**R.D.:** But certainly one of the ways which Southwestern literature written by, somewhat by Anglos and definitely by Chicanos, and by Native Americans, sharply differs from mainstream fiction is precisely because a lot of that social-historical material gets represented. I think of how important the Korean War is in your work, how important World War Two is for Leslie Marmon Silko's *Ceremony* or for Anaya's *Bless Me, Ultima* in different sorts of ways.

**Hinojosa:** Oh, yes. Well, look at the South. The Civil War lives on in American Southern literature, too, don't you see? When you and I were talking about American lit., we were not talking about the South, were we? We're talking about the Northeast, yes? What they read in New York, and New Jersey, and Connecticut.

**R.D.:** All right, so what's the difference? You were in the Korean War, but Silko didn't have any direct experience of World War Two. She wasn't even born yet.

**Hinojosa:** But she was touched and her characters were touched by it. What is it? We do not want to liquidate history. We don't live day to day. I'll give you a Flannery O'Connor story. She was finally convinced by one of her agents during her career to go to New York, and, of course, her mother was aged, and she herself was infirm, but she went. And here's a Southern woman, like us, the Southwesterners, and they said, "Well, what are those people like up there?" And her response was, "They're not from anywhere." That type of answer doesn't need explanations or footnotes, right? It tells it all about her, and about her way of life, and how many millions of Americans who are not New Yorkers or New Englanders feel, right? But it starts earlier than World War Two. It starts with Hemingway. Hemingway's not a European. He could no more describe France, and he could no more describe Spain, *real* Spain, the way a Spaniard could, or the way I, as a Spanish speaker, could probably get there after two or three years. He always wrote about Americans in Africa or in Europe or in certain parts of Europe. Now, I hate to use the word "roots" because I have nothing to do with Haley but—

**R.D.**: A sense of history and a sense of place are concomitant?

**Hinojosa**: Yes, and your own culture. What culture do you belong to?

**R.D.**: So you escape that because you have a sense of history, and because you have a sense of place?

**Hinojosa**: I think so. Absolutely. Having been in the Rio Grande Valley since 1749, when it was first colonized. It isn't New York, and we're not as suave, but if suave writing produces what they're writing, no thank you. But people prefer that, because it's heavy reading, don't you see? Mine is easy reading, but it really is heavy if you start getting into it, as you have, and some of the others. But it isn't a matter of weight. It's a matter of planting your feet. Some American poets do too, and many of us do in the South and Southwest. But over there, they seem to be in a forever-trip of transition.

**R.D.**: It strikes me that the topic of American ethnic literature has almost always been assimilation. And the problem is, once you've assimilated, what else do you have to write about?

**Hinojosa**: Well, they did assimilate. But it cost them a lot.

**R.D.**: A generation ago, I think *the* topic in Jewish writing was assimilation, but that's an impossible act to follow because what do you do after assimilation?

**Hinojosa**: Look at Joseph Heller in *Catch 22*. His protagonist is Yossarian, a lovely Armenian name. What would happen if Joe Heller wrote about a Jewish pilot? He picked "Yossarian" instead. He may say, "Well, I'm writing about America." No, you're not! You're still writing about that one little assimilated thing that didn't quite pan out for all of you.

**R.D.:** So you think someone like him is really evading his real subject?

**Hinojosa:** I think he evades. I think they evade. But also they make a lot of money, which is also very nice for them, you know! I call myself a writer, but I don't depend on writing. So I'm also not compromised by many things.

**R.D.:** But what's different is that many professors who don't need to depend on their writing therefore end up not writing to anyone other than themselves.

**Hinojosa:** Writing the type of stuff that you and I have been talking about.

**R.D.:** What's different about your work is that you're not trying to commercialize your writing, but you're also not making it so esoteric on the other hand.

**Hinojosa:** That's why I said, writing isn't a therapy, and you're not writing for the closet, you're really writing to be understood.

**R.D.:** Yes, it strikes me that that's one of the other ways in which your writing, and some of the work of Chicano writers and Native American writers, links up with world writing in English again. To go back to where we started, one of the differences between the Africans and the Asians, and the Pacific writers, and what I think of as the Anglo-American mainstream is again what emerges from your work: a very strong sense of place, a very strong sense of history, and a very strong sense of politics, a sense of represented content. Though I have never been to the Valley (or your part of the valley as I live near the Rio Grande too), from your work I have a sense of the history, and I get exactly the same sense from a Chinua Achebe in Nigeria, or a V. S. Naipaul in Trinidad, or R. K. Narayan in India. This is not a form versus content question, because some of these writers from around the world play formal games. and I think you play some formal games, but the difference is that your formal games are nonetheless in the service of something, whereas for a John Barth, or—

**Hinojosa:** Cheever.

**R.D.:** They're just ends in themselves.

**Hinojosa:** I think so.

**R.D.:** So it seems to me we're at a real funny moment in American literature, or literature in English, or whatever term you want to use, because it seems to me that being at the center, being completely assimilated into

Anglo culture, now seems to be a handicap. That it's precisely people in situations such as yours, despite some real material difficulties, who have the real advantages.

Hinojosa: Yes, because I don't think that they have any conflicts, do they, up there? And a lack of conflict also betrays lack of blood flowing somewhere. A lot of people who misread may think that that's deep psychological thinking. But it really isn't. They're writing about the same thing now, that they did ten years ago. And I said, "Well, there's less to this than meets the eye," as a New York critic once said. Deep psychological thinking is the ability to read people and the ability to bring them out the ways they say things. They don't have to be as ponderous as a Henry James thing, but actually knowing people, what people say, how they say, how they behave, or do not say, or what they stand for, or won't stand for.

R.D.: So then it's the tensions, if you want, in the world that you depict that gives that world life?

Hinojosa: Yes. That's what's saving us so far, but it'll come to us, too. It has to come to us. We're not in a period of decadence yet. But let's face it, I don't see many other Texas-Mexican novelists down the road either. (*Laughter*) Maybe it's my shortsightedness. Maybe there is somebody writing the way I was writing, and nobody will know about it until twenty years later.

R.D.: So your work may be the product of a very particular moment too.

Hinojosa: It may be, for all I know.

# Sandra Cisneros

Chicano literature, like many other new literatures in English, had a defining moment and generation in which several major talents suddenly emerged. The moment was the early 1970s, when in quick succession Tomás Rivera's *y no se lo tragó la tierra*, Rudolfo Anaya's *Bless Me, Ultima*, and Rolando Hinojosa's *Estampas del valle* were published. Rivera's career was tragically cut short by his death in 1984, but Anaya and Hinojosa have continued their careers, compiling the two most substantial bodies of work in Chicano literature.

The 1980s, in contrast, saw the emergence of Chicana literature, as it was the decade in which a group of strong, younger women writers emerged, including Ana Castillo, Denise Chavez, Gloria Anzaldua, and—most prominently—Sandra Cisneros. There are some strong continuties between the two generations and groups of writers: both tend to use a mosaic of discontinuous forms in place of a continuous, linear narrative, both draw on aspects of Latin American culture, and both write socially and politically involved works. But the social and political involvements of the younger women writers are often considerably different.

The work of Sandra Cisneros shows this most clearly. She was born in Chicago in 1954, and her first book of fiction, *The House on Mango Street* (1984) is about growing up in a Latino—but predominately Puerto Rican—neighborhood in Chicago. This is a milieu very far, both geographically and psychologically, from the traditional centers of Chicano population in the Southwest—Texas, New Mexico, Arizona, and California. These are places Cisneros has had to travel to, in order to see for herself the differences. She argues, however, that the distance between Chicago and Mexico made for a stronger identification with Mexico, and what she says in the following interview about the difference between being Chicano in Chicago and in Texas should dispel any notions about the homogeneity of the Chicano community in the United States. Even the term Chicano is contested, and as always in a colonial or post-colonial situation, there is no neutral, value-free vocabulary for the terms that shape and constitute identity.

Cisneros is the most powerful of the young Chicana writers, the one who has produced work that can clearly stand with the work of Anaya and Hinojosa. She has just published her second book of short stories, *Woman Hollering Creek*, and she has also published a book of poetry, *Wicked, Wicked Ways*. Her training as a poet is something she has put to good use in her ability to capture a multitude of voices in her fiction. But it is as a storyteller, a writer of fiction, that her greatest talents lie, and it is for this reason that her first novel is eagerly awaited. We were able to interview her in El Paso, Texas, when she was there for a week of readings and public appearances. She came to El Paso from Albuquerque, New Mexico, where she was teaching for a semester at the University of New Mexico.

**Reed Dasenbrock:** One of the things that the writers we are interviewing all have in common is that they are bilingual or multilingual. Like most Chicano writers, they may write in English but they know another language well. So I thought we might begin with some questions about language. The new stories you were reading last night—the stories in *Woman Hollering Creek*—struck me as having more Spanish in them than in your first book of stories, *The House on Mango Street*.

**Sandra Cisneros:** Yes. I'm much more conscious of the Spanish now. When I wrote *House on Mango Street*, I didn't know enough about mixing the languages. Also, I thought I was only a product of my English, but now I know how much of a role Spanish plays, even when I write in English. If you take *Mango Street* and translate it, it's Spanish. The syntax, the sensibility, the diminuitives, the way of looking at inanimate objects—that's not a child's voice as is sometimes said. That's Spanish! I didn't notice that when I was writing it. I thought that my father's Spanish was just something that I had at home, but years later, in France when I was writing a letter to someone in Spanish I realized, "This sounds like *House on Mango Street*." I started translating the letter, and I said, "This is *House on Mango Street*. This is where the voice comes from."

I made a conscious choice to move to Texas a few years ago precisely because I realized, "My God! This is what I grew up with in my house, and I hear it everywhere, and I need to live here because this is where I'm going to get the ideas for the things I need to write about." To me, it's exciting to be living in San Antonio, because to me it's the closest I can get to living in Mexico and still get paid. To me, San Antonio is where Latin America begins, and I love it. It's so rich. Everywhere I go I get ideas, something of the language, something in the people's expressions, something in the rhythm of their saying something in Spanish.

**R.D.:** So what does incorporating the Spanish explicitly do? How does it change things?

**Cisneros:** What it does is change the rhythm of my writing. I think that incorporating the Spanish, for me, allows me to create new expressions in English—to say things in English that have never been said before. And I get to do that by translating literally. I love calling stories by Spanish expressions. I have this story called "Salvador, Late or Early." It's a nice title. It means "sooner or later," tarde o temprano, which literally translates as late or early. All of a sudden something happens to the English, something really new is happening, a new spice is added to the English language.

**R.D.:** I noticed that one thing you do in the new stories is translate as you go along. You often give a phrase in Spanish and then quickly give maybe a third of it in English.

**Cisneros:** Sometimes.

**R.D.:** Not all of it.

**Cisneros:** No, I don't have to.

**R.D.:** What kinds of choices do you make there?

**Cisneros:** That's the fun part! See, sometimes you don't have to say the whole thing. Now I'm learning how you can say something in English so that you know the person is saying it in Spanish. I like that. You can say a phrase in Spanish, and you can choose to not translate it, but you can make it understood through the context. "And then my abuelita called me a sin verguenza and cried because I am without shame," you see? Just in the sentence you can weave it in. To me it's really fun to be doing that; to me it's like I've uncovered this whole motherlode that I haven't tapped into. All the expresiones in Spanish when translated make English wonderful. I feel like I haven't finished playing around. I just feel so rich, as though you've given me all this new territory and said, "Okay, you can go in there and play."

**R.D.:** And the source of this is what people actually say?

**Cisneros:** I also look at the written word. I look at a store, a pulqueria named "exquisitas" something or other. They would use the word exquisitas—exquisite—to mean rich, "exquisitas tacos." I like that. All of the sudden it makes me think of a different way of using the word exquisite.

**R.D.:** In English.

**Cisneros:** In English. So I'll start thinking, "How can I put that in a title?"

A word, an English word, will stay with me for a title or for a character or for a phrase. I just love words so much, I love seeing them on the sides of buildings or on menus or written on the floor.

**R.D.:** Do you think of your reader when you are playing back and forth between English and Spanish? Do you have a sense of—

**Cisneros:** Who's going to read it?

**R.D.:** Yes, "I've got an Anglo reader in mind here and therefore I had better translate it, or"—

**Cisneros:** You know who I think of? I think of a world reader. My standards are very high, and I really think of the writers I love the best. I'm trying to match them. And my favorite writers are, right now Merce Rodoreda, Grace Paley, Juan Rulfo, Manuel Puig, Marguerite Duras—these are my favorite writers. I'm trying to reach that world level. I think that we should always aim for that level.

**R.D.:** I was asking in terms of the bilingual situation. In terms of playing with the two languages, do you have an eye on a reader who doesn't know Spanish or are you writing to people who will be able to go back and forth with you from language to language?

**Cisneros:** The readers who are going to like my stories the best and catch all the subtexts and all the subtleties, that even my editor can't catch, are Chicanas. When there are Chicanas in the audience and they laugh, they are laughing at stuff that we talk about among ourselves. And there's no way that my editor at Random House is ever going to get those jokes. But I also am very conscious when I'm writing about opening doors for people who don't know the culture. I try my best. I won't do it for the sake of an Anglo reader. There was one place in my story when, for example, the grandmother cried because she found out I was going to "dar a luz." My editor finally put in the margins, "I think you need to translate this." I said, "I wish I could, but I don't know how without the seams showing, so we're going to have to leave it. People will have to use a dictionary; they can still get it." I really feel that way. I'm not going to make concessions to the non-Spanish speaker. I will try my best everywhere else if it flows into the piece, but if the seam is showing and it's obvious that the character is saying something like, "The grandmother cried because I was going to dar a luz, I was going to give birth," that's clumsy. I'm not going to do that for the person who's monolingual, but I will try to weave it in in such a way in the rest of the story so they don't lose it.

**R.D.:** Could you see yourself writing in Spanish?

**Cisneros:** I have written in Spanish when I've been in Mexico for a little while.

**R.D.:** Do you see that as a creative option for you?

**Cisneros:** Yes, it might happen. But it only would happen if I was living in Mexico. Wherever you put me, that's what I write about. I'm very much a product of my environment.

**R.D.:** So as long as you're living in the States you would see yourself writing in English?

**Cisneros:** Yes, but put me in Texas, I start using the two languages. If you put me in Mexico, I'll write in Spanish. But I won't write as a conscious thing. It'll happen because that's what I hear. I'm so connected to the spoken word. I've always been fascinated with voices since I was in graduate school.

**Feroza Jussawalla:** That's the wonderful thing in your technique. The stories you recently published in *Grand Street* are all letters in different voices. Actually, they're peticiones or little pleading notes that people leave in churches requesting saints to do things for them. How did you come upon that technique?

**Cisneros:** I love listening to people, and even when I was a graduate student at the University of Iowa, I was interested in voices. My first poems were all monologues, all monologues of different people's voices—farmers' voices, Iowa voices—because wherever you put me I write about what I hear. When I was working with high school drop-outs in Chicago after graduate school, I was especially intrigued by what they said because they had a very poetic way of expressing themselves. Street slang is very poetic. So at that point, I was like a linguist roaming around listening to people. Sometimes I was more concerned with the how than the what of what they said. Now it seems funny—I've just made this full circle. I've come right back to what I've always loved. Being in Texas and listening to how people speak in Texas brought me back to my original love, and that is the rhythm of the spoken word.

**F.J.:** And so the voices you caught in those stories are just the voices of the common people, of the Chicano voices all asking for different things—

there is the student asking to pass an exam and the family asking for food in the house—

Cisneros: It was a great feat for me to try to write all these letters as if different people wrote them. It was fun.

F. J.: And you also love personalities. At the reading last night, you said, "I'm not an actress," but when you read, you put yourself in all these roles, you're acting out everybody's different situation.

Cisneros: I'm trying to make you hear what I heard when I wrote it down. I see it all, and I hear it. I'm trying to get you to see on the page what I've heard. But if I'm reading it, then I have the extra advantage of reading it as I heard it and acting it out for you to see it exactly like I saw it.

F. J.: As you were reading the *Grand Street* stories, I was wondering if you would receive the kind of response that Rushdie had, because there seemed to be a voice there that was making fun of the religion and the religious fervor.

Cisneros: I feel like the last speaker. That's me. The monologue. I'm very, very much devoted to the Virgin of Guadalupe, but not exactly the same figure celebrated in Church.

F. J.: Would you be upset or would you find yourself in a kind of funny place if suddenly people were to read the stories and say, "She's making fun of those of us who are devotees and"—

Cisneros: I think my readers can see that the letters vary. There's some that are very emotional and very sad, there are obviously critiques of Mexicans exploiting Mexicans in there. Like the guy who couldn't get paid—that's a true story. In my neighborhood, they were passing around pamphlets saying, "Don't buy tortillas here; we haven't got paid." What are you going to do when stuff like that happens? I'm not only not going to buy tortillas there, I wrote a story. I think the stories range the same way the real letters range from the comic to somebody saying, "Please, I want to pass my test," to the really emotional, "My God, my wife's hemorrhaging." I tried very, very hard to write those with respect, and I think I did.

Now, I'll probably get some people mad at me like the daughters of the Texas Revolution probably with a story about a gay man called "Remember the Alamo." Right? *(Laughter)* But you know, unless I make somebody angry I realize I'm not doing my job. For example, the "Woman Hollering Creek" story was published in the *L.A. Times* and another Latino writer took me to task for writing that story. He actually wrote a letter to the editor saying he was angry and took offense that this is how Mexican-Americans or Mexicans are portrayed. He was saying, "How could you write about us in this manner? We come from a great tradition of humble people, and now writers like this who can afford to go to fancy workshops write about them in such a way that they make fun of them." That's what he was saying.

I had to wonder, though, "Did he read my story?" He felt that I was making fun of Mexican people and the way they talk and that I was being disrespectful of the sweat and blood of these Mexican people who can't help it that they can't speak properly—this is what he said in his letter. But it is through that sweat and blood that I've gone to school and benefited from all the labors of these people and now I'm writing about them. "Woman Hollering Creek" tells a true story, and that's the one that gripped me when it happened to me in Texas. I had to write that story. Obviously our stories are quite diverse. And I wasn't trying in that one story to exemplify all of our experiences, I was just writing one story. His anger, I understand, is because there haven't been other representations of Mexicans in the *L.A. Times* magazine.

F.J.: There is yet another kind of translation you have to do in a sense. For instance, in a story like "Woman Hollering Creek," you draw a lot on Mexican and Southwestern myths and legends. How does that get translated for other readers?

Cisneros: That's why I say the real ones who are going to get it are the Latinos, the Chicanos. They're going to get it in that they're going to understand the myth and how I've revised it. When I talked to someone at *Interview* magazine, I had to explain to him what I was doing with la llorona, La Malinche, and the Virgin of Guadalupe in the story. But he said, "Hey, I didn't know that, but I still got the story." You can get it at some other level. He reminded me, "Sandra, if you're from Ireland you're going to get a lot more out of Joyce than if you're not, but just because you're not Irish doesn't mean you're not going to get it at another level."

F.J.: But you've revised the myth in "Woman Hollering Creek." La llorona doesn't kill the woman or the children as she does in the stories told here along the border, she gives laughter. She frees the Mexican woman who was so bound to her Mexican-American husband—but through the Chicana woman who works at the women's shelter.

**Cisneros:** Yes, this other woman—the Chicana woman—could understand the myth in a new way. She could see it as a grito, not a llanto. And all of a sudden, that woman who came with all her Mexican assumptions learned something. The Chicana woman showed her a new way of looking at a Mexican myth. And it took someone who was a little bit outside the culture to see the myth in a new way.

**F.J.:** You've just touched on something I see as a key theme of yours, which is the conflict of cultures. What is very interesting in this for me is that it isn't between Chicano and Anglo as much as inside "Hispanic" culture. I don't know whether that's the right word to use; I have a lot of students who don't like being called "Hispanic."

**Cisneros:** I hate Hispanic. One day that word just appeared! Just like *USA Today*. One day we were sleeping, we woke up and saw that. "How'd that get there?" *(Laughter)* I don't know where that word came from. It's kind of an upwardly mobile type word. That word to me came out of Washington, D.C. I only use it when I apply for a grant. But something I've learned is not to feel superior when people want to call themselves Hispanic. You have a right to call yourself what you want, and I have to respect that if I want to be called what I want to be called. So, I no longer get so hysterical anymore if someone wants to call themselves that. But you wouldn't find me going out with a Hispanic. *(Laughter)* Anyway, we had a word, no one asked us! I like the word Latino. It groups me with the other Latino groups in Chicago.

**F.J.:** Yet even in *House on Mango Street*, one gets a sense of conflicts within that Latino culture in Chicago. In one of the stories, the male character brings a wife from "back home," as it were. She comes with a baby, doesn't step out, stays locked up and doesn't come out of her apartment, doesn't speak anything but Spanish, and doesn't even try. There seems to be a voice criticizing her.

**Cisneros:** I just wanted to talk there about peoples' fear of the English language and also why they want to keep their own language. The language, for a lot of people, was a link back; it meant that you were going to get back eventually. That's why some people refused to learn English because they were assuming, as so many immigrants did, that there was a road back. And it's a frightening thing when you let go of a language because you've let go your tiny thin string back home.

F.J.: So, do the three mix? Do they ever come together or are they three separate cultures?

Cisneros: What are the three cultures you mean?

F.J.: The Mexican, the "Hispanic" of the Chicago neighborhood, and the Chicano.

Cisneros: The Chicago neighborhood to me is the Mexican neighborhood.

F.J.: So it's just Mexican. It's not Chicano, it's not Hispanic—

Cisneros: It's Latin American; it's Mexican. And even if it is Chicano the people don't identify it as Chicano. They say, "We're Mexican." We say we're Mexican in my mother and father's house. And I like what Anzaldua says: "Los Mexicanos." She's talking about a race, not a nationality. That, I think, is perhaps the best way to phrase what we are in Chicago. We mean the race, la raza. We do not mean what side of the border you are from, as they do here in El Paso where some are U. S. citizens and others are Mexican.

R.D.: So then what's the difference between the ambiente in Chicago and what you encountered in Texas?

Cisneros: Very different. In Texas, they are physically closer to the border, but emotionally they're far away. We in Chicago were physically farther, but emotionally closer to Mexico. We had relatives in the interior. We had ties to Mexico in a way we did not have ties to Illinois. When I came to Texas, the Texans assumed that I was going to show them up and that I thought I was better because I was from the Midwest. And that always confused me, because I didn't have any allegience to Illinois. I was just born there. I did not feel towards Illinois what they felt towards Texas. We didn't feel for the land. And it took me awhile to figure out that the Texans had been here in Texas for hundreds of years. They were Texans first, and I didn't understand that.

R.D.: Do you feel that in New Mexico also?

Cisneros: I've only lived in New Mexico for three weeks, so I don't know the New Mexicans yet. The Texans are a whole different people, they were new to me. I get emotional when I hear the Mexican national anthem. The Texans don't. Today when the children in the elementary school I visited were playing the Mexican national anthem, "me emocionio," it emotioned me, that's the only way I can phrase it. It "emotioned me"—it moved me— to hear them sing that Mexican national anthem. I feel very Mexican, but the Texans don't feel Mexican. They're not Mexican, they're Texan. And that's a real distinction, a different relationship.

**F. J.**: So what did you experience when you moved to Texas?

**Cisneros**: Well, I wasn't Chicana, I was Mexicana! But in Texas I had to start saying I was Chicana, because when I said I was Mexicana they thought I was from Mexico! And I was, kind of. *(Laughter)* And then I would go to Mexico. If I said I was Mexicana, people would look at me. I have a poem about that called "Original Sin." It's about going on the plane to Mexico and I have to run after the stewardess to explain that she had given me the wrong national identity form. It's a true incident. Then I went into the bathroom and shaved my underarms, because in Mexico they don't like hair under your arms, and I was going to meet my father's family. I'm like this woman caught in mid-air with my own identity and the one I'm going to get over there. So, in Texas I had to start calling myself Chicana even though my family doesn't like it because it moves me one step further away from the country they don't want to lose identity with. My brother always says that "We're Mexicanos." I never deny that I am; I feel very Mexican. But I had to start using Chicano so as not to confuse my audience.

Actually, I feel lucky that my father was Mexican and my mother Mexican-American, because a lot of Chicanos don't have the relationship with Mexico that I do. They don't have those childhood memories, they don't have those recuerdos, they don't have those nuances of popular culture that I grew up with as a result of having a Mexican father. And that clash of the Mexicans with the Mexican-Americans, the clash of my father's class and my mother's working class is the subject of my next book. I couldn't write about that in *House on Mango Street*, because I was too young as a writer. I couldn't handle the cast of characters that is in the novel I'm writing now. That clash of being a child, where when you went to Mexico the grandmother would just get so angry because of your American barbaric ways. You know, Mexico looking at America as the barbaric country! That's my next book.

**R. D.**: What are the differences in background between your parents? How does that play into the novel?

**Cisneros**: My father was raised by an absent father and a not very well-educated mother. My grandfather was educated, but my grandmother was not. My father was born in some town in Oaxaca, because my grandmother was following my grandfather with his troops. But he never says that, he's ashamed to say that, because you know how people from the D. F. [Districto Federal] are—he says Mexico City. But if you really look on the books, it's Oaxaca. My grandfather was a cadet in the Mexican West Point, and he fled during periods when it was not fortunate to be a cadet during the Mexican revolution. So he spent some time in Philadelphia. But he was from a home that had some money to send him there. My father had the privilege to go to school and threw it away. He went to school and he spent that first year gambling, and going after ladies, and having a good time. And when his grades came, he was so afraid of my grandfather who, when he was home, was a very, very strict military man that my father ran away from home rather than face his father. My father was the favorite son in the family of five, and he ran away like a prodigal son. Out of terror. He took off to the United States with the black sheep uncle, and they traveled around the United States together. They were just traveling around, vagabonding. My father came to the U. S. during World War II, and then they picked him up and said, "you can either be deported or you can enlist!" He became a U. S. citizen, served in the Army, but he didn't speak any English. He used to have to ask the Puerto Ricans or any Spanish speakers in the Army what was going on. He has all kinds of stories from that period when he was in the Army. I have to do my research now to write my novel because though the foundation of it is that, it's going to become something else.

My mother's family, on the other hand, came from Guanajuato where no one in the family has been, except me. I just went back there last week to check it out. During the time of the revolution, if you were poor, as my grandmother said, it didn't matter what side you were on. The federales would steal your chickens and rape your women, and the revolucionarios would do it too. So they left. If you follow the railroad maps, which I have been following, you can see how my grandfather came up with the railroad, worked in Flagstaff, worked in different cities, saved money and sent for my grandmother and her family, her brothers and her mother and brought them all up.

R.D.: So they fit more the classic pattern of Mexican immigration?

Cisneros: Yes. My grandfather worked on the railroads all his life. Following the railroad lines, like a lot of migratory patterns of people, they eventually all came up to Chicago. And he worked on the railroads there. While they were in Chicago, they lost ties with the Mexican relatives. Some of my mother's brothers and sisters had been born in Mexico or Flagstaff but most of them in Chicago, with two Spanish-speaking parents in a very poor Mexican neighborhood in Chicago. My father and my black sheep uncle were passing from New York. It was getting too cold, they were on their way to California on the bus, and the bus stopped in Chicago. And he said, "Well, I've heard there's lots of Mexicans here. Let's get off here for a little while." They stayed there the rest of their lives. My father met my mother at a dance. My mother didn't like him at all because my father came from a middle-class family and here he was with Chicanos. He was trying to show off. He would tell my mother all these things, how much money he made. She always said she couldn't stand him because he was such a show-off. I don't know why she married him. *(Laughter)*

F.J.: It strikes me as you are describing your new novel that one of the things it is about is class politics. What would you say your politics are now?

Cisneros: I have lived in socialist countries, so I can't call myself a socialist, because I know that doesn't work. When I travelled in Europe for a year, I went from country to country and I met women and men, and women helped me and men helped me, but it turned out to be too expensive when you got anything free from a man *(laughter)*, so I realized I'd only depend on women. Women helped me and they asked for nothing in return, and they gave me great compassion and love when I was feeling lost and alone. I, in turn, listened to their stories, and I think I made so many friendships that crossed borders. It was like we all came from the same country, the women; we all had the same problems. I don't know what my politics are, except my stories tell it to you. I can't give it to you as an -ism or an -ist.

F.J.: How about as feminist?

Cisneros: Well, yes—it's a feminism, but it's a feminism that is very different from the feminism of upper-class women. It's a feminism that's very much tied into my class.

R.D.: What would be the difference?

Cisneros: I guess my feminism and my race are the same thing to me. They're tied in one to another, and I don't feel an alliance or an allegiance with upper-class white women. I don't. I can listen to them and on some level as a human being I can feel great compassion and friendships; but they have to move from their territory to mine, because I know their world. But they don't know mine. Then I moved to Texas, and that made me so angry. I don't know why Texas did that to me. Texas made me angry. In some way that I never had before, I started getting racist towards white people. I was wandering around like this colonized fool before, trying to be like my women friends in school. I didn't have any white women friends when I was in Texas. Once, Norma Alarcón came to visit me when I was working in San Antonio and she said, "Don't you have any white friends?" It suddenly occurred to me that she hadn't met one and I thought, "I don't!" You know, that's because I was working in the barrio, I was doing community arts, I didn't have time. White people never came to the neighborhood where I worked. I wasn't about to go into their neighborhood and start telling them about Chicano art. I was creating Chicano art, and I was bringing Chicano writers to the neighborhood. I was up to my elbows in work. I didn't have time to be going off to UTSA [University of Texas, San Antonio] telling them where Chicano writers are.

I was committed to the neighborhood; I was committed to creating a small press book fair—the first one that was there. And if people were scared of my neighborhood, well, they better start thinking what our cultural center was all about to begin with and who we were supposed to serve first. Something ugly happened during that time that I didn't realize. I have to say now that I'm in a more balanced place than I was at that period. And so my politics have been changing, and some of my white women friends who have come into my life—I think it was divine providence that put them there—have taught me a lot. Those white women friends who have bothered to learn about my culture have entered into my life now and have taught me something. Maybe a little sliver of glass of the Snow Queen in my heart has dissolved a bit. But I'm still angry about some things, and those issues are going to come up in my next book.

F.J.: What are those?

Cisneros: I'm really mad at Mexican men, because Mexican men are the men I love the most and they disappoint me the most. I think they disappoint me the most because I love them the most. I don't care about the other men so much. They don't affect my personal politics because they're not in my sphere whereas Latino men, and specifically Mexican men, are the ones that I want to be with the most. And they keep disappointing me. I see so many intelligent Mexican women in Texas and they can't find a Mexican man because our Mexican men are with white women. What does that say about Mexican men? How do they feel about themselves if they won't go out with Mexican women, especially professional Mexican women? What does that say about themselves? They must not love themselves or, like someone said, "You must not love your mama." You know? You must not. That's an issue we talk about only among ourselves—the Latina women. That's really hard for me to tell my white women friends and make them understand without offending them. And these issues have to come up, and they will come up. Now these are some of the things on my agenda that I didn't get to in this book, but I'll get to in the next one.

F.J.: Could it be that you are an exception among Latina women?

**Cisneros:** No! I'm not the exception! I came to Texas, I met so many major mountain movers here, especially in Texas. The Chicanas I met in Texas, my God they're something! They're like nopalitos. And I think it's because they're like the landscape. But it's hard to be a woman in Texas.

F.J.: They are not women who want to assume the traditional Mexican female role?

**Cisneros:** I have to say that the traditional role is kind of a myth. I think the traditional Mexican woman is a fierce woman. There's a lot of victimization but we are also fierce. We are very fierce. Our mothers had been fierce. Our women may be victimized but they are still very, very fierce and very strong. I really do believe that.

R.D.: Is the same kind of gender politics involved in writing?

**Cisneros:** How specifically?

R.D.: Certainly, male Chicano writers were recognized and published before the women. Do you think that's a function of some of the same kinds of things you've been talking about?

**Cisneros:** The men who were published first, Tomás Rivera, Rudolfo Anaya, Rolando Hinojosa, they were all in universities, no? Whereas with the women, it's taken us this long to get educated. Or some of them have educated their husbands first. It's taken us a while to get to this level where we are educated enough so that we can feel confident enough to even compete. It's taken us this long to take care of our sense of self. There's a lot of stuff going on with women, as far as getting your education, and as far as figuring out you don't have to go the route that society puts on you. Men are already in a privileged position. They don't have to fight against patriarchy; it put them in a great place. But the women did; it took us a little while to figure out, "I don't have to get married just yet," or "Wait a second, I don't have to have a baby now." And some of us figured it out a few babies later.

I think it took a little while for the women who wanted to get their education, and to fight for that education, because our fathers didn't want us to go to school or they wanted us to go to school to get married. As for me, I went through great trauma in my twenties trying to figure out that my life had no role model, so I had to invent that. I don't know if Rolando Hinojosa went through the trauma of wondering if he should have children in his twenties and should he get married. I don't think he did. He had other pressures, supporting his family, sure, but I had pressures too. You know, we all did. I wasn't even applying for a job in a university with an MFA. Imagine that. With an MFA from one of the famous writing schools, and even with an NEA I didn't dare apply for a job at a university. I was making $12,000 a year working at an alternative high school in inner-city Chicago when I came out of Iowa. Why? Because as women, we think we're not good enough. Because as people of color, we have been led to believe, we're colonized to think, we're not smart enough, we're not good enough, we have nothing to share at the university. And where would I have gone at the university had I gone into the schools that I left? Would I be teaching *Moby Dick*? You know I don't want to teach *Moby Dick*! (*Laughter*)

F.J.: You said yesterday in your talk that your consciousness of yourself as being a thoroughly colonized person developed while you were working in Chicago with underprivileged students. I'm trying to think of what it means to you to have been a thoroughly colonized person.

Cisneros: My consciousness of growing up, the consciousness of myself, the subjects that I write about, the voice that I write in—I suppose all of that began in Iowa in a seminar class. The madeleine—to use Proust's term—was Bachelard's poetics of space. The house. The house! Everyone was talking about the house the way they'd always been talking about everything. It was at that moment I realized, "I don't have a house—these things don't matter to me!" (*Laughter*) I don't have a house, how could I talk about house! With people from my neighborhood, you'd be talking about a very different house than the one Bachelard was talking about—the wonderful house of memory. My house was a prison for me; I don't want to talk about house.

F.J.: You treat that in *House on Mango Street*. There is a little interlude where the child runs into one of the nuns who teaches at her school and the nun points up to a window and asks, "Do you live there?"

**Cisneros:** I used to be ashamed to take anyone into that room, to my house, because if they saw that house they would equate the house with me and my value. And I know that house didn't define me; they just saw the outside. They couldn't see what was inside. I wrote a poem that was a precursor, or perhaps the same story—about an apartment, a flat. I wrote it for the workshop after that experience of being in that seminar, and *House on Mango Street* began that night, that same night. It was an incredible moment. It all began at that same time. I can't tell you whether the poems came first or the stories; they all came like a deluge. It had been as if all of the sudden I realized, "Oh my God! Here's something that my classmates can't write about, and I'm going to tell you because I'm the authority on this—I can tell you."

F.J.: So after the seminar you were not ashamed of that house anymore. You wouldn't be ashamed of your background, you'd say, "This is the background that empowered me."

**Cisneros:** At that moment I ceased to be ashamed because I realized that I knew something that they could never learn at the universities. It was all a sudden that I realized something that I knew that I was the authority on.

R.D.: What was that?

**Cisneros:** It was the university of the streets, the university of life. The neighbors, the people I saw, the poverty that the women had gone through—you can't learn that in a class. I could walk in that neighborhood, and I knew how to walk in that neighborhood, and they didn't. So to me it began there, and that's when I intentionally started writing about all the things in my culture that were different from them—the poems that are these city voices—the first part of *Wicked Wicked Ways*—and the stories in *House on Mango Street*. I think it's ironic that at the moment when I was practically leaving an institution of learning, I began realizing in which ways institutions had failed me. It was that moment in Iowa when I realized my difference from the other classmates as far as our class differences, our cultural differences, my color difference—all of which I had acknowleged but I couldn't articulate as such until that moment in that seminar class: I began intentionally addressing the issues and using the voice that I'm now known for; I began searching out writers who were writing the types of stories that I wanted to read; I began, in essence, trying to piece together those parts of my education that my education had missed, to fill that void so to speak. I can't pretend that I came out of the Iowa corn fields whole and complete like an Athena from Zeus' head. But I knew where I wanted to go.

**R.D.:** Who are the writers who have influenced your work significantly?

**Cisneros:** A whole generation of the Chicano writers were influenced by the Latin American male boom because that's all we got. Borges was an influence, but the ones I really stay with are Manuel Puig and Juan Rulfo, Rulfo obviously for his rhythms and what he's doing with voices. And, of course, you know Rulfo influenced that story I wrote last night, very much so. Manuel Puig for his compassion, always looking out for these under-dogs. So I have to say we were influenced by the Latino male writers, and it's only recently that we are gaining access to the women's work and that we're getting influenced by the women. I think the writers that influenced me the most in this last collection were—well the one I can name the most is Merce Rodoreda. She's Catalan. She's taught me a lot about voices and monologues and following that kind of emotions that she does. Her writing is very emotional and I like that. She taught me a lot in writing this last book.

But there are also a lot of American working class women writers. They can be white women writers if they're working-class women writers—Pat Ellis Taylor in Austin, Texas, I love her work very much.

**F.J.:** And the Asian women?

**Cisneros:** I love Maxine Hong Kingston. *The Woman Warrior*—what a wonderful book that was for me. That gave me permission to keep going with what I'd started with *House on Mango Street*.

**R.D.:** So not just Latino writers, but also other minority writers—

**Cisneros:** Yes. I'm not that familiar with the black women writers, but I'm much more interested in some black feminist women writers as opposed to the mainstream black women writers.

**R.D.:** Why is that?

**Cisneros:** I'm not saying that I prefer one over the other, but I think that small presses are more fearless about things that they take.

**F.J.:** And that's why you say your neighborhood then is among those people who are publishing with the women's presses and the minor presses rather than the major—

**Cisneros:** I didn't realize that was my neighborhood until I was serving on an NEA panel. Anytime a book came up that was by a women's press or a feminist press or a working class press, I knew those writers. When they mentioned the writers who were publishing with New York I didn't know who they were *(laughter)*, but anytime a name that was from a small press or Southwest or minority came up, I usually knew it.

I just have to say personally I haven't read the black women writers to the degree that I've read some of the smaller presses. And that's because I'll read their works, but I haven't kept up with them. For some reason, they're not making me do mental backflips like some of the other writers I'm reading. They're wonderful writers, but we have to work as writers to the ones that are somehow doing something for us in our own agenda. My companera, Helena Maria Viramontes, loves the black women writers—the big press ones that we're talking about, the handful.

**F.J.:** You mean Gloria Naylor and Paule Marshall—

**Cisneros:** Naylor, Paule Marshall, Toni Morrison, Alice Walker. I'll read their stories, and they don't do to me what Merce Rodoreda does to me. Something happens when I read Rodoreda and Puig. I don't know what it is. And I think that you have to stay with those writers that are somehow touching those passion buttons in you. I don't know what it is that they do for me.

And it may be that I'm just not taken by the linear novel form, that I'm much more interested in something new happening to the literature. I'm saying this all now, as I'm speaking to you, for the first time. That may be why some of the black women writers who are working in traditional forms, even though I can recognize the craft—but that's not the kind of story that appeals to me. I'm much, much more excited by a writer who is doing something with the form, like Rulfo or Borges or Puig. Just from my own personal taste, I like somebody doing something new.

**R.D.:** So now you're writing a novel, your first novel. Many Chicano writers seem to have taken small forms and built up a kind of mosaic, have worked with a group of short stories rather than a continuous narrative. This is true, of course, of *House on Mango Street*, but I'm also thinking of Tomás Rivera's *y no se lo tragó la tierra* and Ana Castillo's *The Mixquiahuala Letters* and Denise Chavez's *The Last of the Menu Girls*. Why do you think this is so?

**Cisneros:** For one thing, you have to talk about where we are as far as our careers as writers. We're young writers, and you don't start out by building a house if you haven't learned how to build a room. Some writers have done that, and I don't think that they've done a very good job of building their houses. I'm much more interested in carpentry and getting my walls done so that all the joints meet. I'm a very, very meticulous carpenter. So, I think that at this point in our career and our craft we're learning how to build the rooms before we can build a house. And also, maybe we don't want the house—

**R.D.:** Yes, that would be my question—

**Cisneros:** I didn't know what I was writing when I wrote *House on Mango Street*, but I knew what I wanted. I didn't know what to call it, but I knew what I was after. It wasn't a naive thing, it wasn't an accident. I wanted to write a series of stories that you could open up at any point. You didn't have to know anything before or after and you would understand each story like a little pearl, or you could look at the whole thing like a necklace. That's what I always knew from the day that I wrote the first one. I said, "I'm going to do a whole series of these, and it's going to be like this, and it'll all be connected." I didn't know the order they were going to come in, but I wasn't trying to write a linear novel.

**R.D.:** But now you are?

**Cisneros:** Well, no. I'm writing a novel; I don't know if it's linear. I don't decide the shape. It really decides itself. I don't know the shape of this novel. I don't know it yet. All I have is pages of it, and I have some parts of it, and I know some of the agendas and the issues, and I have some parts written— but I don't know the shape.

**F.J.:** It's going to be about your family, right?

**Cisneros:** Yes, it'll start out with that foundation, but it's not going to be autobiographical. It'll start out with an autobiographical foundation of taking my father and my mother and their situation at that time in history, but

I have to do research about that time so I can fill in the gaps of what family doesn't speak about or what my father doesn't know. And it's going to be my agenda, you know?

**F.J.:** You keep saying agenda; it's almost as though you were doing some cause writings. Starting with a position—

**Cisneros:** That's right! That's right, we do. That's how fiction is different from poetry. I don't have an agenda when I write poetry. I don't know what I'm going to write about.

**R.D.:** But you do when you write fiction?

**Cisneros:** Absolutely. Absolutely. I've got some things that have got to get said, and this is how I'm going to get it out. I have to sometimes ask my two editors, my Random House editor and my personal editor, is my axe too sharp here? Do I need to hold back? Because I do have some things I really want to do.

**R.D.:** Do you see that as a difference between minority writers and Anglo writers, white writers?

**Cisneros:** I think that the work of women and minorities and working-class people has spiritual content and political content, and that's their strength. I really do. I see so much writing by mainstream people that is well written but it doesn't have anything to say. So, it's not going to be substantial, not going to stand. And I would much rather have work that's not quite as clean and finished, but that has some spiritual content. I see the spiritual and political in some ways being the same thing.

# Index